D0983965

Unless Recalled Earlier
DATE DUE

Demco, Inc. 38-293

TOTAL
CAPACITY
MANAGEMENT
Optimizing at the
Operational, Tactical,
and Strategic Levels

TOTAL CAPACITY
MANAGEMENT
Optimizing at the Operational, Tactical, and Strategic Levels

C.J. McNair
Richard Vangermeersch

RECEIVED

MAY 2 7 1999

MSU - LIBRARY

FAR ‖ The IMA Foundation for Applied Research, Inc.
An affiliate of the Institute of Management Accountants

S_L^t

St. Lucie Press
Boca Raton   Boston   London   New York   Washington, D.C.

HD
69
.C3
M39
1998

Library of Congress Cataloging-in-Publication Data

McNair, Carol Jean.
  Total capacity management : optimizing at the operational,
tactical, and strategic levels / C.J. McNair, Richard Vangermeersch.
      p. cm.
    Includes bibliographical references and index.
    ISBN 1-57444-231-7 (alk. paper)
    1. Industrial capacity--Management. I. Vangermeersch, Richard G.
J. II. Title.
  HD69.C3M39 1998
  658.5—dc21
                                           98-7180
                                           CIP

This book contains information obtained from authentic and highly regarded sources. Reprinted material is quoted with permission, and sources are indicated. A wide variety of references are listed. Reasonable efforts have been made to publish reliable data and information, but the author and the publisher cannot assume responsibility for the validity of all materials or for the consequences of their use.

Neither this book nor any part may be reproduced or transmitted in any form or by any means, electronic or mechanical, including photocopying, microfilming, and recording, or by any information storage or retrieval system, without prior permission in writing from the publisher.

The consent of CRC Press LLC does not extend to copying for general distribution, for promotion, for creating new works, or for resale. Specific permission must be obtained in writing from CRC Press LLC for such copying.

Direct all inquiries to CRC Press LLC, 2000 Corporate Blvd., N.W., Boca Raton, Florida 33431.

Trademark Notice: Product or corporate names may be trademarks or registered trademarks, and are used only for identification and explanation, without intent to infringe.

© 1998 by IMA Foundation for Applied Research, Inc.
St. Lucie Press is an imprint of CRC Press LLC

No claim to original U.S. Government works
International Standard Book Number 1-884015-38-7
Library of Congress Card Number   94-46301
Printed in the United States of America   1 2 3 4 5 6 7 8 9 0
Printed on acid-free paper

THE IMA FOUNDATION FOR APPLIED RESEARCH, INC.
TRUSTEES, 1997–98

Foundation Officers

President
James C. Horsch, CMA
Consumers Energy Company
Jackson, Michigan

Treasurer
John F. Pope, CMA, CFM, CPA
IMA Vice President of Finance
The Quantum Group, Inc.
Marina Del Rey, California

Trustees by Virtue of the Bylaws

Keith Bryant, Jr., CMA
IMA President
Formerly with University of
   Alabama at Birmingham
Birmingham, Alabama

Clair M. Raubenstine,
   CMA, CPA
IMA Chair
Coopers & Lybrand, LLP
Philadelphia, Pennsylvania

John F. Pope, CMA, CFM, CPA
IMA Vice President of Finance
The Quantum Group, Inc.
Marina Del Rey, California

Pamela Prinz Stewart
IMA President-elect
Robert Half International
Orlando, Florida

Appointed Trustees

Donald B. Christensen
J. C. Penney Insurance
   Group, Inc.
Plano, Texas

Paul P. Danesi, Jr.
Texas Instruments, Inc.
Attleboro, Massachusetts

Henry J. Davis, CMA,
   CPA, CIRM
Dodge-Rockwell Automation
Greenville, South Carolina

Sandra M. Denarski, CMA
Johnson & Johnson
New Brunswick, New Jersey

James C. Horsch, CMA
Consumers Energy Company
Jackson, Michigan

Robert C. Miller
Formerly with Boeing
   Commercial Airplane Group
Seattle, Washington

Michael D. Shields
Michigan State University
East Lansing, Michigan

Gary H. Siegel, CPA
DePaul University
Chicago, Illinois

FOREWORD

Practitioners and academics have struggled for a hundred years to understand, identify, measure, and report capacity. Today, we still are seeking models that fit our particular environment. Why is it so difficult to arrive at an approach that is generally accepted? After all, management accountants, financial managers, and operational managers have a common goal—to eliminate waste and reduce costs while creating products and services customers want to buy. Yet there is lack of consensus when we talk about unused, excess, and idle capacity. Some say it is good, some say it is bad.

Now we have the cost accounting view, presented by two highly respected management accounting researchers. Dr. McNair has devoted more than 10 years of research to the subject of capacity while Dr. Vangermeersch, a noted accounting historian, has traced the literature from inception. *Total Capacity Management* is really two books in one. Chapters 1 to 6 and Chapter 11 are on capacity cost management, including a discussion of 12 capacity models, while Chapters 7 to 10 cover the history of the accounting treatment of capacity. From an historical perspective, ideas about capacity have come full circle, from a high point in the 1920s through the "dark ages" of 1953–1978 to a rediscovery of the relevance of capacity in our day.

FAR's research has already stimulated lively dialogue among IMA and APICS (American Production and Inventory Control Society) leaders. IMA's traditional cost world and APICS's operational throughput world need to be aligned. We can accomplish this alignment if we take the time to understand varying perspectives. To this end, we encourage the submission of articles and letters to IMA's official magazine, *Management Accounting*, addressing differing viewpoints, such as the operational viewpoint espoused by APICS, a throughput accounting and constraint management viewpoint, and others.

Total Capacity Management is truly comprehensive and ranks as a major work on the subject. For the most benefit, read it in conjunction with IMA's Statement on Management Accounting 4Y, "Measuring the Cost of Capacity" (SMA 4Y/$7.50), and *Capacity Measurement & Improvement: A Manager's Guide to Evaluating & Optimizing Capacity Productivity* (C2/$35), from CAM-I (Consortium for Advanced Manufacturing-International). McNair and Vangermeersch wrote SMA 4Y and conferred with CAM-I on its book.

To learn more about throughput accounting, refer to *Synchronous Management: Profit-Based Manufacturing for the 21st Century*, Volumes 1 and 2 (SPECTRUM 3/$65). The authors of this book define total capacity at a resource as: total capacity = throughput capacity + protective capacity + excess capacity. Wasted capacity is lost throughput when nonsynchronous conditions exist. Readers are encouraged to explore capacity issues from an operational perspective by reading this work.

Publications referenced in this foreword are available from IMA's Customer Orders & Information Department, (800) 638-4427, ext. 278. Visit IMA's website, http://www.imanet.org for a description of each title.

Guidance in the preparation of this monograph was generously provided by the IMA Project Committee:

Paul P. Danesi, Jr.
Texas Instruments, Inc.

Henry J. Davis, CMA, CPA, CIRM   Lou Jones
Dodge/Rockwell Automation   Caterpillar Company

This report reflects the views of the researchers and not necessarily those of the IMA, the trustees of FAR, or the Project Committee.

Julian M. Freedman, CMA, CPA, CPIM
Director of Research
The IMA Foundation for Applied Research, Inc.

About the Authors

☐ C. J. McNair, CMA, Ph.D.

C. J. McNair is a professor of management accounting at Babson College, Wellesley, Massachusetts. Since graduating from Columbia University in 1986, she has become a noted expert in the design and development of cost management systems. Dr. McNair has published numerous books and articles in this area, including *The Profit Potential: Taking High Performance to the Bottom Line, World-Class Accounting and Finance,* and *Benchmarking: Tool for Continuous Improvement.*

Other recent writing includes several management accounting guidelines for the Society of Management Accountants of Canada: *Measuring the Cost of Capacity, Redesigning the Finance Function,* and *Implementing Process Management: A Framework for Process Thinking.* Current work includes development of value-based accounting models and field work on applications of capacity cost management in various industries.

☐ Richard Vangermeersch, CMA, CPA, Ph.D.

Richard Vangermeersch is a professor of accounting at the University of Rhode Island. He received a Ph.D. in accounting in 1970 from the University of Florida. He was president of The

Academy of Accounting Historians in 1987 and has been presented with two Hourglass Awards by that organization.

Dr. Vangermeersch has been a member of the IMA since 1970, starting with the Bangor-Waterville Chapter and then the Providence Chapter. He has been both manuscript director and CMA director for the Providence Chapter. He has published many articles in *Management Accounting,* four of which received Certificates of Merit, and many other items in various IMA publications, as well as the three-volume set of *Relevance Rediscovered.* Dr. Vangermeersch also has been graciously acknowledged in *Proud of the Past: 75 Years of Excellence Through Leadership, 1917–1992,* and in *IMA's Legacy: Creating Value Through Research.*

ACKNOWLEDGMENTS

This 10-year project is the product of the efforts of many people and many organizations. The project started when the authors were in adjoining offices at the University of Rhode Island. At that point they were assisted greatly by a very focused graduate assistant, Mike Baruch, and the departmental secretary, Lois Pazienza.

The original work was shared with Julian Freedman, IMA director of research, who started the more formal part of the project and has stayed with it to completion. Thanks, Julian, and also thanks to Claire Barth, IMA senior editor, for her excellent help.

The authors also shared their findings with Al Vercio from Texas Instruments as a part of an exchange with the Consortium for Advanced Manufacturing-International (CAM-I). Peter Zampino, then with CAM-I, traveled to Kingston, R.I., to exchange thoughts with the authors.

Denny Neider from Price Waterhouse chaired the IMA Committee on Research that awarded the authors the contract to write the study. Denny was an extremely positive source of inspiration, as were the other members of that Committee. Bob Miller from the Boeing Company helped as the president of the IMA Foundation for Applied Research, Inc. (FAR). He appointed

Paul Danesi of Texas Instruments as the liaison between FAR and the authors. Paul has done a great job, along with other members, Hank Davis from Dodge-Rockwell Automation and Lou Jones from Caterpillar Company.

Julian asked the authors to work with Randolf Holst, manager of Management Accounting Guidelines of the Society of Management Accountants of Canada, on a similar project. Thanks to his help and the kind assistance of a focus group on the topic, MAG #42, "Measuring the Cost of Capacity," was issued in 1996. (It was published by IMA as SMA 4Y.) The focus group consisted of Dennis Daly, Metropolitan State University; Sally Claybourn Evans of IBRD Rostrum Global; Dan Hauschild, AMPros Corporation; Randolf Holst; Lou Jones; Al King of Valuation Research Corporation; Teresa Malarky of Hills Pet Nutrition, Inc.; and Al Vercio. The comments of the focus group greatly sharpened the thinking of the authors on the topic.

The authors owe a special debt of gratitude to Al King for his moral support and long-term interest in the history of management accounting. Joel Dirlam, a noted emeritus professor of economics at the University of Rhode Island, provided both his thoughts and his file on the economic literature about capacity. Thanks again, Joel. Mike Lythgoe of the APICS Educational and Research Foundation gave the authors a chance to exchange ideas with APICS members in Denver in August 1996. This meeting provided many useful ideas on both sides. Thanks, Mike.

The authors are continuing their work on accounting and capacity cost management in historical research, in managerially accepted accounting principles, in further field studies, and by surveys. They look forward to communicating with readers. The authors believe that the widest possible dialogue about accounting and capacity cost management within organizations, industries, and society will yield great benefits. Most of all, the authors acknowledge you, the readers, for your attention. Thanks.

EXECUTIVE SUMMARY

Capacity is a many-splendored phenomenon and is truly a "movable feast." This IMA publication takes the reader through many varied ways of viewing capacity and, therefore, capacity cost management. There is no one easy answer. There is no one easy time frame for viewing capacity. There is no one field of knowledge that can encapsulate capacity and capacity cost management. But there have been many aids to the development of a workable answer to a specific organization for a given time period. This monograph describes these aids in depth so that readers can receive help in battling out their solutions.

The IMA and its predecessors, National Association of Cost Accountants (NACA), 1919–1957, and National Association of Accountants (NAA), 1957–1991, have supplied accounting practitioners with much information about capacity cost management. This monograph is a continuation of IMA research into the topic and stresses the rich contributions of IMA members, starting almost from the beginning. While perhaps the best IMA work was *Accounting for Costs of Capacity* (1963), IMA debates on this topic at the annual meetings in 1921, 1923, 1926, and 1945 were also very rich. One of the important findings of this monograph is the current need to debate and discuss the topic of capacity cost management within organizations, industry groups, and society.

This monograph draws from very much more literature than only that of accounting practitioners. It draws from literature in engineering, accounting theory, accounting texts, management, production and inventory control, and government. One of its important contributions is to show the participation of writers other than just accounting practitioners. The authors lead by example and urge readers to engage in selected readings in the course of doing research on this many-splendored topic. There are no easy answers.

Another important contribution of this monograph is its use of three economic time periods—short run, intermediate period, and long run—in discussing the various models of capacity cost management. These three time periods are matched with the management time frames of operational, tactical, and strategic. The stress of the intermediate period is especially significant, as this time period has rarely received coverage in writings on capacity cost management. Hence, these different time periods become a part of the movable feast.

Related to this overriding theme of the movable feast is the development of 12 different models of capacity cost management. These 12 models allow readers to pick and choose and create their own models. These models cover the 20th century and illustrate the richness of thinking that has not been captured before publication of this book. In addition, the authors have brought the notion of "ideal capacity" to all these models of the movable feast.

The authors bring a unique mix to this timely and timeless project. C. J. McNair, CMA, has much experience in field studies, including some of the aforementioned 12 models. She has written numerous books and articles on her findings. McNair has presented seminars on capacity cost management in many different forums.

Richard Vangermeersch, CMA, has written numerous books and articles on the history of cost/management accounting, especially in the 20th century. This mix of backgrounds has given this book much depth.

The authors have been very successful in selling their ideas. Along with a focus group, they prepared Management Accounting Guideline (MAG) #42, "Measuring the Cost of Capacity," for the Society of Management Accountants of Canada; the IMA published it as Statement on Management Accounting (SMA) 4Y in 1996. Hence, the monograph has a solid practitioner base as well as a rich research base. It is solution driven.

The monograph has three parts. In Part I, after an overview in Chapter 1, Chapters 2 through 5 present the first level of the various aids for accounting and capacity cost management. Chapter 6 serves as a bridge between Part I and Part II. Part II (Chapters 7 through 11) presents the second or deeper level of the various aids by delving into the historical explanations for the tools mentioned in Part I. Part III, "An Annotated Bibliography: Overview of Capacity Literature," presents the material for much more in-depth research into these aids by academics and other researchers.

Managing capacity is truly a movable feast, one that brings a company and its management into close proximity with every major business issue possible. Whether focused on maximizing the velocity of materials through the plant in the short term or redeploying resources to improve the value-creating ability of the firm, capacity cost management is the key to gaining and maintaining a competitive advantage.

The models, examples, and historical analysis developed in this monograph span almost 100 years of practice and theory in capacity cost management. What is striking in the end is that almost every idea, every model, every approach was envisioned by the early thinkers.

Only in the area of strategic capacity management can it be argued that the term "new" may be applied to the models, techniques, and practices that are emerging. As companies turn to horizontal or process management structures, as organizations begin to take on the appearance of networks embedded in larger networks, and as computers and other telecommunications technologies pave the way for the virtual corporation, the concept of capacity in the traditional sense may fade. Even so, will better utilization of a machine or a plant always matter? The answer clearly is yes.

But will better capacity utilization mean superior company performance? The answer to that question is more doubtful in the future than ever before. Reducing excess resources, eliminating waste, and striving for continuous improvement remain as essential today as ever, but the definition of value, and where that value is created, is forever being changed.

In the end, it is the company that understands its value-creating abilities, as defined by the customer, that will prosper. Using these external signals of value to guide its capacity decisions, firms likely will find that capacity in the "soft" sense (people/process capability) will assume ever greater importance over capacity in the "hard" sense (machine utilization). But capacity cost management will remain, with the feast consumed in a different location but available nonetheless.

TABLE OF CONTENTS

PART III
ANNOTATED BIBLIOGRAPHY

FIGURES AND TABLES

Part I

Modern Practice in Capacity Cost Management

1

THE MOVABLE FEAST

The work of organizations includes taking stock of the resources at one's command and planning the fullest use of
them all.[1]

Capacity is the value-creating ability of an organization, an ability that takes form in a wide variety of resources. Lying at the
heart of the management process, capacity shapes and defines
cost systems.

Every cost estimate used by an organization has an implicit
assumption of capacity built into it; every decision made has an
impact on this potential to create value. Problematic in nature,
capacity and its measurement are topics that have been debated,
hotly at times, throughout the 20th century. It is this elusive
concept—the capacity of a process, system, or organization to
do work—that this monograph is about.

The essence of the capacity issue is the unavoidable fact
that resources not used to their fullest represent *waste*. Waste
erodes profits and shortens the life of an organization. Waste
is the entropy of business systems, the drag on their current
and future performance. Effectively managing an organization

starts with making the fullest use of every resource at the company's command, that is, its theoretical capacity. Using this capacity productively, maximizing its value-creating potential, starts with eliminating resource waste, which is idle or excess capacity.

Capacity is a core issue in cost system design and analysis; capacity has to be defined for every resource or process. Capacity, in essence, defines the denominator in the cost equation. For every cost pool there has to be a *driver* and for every driver a *capacity*. The combined results of the historical and empirical analysis detailed in this monograph suggest, then, that while the precise definition of capacity has always been elusive, the motives of business and academe in attempting to define it are more concrete. Understanding and effectively managing capacity is, as suggested by the citation from Whitmore, the key to minimizing waste and ensuring that resources are used to their fullest.

This chapter presents an overview of the findings from an eight-year research project on capacity cost management. As with the concept of capacity itself, the presentation of the results of this study represented unique challenges. Specifically, in contrast to the sequence of the actual monograph, this chapter begins with a summary of the historical development of capacity cost management, which is presented in more depth in Part II.

The historical summary is then followed by a discussion of current trends in the field, based on the results of both archival and field research. These results are more fully detailed in Part I. The motivation for this departure from the "normal" method of introducing and presenting the results of a study is quite simple: this document is intended to serve multiple readers with multiple interests. The results from the field, which represent an overview of best practice in capacity cost management, will likely be of interest to all readers, while the historical analysis may appeal to a smaller, though equally important, audience. The resulting structure is truly a movable feast.

Historical Overview
of Capacity Cost Management

☐ The Age of Discovery

The history of capacity cost management can be broken into five separate eras, as suggested by Table 1-1. The Age of Discovery, bridging the years 1900 to 1919, was a watershed period when many of the ideas and techniques shaping modern management were born. As detailed in Chapter 7, the Age of Discovery was dominated by the Scientific Management school and one of its strongest proponents, Henry Gantt. Gantt had little time for accountants and their focus on transactions and financial statements; costs were to serve management, not the financier. Gantt's position brought him into direct conflict with A. H. Church, the father of modern cost accounting. Their 1915 debate, spanning five months and six issues of the then-popular magazine *American Machinist*, created intense discussion among managers, accountants, and industrial engineers over the "proper" treatment of expense burden.

Gantt's position in the 1915 debate is summarized in the opening pages of the first "round" in this memorable dialogue:

> It has been common practice to make the product of a factory running at a portion of its capacity bear the whole expense of the factory.... Mr. Gantt offers the theory that the amount of expense to be borne by the product should bear the same ratio to the total normal operating expense as the product in question bears to the normal product, and that the expense of maintaining the idle portion of the plant ready to run is a business expense not chargeable to the product made.[2]

Church did not disagree with the thrust of Gantt's argument and the logic driving his position—that idle capacity costs needed to be isolated in management reports. Church's main disagreement centered on the placement of idle capacity expense on the

Table 1-1. Eras in Capacity Cost Management

Period	Focus of Reporting	Treatment of Idle Costs	Key Features of the Period
The Age of Discovery 1900-1919 (Chapter 7)	Management	No agreement	Opening period is shaped by the Scientific Management movement and the efforts of its key spokesman, Henry Gantt. Gantt, debating A. H. Church, argues for a simple percentage approach to splitting idle capacity costs between the balance sheet and income statement. Church holds fast to the supplementary rate method. No agreement is reached during the era.
The Golden Era 1920-1932 (Chapter 8)	Management	Charge to P&L	A period of debates, the Golden Era is marked by a search for "true costs." GAAP suggests P&L treatment of idle costs, which are equated to unearned burden. Era is dominated by industrial engineering. Management held accountable for idleness. Focus is on decision support and behavioral impact of capacity reporting.
An Era of Crisis 1933-1952 (Chapter 9)	Government	Charge directly to product	Recovery and response to crisis (Depression, World War II). Accounting serves a constituent role in upholding regulations. Idle costs are buried in product costs. Period is dominated by financial accounting. No one held accountable for idle costs. Focus is on external reporting and adherence to governmental regulations.
The Full Cost Era 1953-1978 (Chapter 10)	External reporting	Charge directly to product	Managing prosperity. Full costing is accepted as best, perhaps only, acceptable costing method, with no formal promulgation to support this position. Direct costing attempts a brief stand but is soundly defeated, resulting in GAAP and IRS rulings preventing this costing method for inventory valuation. Era is dominated by financial reporting. Idle costs are all but ignored.
The Era of Questioning 1979-present (Chapter 11)	Management	Open to debate and experimentation	Search to regain relevance in management accounting. GAAP treatments of idle capacity costs once again debated. Concensus is reached by SMAC, IMA, and CAM-I to charge at least some forms of idle capacity costs directly to P&L. Period is dominated by management experts. Focus on decision support information. Many models emerging for managing capacity and its costs.

published financial statements. Contrary to Gantt, Church wanted ultimately to charge idle capacity costs to product using a supplementary burden, or overhead, rate. Church felt this treatment would provide management with the information it needed, while reflecting the traditional accounting solution to the problem.

☐ The Golden Era

The subsequent Golden Era, spanning the period from 1920 to 1932, was marked by lengthy debates and discussions about capacity and the "proper" treatment of the costs it represents. During the Golden Era, the cost of capacity was equated to the burden or total overhead of a plant or process. Reflecting a recognition that the only reason to have burden was to provide the company with the capacity to do work for its customers, the controversy focused on the choice of baseline capacity measures and the treatment of the idle capacity costs that were an inevitable part of business.

By 1926 a consensus appeared to emerge on the "proper" treatment of the burden caused by idle capacity, as reflected in the *NACA Bulletin* for the 1921, 1924, and 1926 annual meetings of the National Association of Cost Accountants (NACA— now the Institute of Management Accountants). On each of these occasions, the NACA debated the topic of idle capacity costs and their treatment, culminating in a MAAP[3] that supported Gantt's earlier position. Best practice in capacity cost management, as defined by the NACA debates during the Golden Era, included two factors.

- "Normal" capacity, or total possible time less reasonable allowance for breakdowns, repairs, inefficiency, lack of operators, and all other normal delays outside of orders, should be the baseline capacity measure;[4]
- Any over- or under-absorbed burden resulting from a difference between actual capacity utilization and normal capacity should be charged directly to the profit and loss statement at the end of the year.

Representing a marked departure from the tenets of full absorption costing, this MAAP reflected an overarching concern with providing management information that would lead to a reduction in idle capacity and the waste it entailed.

The two periods from 1900 to 1932 were the defining periods in capacity cost management because of the depth and focus of the debates that characterized them. This high-water mark in the analysis and treatment of capacity and its costs remains unmatched in its clarity and decisiveness. Part and parcel of the ongoing quest for "true" cost, the debates of the Era of Discovery and the Golden Era placed logic before politics, objectivity before conservatism, and relevance before precision.

☐ The Era of Crisis

One of the most interesting elements of historical analysis is the clear demarcation of practice apparent in retrospect, yet undetectable at the moment of change. The development of New Deal programs and policies in the United States is such a point of demarcation, representing a period of immense economic and social change whose effects are still being felt today—the Era of Crisis. For the study of capacity cost management, 1933 was a critical year, marking events that served to set aside the capacity cost MAAP of the 1920s in favor of numerous uniform industry cost codes. In tracking this change, it is apparent that accounting practitioners no longer placed a premium on providing relevant management information.

While various programs were developed and implemented between 1933 and 1936, the National Industrial Recovery Act (NIRA) ended up having the greatest impact on costing practices and capacity cost management. The NIRA's focus was on the development of financial reporting models that would neutralize what Franklin D. Roosevelt felt to be unhealthy competitive practices born of laissez-faire capitalism, practices he deemed responsible for the Depression. The NIRA was the tool used to undo the market mechanism; uniform costing and cost-plus pricing were created to replace Adam Smith's "invisible hand of the market" with a visible and enforceable alternative.

The essence of the NIRA was a quid pro quo for business. In exchange for agreeing to hire additional workers and for ensuring that all employees would be paid a solid, living wage, a company would be allowed to pass the resulting increase in cost through to the government and the market at large. Built into the structure of the cost codes was a full cost recovery model that guaranteed a *fair and reasonable profit* to any company supporting the New Deal policies and programs designed to repair the damaged economy. Excess capacity, like all forms of excess cost, was to be recovered through increased costs and prices.

It is difficult to believe that consumers would willingly pay a higher price for goods, but the NIRA had a deal for everyone involved. Companies that signed the cost code for their industry would be awarded a Blue Eagle insignia that could be placed on letterheads, in shop windows, and on products. FDR, in his fireside chat of July 24, 1933, asked housewives and families to help the nation recover by patronizing companies that displayed the Blue Eagle and to boycott those that did not. Paying a higher price was turned into a patriotic act, a symbolic joining of hands in the drive to help the nation help itself.

Based on a Supreme Court ruling on the Schecter Poultry Case, the NIRA was declared unconstitutional in 1935. Even though the NIRA was disbanded, the Blue Eagle continued to serve as a basis for receiving government contracts and for enlisting the support of consumers in the active boycott of "recalcitrants" such as Henry Ford. U. S. Steel, among other corporate giants, publicly stated in its annual reports its ongoing adherence to the industry cost codes of the NIRA long after the act was officially overturned. It was, after all, in everyone's best interest to disengage from the market.

Between 1933 and 1952, concern over and debate about capacity cost management practices dissipated. Accounting, serving a constituent role in upholding government regulations, shifted its emphasis to external reporting and compliance. Idle capacity costs, which only a few years earlier had been segregated and reported as a period expense on the income statement (based on unanimous agreement at the NACA annual meeting), were buried in product costs. No one was held accountable for idleness and waste; everyone was driven to support full cost recovery and the pricing system that grew from it. Costs were to be covered, not analyzed and minimized.

The NIRA, with its legacy embodied in the Blue Eagle, appears to be the most significant singular event shaping cost practices in the United States. It was the only time in documented history when government intervention in business practices went beyond regulating market transactions to interfering with the internal operations of the firm. The impact of the NIRA on accounting remains today, embodied in the full cost model and the reporting practices it comprises. A legacy of Roosevelt's New Deal, the full cost model and the cost-plus mentality it fostered continue to serve as an insidious but effective roadblock to change in management accounting.

☐   The Full Cost Era

Between 1953 and 1978, external reporting concerns defined the field of accounting. The Full Cost Era was a time of economic prosperity, as the United States dominated the global market. With the productive capability of Europe and Japan effectively destroyed, there was little competition to American companies. Devoid of economic threat prior to the mid-1970s, it was an economy of promise. There was little demand for cost models that supported cost minimization and analysis. In this unique setting, full cost recovery and the logic and techniques that supported it became the mainstay of accounting education and practice.

Two topics dominated the management accounting literature during this period: the direct cost/full cost controversy and variance analysis. The direct cost/full cost debate spanned the period from roughly 1950 to 1964. The "direct costers" argued that the only logical costs to attach to products were those that could be clearly and unambiguously traced to them. Fixed overhead, which consisted of a wide range of indirect costs that often had no causal relationship to the actual units produced, was seen as a period expense chargeable directly to the income statement.[5] Focused on supporting management reporting by removing the fluctuation in product costs caused by fixed or "uncontrollable" expenses, direct cost methods were presented as a logical alternative to the full cost model.

Full costing and its proponents placed little emphasis on separating fixed and variable overhead costs, intent instead on assigning "all expenses for activities provided for the benefit of manufacturing"[6] to period production. All expenses were to be absorbed by current production, regardless of the level of capacity utilization involved. The resulting cost estimates, subject to the vagaries of volume shifts and their resulting impact on average cost of production, had to be translated through variance analysis and related tools into numbers management could use.

Direct cost methods advocated conservative inventory costing methods that placed primary emphasis on developing reliable or stable cost estimates. Full costing, on the other hand, emphasized capitalizing fixed costs to inventory and supporting external reporting requirements. Backed by the IRS ruling disallowing direct costing for tax purposes, full costing won out in the end. The debate effectively put the last nail in the capacity cost management coffin as an alternative costing method. Full costing was *the* product costing method. Little room or patience was left for debating capacity issues or capacity costing approaches in the accounting literature.[7]

The negative impact of the direct cost/full cost controversy on accounting thought and practice is hard to overstate. While the NIRA appears to be the origin of the dominance of full absorption costing logic, the direct cost/full cost debate closed down all meaningful discussion of alternative accounting approaches to product costing. In addition, the fine but critical difference between the terms "variable cost" and "direct cost" was lost.

Direct costers were, in the end, variable costers, but that did not mean that variable costs were the only direct costs. Adhering to this illogical, indefensible position may have lost the debate for the direct cost proponents, but it cost management accounting far more. Lost in the process was the driving concern with causality and traceability as the basis for product costing, as well as the ability to debate the logic and impact of full cost methods.

The second half of the Full Cost era is the best testament to this argument. In the literature, concerns moved away from capacity cost management and idle capacity costs to variance analysis as the basis for management reporting. "How many variances can dance on the head of a pin" is a fitting description of the literature from 1965 to 1978. When capacity issues came up, if at all, the logic was that changing depreciation methods[8] would alleviate the problem. Implicit in this shift was a movement away from the prior position—that the capacity of a plant or process included all the resources required to keep it in a state of preparedness. Capacity was narrowed down in this period to machine utilization and the treatment of depreciation expenses.

Overhead variance analysis, however, received a much deeper examination. Discussions and examples of two-, three-, four-, and even five-way analysis of overhead variances appeared, promoted as improvements in the relevance of accounting information for decision making.[9] Capacity baselines were discussed but with an emphasis on the competing objectives of planning and control versus product costing. While the motto "different costs for different purposes" reemerged as the defining feature of management accounting, these different costs in reality were reduced in most cases to full costs and variations on variance analysis of the difference between actual and standard costs.

This is not to say that all practitioners and academics were tightly locked into the full cost model and its universal applicability but rather to note that the full cost model dominated in the accounting literature. As the discussion in Chapter 10 suggests, a core group of accounting professionals remained concerned with the choice of capacity baselines and the treatment of the volume variance that is an inevitable outcome of the full cost model. In general, however, the literature and discussions of the 1953–1978 period appear to have been concerned primarily with finding ways to adapt financial accounting data to meet management's needs for information. One accounting system could serve all users if it was adequately developed and analyzed.

□   The Era of Questioning

The complacency of the Full Cost era was shattered in the 1980s by a series of increasingly aggressive critiques of management accounting practice. The best known of these critiques is the book *Relevance Lost* by Johnson and Kaplan.[10] They shifted the attention of accounting back to management reporting and the relevance of accounting data for decision making in modern organizations. Noting that little decision relevance exists in the full cost, historical accounting model, these authors refocused the profession on debating and understanding the role of accounting in modern organizations.

Johnson and Kaplan's work opened a relative floodgate of pent-up frustration in business circles on the usefulness of existing accounting information. Accounting was seen as a dinosaur, unchanged in its practices since the early 1920s. The blame for this sad state of affairs was laid at the feet of the Securities and Exchange Acts of 1933 and 1934, in the belief that these acts forced accounting to assume a new role in the economy: ensuring the validity of external financial reports through the audit process.

As noted above, Johnson and Kaplan were correct about the source of the radical change in accounting (Roosevelt's New Deal program) and the critical time period (1933–1935) but perhaps not about the reason for the cataclysmic shift in accounting practices. In 1933 the field of accounting did more than shift its attention away from supporting the needs of management for information; it abandoned the natural logic and functioning of the market, in the process seemingly redefining the rules and nature of competition. This shift in focus was driven by the NIRA and was actively reinforced by the development of the audit programs required by the SEC Acts.

As attention in accounting today begins to shift back to supporting analysis and decision making prior to taking action (and creating costs), debates are reopening the search for the "best" method for determining product costs. Activity-based costing emerged early in this period of questioning. Inherently full cost in nature, early ABC models focused on sorting costs into activity-based pools. Through the use of drivers, the costs of an activity then were attached to the products and services that benefitted from them. ABC met with early acceptance as a more refined costing model that recognized that indirect costs have a purpose and that the role of accounting is to identify and measure the costs and benefits of these expenditures.

New journals were born of this renewed interest in the costing problem. *Journal of Cost Management, Journal of Management Accounting Research*, and *Advances in Management Accounting* emerged as additions to the ongoing publication *Management Accounting*.[11] Strategic cost management, target costing, life-cycle costing, and activity-based management, to name just a few models, had their birth in this period of renewal and self-reflection for the accounting profession. Debate on the purpose and nature of costing reappeared, signaling an end to the placid acceptance of full cost logic.

Behind this marked shift in the nature and focus of management accounting was the global market and its impact on the world of business. New demands for information gave way to new techniques, not because the value of this knowledge was just being recognized but rather because the need for it was so strong. The global market, laissez-faire in nature, proved to be a harsh disciplinarian, removing the comfortable buffer provided by the managed economy born of Roosevelt's New Deal. The impact of global competition and the loss of supremacy in the world market lay behind the renewed pressure and demand for relevant cost information—information that arrives before action, not after it.

As the full cost model was increasingly contested and the role of management accounting shifted away from serving as a "feeder" to the external reporting process to being an integral part of the management information system, capacity and capacity cost management issues began to reappear in the literature. As detailed in Chapter 11, the 1990s saw an exponential increase in the articles, books, and debates on capacity and its impact on the costing process.

This burgeoning interest is reflected in the results of the empirical analysis detailed in Part I of this monograph. As seen in Chapters 3 through 5, companies are once again experimenting with various tools and techniques for analyzing and managing capacity *and the costs it causes.* Having gone full circle, capacity is once again being defined as the capability to do work, as the cost of preparedness. This cost includes all the resources a company obtains to support the productive process. Overhead has reemerged, not as a cost to be tallied and spread across products but as the critical component in the value-creating process. In its rebirth, capacity cost management is proving to be the critical link between accounting information and the decisions it supports.

The Present State of
Capacity Cost Management Practice

The reemergence and proliferation of capacity cost management models appear to be logical outgrowths of the renewed interest in cost models. For instance, Cooper and Kaplan have discussed capacity as it is defined and managed within an activity-based costing framework.[12] Goldratt's theory of constraints is, in reality, an elaborate capacity management system. Organizations such as CAM-I (Consortium for Advanced Manufacturing-International) and Sematech are developing elaborate capacity cost management systems for use by member firms. It would appear that, after a long and interesting history, capacity cost management is once again taking center stage in the ongoing discussion of cost and its meaning.[13]

The magnitude and type of interest in capacity cost management appear, based on the results of this study, to be tied ultimately to two primary factors: macroeconomic trends and the degree of consensus on cost practices. Specifically, as macroeconomic pressure on a company increases, reducing its short-term profitability and performance, managers are more likely to reassess the nature and total amount of resources the company is currently consuming. In a related aspect, as the nature and definition of the cost of various outputs and activities are questioned, attention appears to be drawn to the assumptions and definitions of the capacity or amount of work this cost represents. Conversely, when economic times are more bountiful, capacity and the costs it creates appear to fade from view. Interest in cost and capacity appears to be linked to the economic reality of the marketplace (see Figure 1-1).

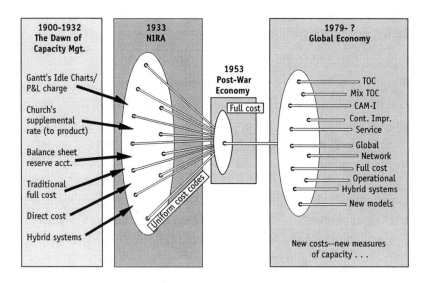

Figure 1-1. The Historical Development of Capacity Cost Management

While it is impossible ever to state with finality that any one force or any one event creates change at a macroeconomic or microeconomic level, it is logical to suggest that changes in the role of accounting in the macroeconomic arena would shift the nature of core practices and techniques within the field. Capacity, an essential component of the cost equation and the information it provides, appears to be debated only when the concept of cost itself is being questioned. Today as in the early 1900s, there is little certainty about what defines best practice in costing or what constitutes a relevant cost estimate. The models and techniques being developed and implemented today in companies around the globe reflect this renewed curiosity and a contingent view of the concept of cost and the capacity to create value it provides.

☐ Emerging Capacity Cost Management Practices

Proof that the issues surrounding capacity cost management are playing a central role in the cost debates of the day can be found in the plethora of articles, workshops, and capacity cost models emerging in the management literature. As detailed in Part I of this monograph, numerous new and unique approaches to capacity cost management currently are being debated, promoted, and used by companies in North America. The Institute of Management Accountants, the Society of Management Accountants of Canada, and CAM-I have joined hands, taking a decisive position on best practice in capacity cost management by carrying out a joint research project. The results were published by the IMA as Statement on Management Accounting 4Y.[14]

Table 1-2 provides a summary description of 12 of the models identified during the course of this study. Of these 12 models, seven were studied in more depth through case studies and discussions, specifically:

- Normalized costing,
- Mix-adjusted capacity reporting,
- Resource effectiveness model,
- Capacity variance model,

- CAM-I model,
- CUBES model,
- Cost containment model.

The ways these models are being defined, applied, and used by companies are described in Chapters 3 through 5. These case studies provide evidence of the diversity of issues and approaches that make up modern capacity cost management practices.

Implicit and at times explicit in all these models is the ghost of the 1926 debates and their single-minded focus on creating usable, stable, relevant cost estimates for decision making. The cost of idle capacity and its sundry causes are once again being highlighted in management reports, not hidden in product costs. As attention shifts toward planning and away from control re-

Table 1-2. Capacity Cost Management Models

Features / Model	Primary Time Frame	Organizational Level	Capacity Baseline Emphasized	Suggested Treatment of Idle Capacity Costs	Primary Focus of Model
Gantt idleness charts	Short-term	Process	Practical	Charge to P&L	Efficiency/utilization
Supplemental rate method	Short-term	Process/plant	Practical	Charge to product	Idle capacity costs
Normalized cost	Intermediate	Process/plant	Normal	Charge to P&L	Decision analysis
Theory of constraints	Short to intermediate	Process/plant/company	Practical (marketable)	None suggested	Throughput
Mix-adjusted model	Short-term	Process/plant	Theoretical	Charge to P&L	Throughput
Resource effectiveness model	Short- to long-term	Process/plant/company	Theoretical	Charge to P&L	Resource utilization
Capacity utilization analysis	Short to intermediate	Process/plant/company	Theoretical	Charge to P&L	Resource utilization
Capacity variance model	Short to intermediate	Process/plant	Theoretical	None suggested	Causality/analysis
Activity-based cost model	Short to intermediate	Process/plant/company	Normal	Charge to P&L	Cost of resources used
CAM-I model	Short- to long-term	All levels (potential)	Theoretical	Charge to P&L	Communication
CUBES model	Short to intermediate	Process/plant/company	Theoretical	None suggested	Process utilization
Cost containment model	Intermediate	All levels (potential)	Implicit theoretical	None suggested	Total cost/resources

porting, companies and the cost systems that support them are again emphasizing responsibility for minimizing this costly drain on profitability and long-term performance.

The future of capacity cost management appears brighter than it has been at any time in the past, as new models, new logic, and new capabilities are added to the management accountant's tool kit. No longer concerned with finding the "right" answer to the capacity question, companies are turning their attention toward identifying and measuring capacity and capacity costs from many different perspectives for many different time frames and uses. The present state-of-the-art in capacity cost management is, as it was in the early 1900s, best summarized as a period of analysis and exploration, as companies search for ways to improve their performance in the short, intermediate, and long term.

☐ Key Issues in Capacity Cost Management

A variety of methods were used in completing the research contained in this monograph, including historical analysis, case-based field research, and Delphi methodologies. Each element of the research design yielded significant, unique insight into the complex area of capacity cost management. The historical analysis defined the range and nature of change in capacity reporting practices, the field study provided details on current practice in the area, and the Delphi approach served to identify and define key issues surrounding capacity.

Attention now turns to the results of the Delphi segment of the study. The essence of capacity cost management, as defined by a Delphi group of capacity experts,[15] is "to profitably manage the value generating competencies, processes and capacities of an organization in ways that support the strategic direction of the business."

Capacity cost management appears to mean more than measuring and directing short-term capacity utilization; in the minds of these experts it seems to be intricately tied to the future of the firm. This forward-looking view of capacity cost management is reinforced by the list of objectives developed during the Delphi process. Specifically, the objectives of capacity cost management as agreed upon by these experts included:

- In the short run, to optimize capital decisions and the effective and flexible use of investments that have already been made;
- To maximize the value delivered to customers;
- To help minimize requirements for future investment;
- To support effective matching of resources with current and future market demands;
- To eliminate waste in the short, intermediate, and long run;
- To support the establishment of capacity measurements that identify the cost of capacity and its impact on business cycles and overall company performance;
- To identify the capacity required to meet strategic and operational objectives as well as estimate currently available capacity;
- To detail the cost of unused capacity and suggest ways to account for that cost;
- To create a common language for and understanding of capacity cost management and the issues that define it.

As defined by the Delphi group, attaining these objectives is the essence of an effective capacity cost management system. These objectives provide the basic framework for defining and utilizing capacity cost management. The framework requires that decisions be made concerning:

- Resource capability;
- Baseline measures of capacity;
- Estimated cost of capacity under different levels of utilization;
- Capacity management objectives in the short, intermediate, and long term;
- Capacity issues and objectives at different organizational levels (i.e., process, unit, company, and total value chain);
- Analysis and choice of appropriate capacity cost management tools given the existing company strategy and core objectives;
- Analysis and improvement in actual capacity utilization.

It is this range of issues, objectives, and decisions that shapes the structure and conclusions on the capacity cost management framework presented in this monograph.

In its totality, then, this study details the historical development of capacity cost management practices, samples the range of approaches being used by companies to deal with capacity issues today, and integrates these findings with the information gathered during the final phase, or Delphi group, to suggest a model for the future development of capacity cost management (see Chapter 5). Throughout this discussion, the focus will be on the many different thoughts and approaches that can be used to understand and manage capacity costs in a wide variety of settings.

The ultimate goal of the analysis and discussion of capacity cost management presented here, then, is not to suggest one "right" way to measure and manage capacity costs but rather to present the many different views and models that have evolved to date and that can be used to support improvement in current and future utilization of this capability. Underlying this approach is one core belief: effective capacity cost management is not a destination, it is a journey—a *movable feast*.

> When there is no difference, there is only indifference.—
> Louis Nizer

☐ References and Notes

1   J. Whitmore, "Factory Accounting Applied to Machine Shops," Part VI, *Journal of Accountancy*, January 1907, p. 213.
2   H. L. Gantt, "The Relation Between Production and Costs," *American Machinist*, June 17, 1915, p. 1055.
3   Within this monograph, the term "MAAP," managerially accepted accounting principle, will be used to designate agreements made on accounting issues based on best management practice rather than traditional accounting concerns. The MAAP on idle capacity costs discussed here is developed in more depth in Chapter 8.
4   In modern terminology, this form of capacity would be called "practical." Throughout this monograph, the shift in the use of "normal" away from its practical roots remains, as it is embedded in the historical text.
5   The comments in this section are based on a concise and well-prepared article, "Why Not Capacity Costing?" by R. K. Jones, *NAA Bulletin*,

November 1957, pp. 13–21. Arguing for capacity costing as a mid-range solution in the direct cost/full cost controversy, Jones provided clear descriptions of the key positions of the two dominant schools of thought and how capacity costing would mediate many of their seemingly unreconcilable differences.

6   Ibid., p. 13.

7   Jones's 1957 article (op. cit.) states that "capacity costing absorbs all variable costs, as in direct costing, plus the portion of fixed expenses which the volume of production bears to the attainable capacity" (p. 14). This logical mid-range solution is lost in the literature of the day but seems prophetic, given the nature and focus of capacity cost management practices today.

8   Ferrara was a primary proponent of the logic that idle capacity was a myth. Focusing solely on the utilization of machines, he argued that changing to units of production depreciation would eliminate this issue. Ferrara's logic went deeper than this position, though, as he argued for a "cycle" overhead concept, similar to the normalized cost found during the field work being used at Caterpillar. For further details see "Idle Capacity as a Loss: Fact or Fiction?", *Accounting Review*, July 1960, pp. 490–496. Ferrara, in discussions with the authors, has since substantially modified the position taken in this earlier work.

9   A prime example of this approach is P. Johnson's "Decision-Making Aspects of Overhead Variance Analysis," *Cost and Management*, November-December 1976, pp. 49–53.

10   *Relevance Lost: The Rise and Fall of Management Accounting,* H. T. Johnson and R. S. Kaplan, Boston: Harvard Business School Press, 1987.

11   *Management Accounting* is the most recent title given to the continuous publication of management accounting issues begun with the birth of the National Association of Cost Accountants (NACA) in 1919.

12   R. Cooper and R. S. Kaplan, "Activity-Based Systems: Measuring the Costs of Resource Usage," *Accounting Horizons,* September 1992, pp. 1–12.

13   Capacity cost management is the field of management accounting that addresses capacity measurement and management issues. The objective of capacity cost management is to provide information to management about the potential impact of its decisions to change the amount or nature of available capacity. Whether this change involves physical resources or the processes and people that bring these resources to life, the goal is the same: to improve profitability and long-term performance.

14   This Statement (SMA 4Y, "Measuring the Cost of Capacity"), written by the authors of this monograph, is available from the Institute of Management Accountants, Montvale, NJ.

15   In the process of completing this study, the Society of Management Accountants of Canada conducted a day-long meeting of experts from industry and academe in the area of capacity cost management. The group of 10 practitioners and academics debated topics such as the definition and focus of capacity cost management, providing much of the detail in this section.

2

MEASURING AND MANAGING CAPACITY COSTS

...management has two controls over the amount of work in a system: input into the system and output from it. Whenever the input rate exceeds the output rate, the work in the system increases, and vice versa....to be able to get the right work out, one must first get enough work out; that is, capacity planning must precede priority planning.[1]

Business planning starts with defining, measuring, and determining the management policies that will shape the *capacity* of a firm. Capacity, the value-creating ability of the resources accessible to an organization, is an assumption, a concept that is neither easily measured nor managed.

Systemic in nature, capacity and capacity costs defy simple methods of analysis. While few would argue that capacity and its management are essential to the creation of a sustainable, profitable enterprise, few can agree on what capacity really is, how best to measure it, and the most appropriate way to track its use. Capacity cost management is a movable feast because it is such an illusory concept.

Yet managers live in the world of facts, figures, and consequences, all very real and very measurable in the coin of the realm: corporate profits and shareholder value. The recognition that measurements drive performance creates the need to grapple with the basic issues of the capacity cost management problem and potential solutions to it. In this chapter, the issues shaping capacity measurement and management will be discussed, laying the foundation for probing the impact of changing time frames and management focus on capacity management, in the remainder of Part I.

Basics of Capacity Cost Management

The first step in capacity cost management is reaching a consensus within an organization on what capacity is and the baseline measures used to capture this capability. Having agreed on the basic capacity of the firm or process, attention turns to making estimates of the cost of a unit of capacity, how to track and report the utilization of existing capacity, and how to improve company performance in this key area. Unutilized capacity that cannot be ·stored is *waste*; on this fact capacity experts agree. Minimizing wasted capacity, whether that waste is stored in unnecessary inventory, reflected in pure idleness, hidden by rework, or buried in standards, is the ultimate goal of capacity cost management.

The basic economics of business drive the capacity cost management practices of a firm (see Figure 2-1). Specifically, a company faces a market-defined price barrier that constrains the amount of resources it can profitably consume in creating products and services for customers. The market price barrier is based on an assessment by customers of the *value* of the product/service bundle offered by the company. This value assessment takes into account the core product attributes,[2] including functionality, quality, reliability, availability, and the total economic worth of the resources sacrificed to obtain it.

A shorthand view of Figure 2-1 and its implications is that the market price for a product is based on a core set of value-

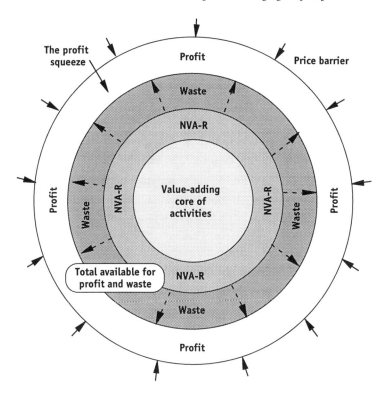

Figure 2-1. The Basic Economics of Business

adding activities (VAC), transformations and transactions performed by the company to meet customer requirements. If the
VAC is reduced in the customer's eyes, the market price com-
manded by the product will drop. Relatedly, as the VAC is expanded, the defined market price increases. This phenomenon
is reflected in the growing trend by manufacturing and service
companies toward "enhancing," that is, bundling several products and services and so creating a higher-value product that
meets multiple needs or provides superior service and satisfaction for the customer.

Profit, waste, and nonvalue-adding activities and the resources
they consume complete the picture of the firm suggested here.
Effective management of the entire set of resources available to
the firm—its capacity—enhances profitability. Ineffectiveness

and waste reduce profit. Given this perspective, then, the essence of capacity cost management is *to manage profitably the value-generating competencies, processes and capacities of an organization in ways that support the strategic direction of the business.*[3]

A company achieves this objective by pursuing the following goal: *minimize the unit cost of production within the VAC and minimize waste by establishing appropriate benchmarks, improving related processes, and utilizing resources more effectively.*

Managing capacity is not a one-time event or confined to the moment a resource is used. In fact, the impact of capacity cost management practices starts at the moment a product or process is designed. The structure of a process and the effective and efficient use of this capability by the firm's mix of products and services intertwine to affect the overall profitability and competitiveness of the company.

Capacity cost management, then, begins with the planning of products and processes and continues on through subsequent disposal and reassignment of these resources downstream. Driven by the life cycle of the firm and its ever-changing mix of products and services, effective capacity utilization is a primary goal of the operational, tactical, and strategic decision-making processes.

Capacity cost management creates a number of challenges at all levels of the enterprise. The actual costs and implications of current capacity utilization levels and idleness are baseline issues that have to be dealt with by every firm, regardless of what products and services it offers. Only effectively used capacity results in profits; all other uses of capacity actually reduce the company's profits. The capacity cost management system has to make this basic economic fact visible as well as providing the basis for taking action to improve performance.

The Basic Language of Capacity

Developing a comprehensive approach to capacity and its management requires the creation of a common language for discussing and measuring capacity utilization. While different contexts and strategic objectives shift the focus and importance of specific elements of the capacity puzzle, the basic definitions and concepts that guide best practice in capacity cost management remain unchanged. Specifically, six key issues combine to create the basic language of capacity cost management:

- Resource capability,
- Baseline capacity measures,
- Capacity deployment,
- Capacity utilization measures,
- Time frame of analysis, and
- Organizational focus or strategy.

The definitions and issues encompassed by each of these six points reflect current best practice, as defined by the joint efforts of capacity experts from the Institute of Management Accountants, CAM-I, the American Institute of Certified Public Accountants, and the Society of Management Accountants of Canada. In the ever-changing, ever-maturing area of capacity cost management, best practice is the best if not the only guideline for establishing company policies.

☐ Resource Capability

To survive and prosper, a business requires resources and the ability to use them effectively. These resources provide the capability to create value for the customer and therefore to support the revenue-generating efforts of the firm. Due to the central role played by resources and resource capability in capacity cost management, their flexibility and match to current company and customer requirements is a critical element of capacity cost management.

Resources are *the potential for creating value that an organization buys and uses to support its activities and outputs.* Resource capability, then, is the amount and type of work a resource can support. Resource capability is affected by the storability, flexibility, and useful life of a resource. For instance, a multifunction machine such as a universal drill press is a resource whose capability to create value can be stored for an indeterminate time period, can be used in a variety of ways and on a variety of products, and has a definable and significant useful life. In contrast, the capability of a human being at any point in time, while flexible, is short-lived in nature and cannot be stored. While the individual's capability can be retained and perhaps enhanced over the long term, the enterprise purchases, measures, and manages the value-creating potential of any individual in minutes and hours.

Resource capability requires the investment of time, money, and effort at several points. First, there is the *cost of preparedness,* the initial and continuing costs of readying resources for activity or use. A related factor is the *estimated cost,* the total economic value of all resources consumed in performing an activity over a period of time. Estimated costs include the purchase price of the resource, the preparedness and operating costs required to reap the benefits the resource can provide, and the downstream costs of disposing of the resource once its useful life has expired.

Accurately capturing the patterned matching of these costs or inputs and the outputs they provide to the enterprise and its stakeholders (i.e., the *behavior* of costs) is the major challenge in creating and using any cost system. A capacity cost management system is not exempt from the conundrums created by the *variability* of costs or the relationship between the amount of work done and the units or amount of resources this activity consumes (that is, fixed, variable, semifixed, or semivariable costs). In fact, cost variability is of major concern in creating and using capacity cost estimates. Coupled with the nefarious *relevant range,* the set of assumptions over which the defined cost patterns and capacity estimates are believed to be reasonably accurate, cost variability shapes the behavioral and organizational impact of capacity cost management systems.

In creating a capacity cost management system, the designer has to understand the core nature of the company's existing and potential resources, as well as how flexible, adaptable, reliable, and long-lived this value-creating potential is. Capacity is, after all, the denominator in the cost equation. Detailed knowledge regarding what the company's resources can do and are doing to create value for customers, as well as how readily their value-creating nature can be tailored to specific needs at any point, lies at the heart of the capacity problem. Mastering capacity management begins with understanding resource capability and how the company's activities consume it.

☐ Baseline Capacity Measures

Resources represent a company's capability to do work. The amount of work these resources can support, their *available capacity*, is the second major assumption made in creating a capacity cost management system. While many different views exist about which baseline or maximum capacity estimate is most logical, the core definitions of these options are less disputed.

Five basic measures of baseline capacity can be used in creating the capacity cost estimate: theoretical capacity, practical capacity, normal capacity, budgeted capacity, and actual capacity utilization (see Figure 2-2). *Theoretical capacity* is the optimum

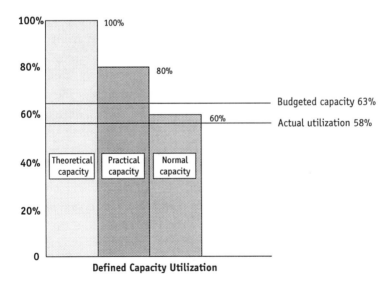

Figure 2-2. Baseline Definitions of Capacity

amount of work that a process or plant can complete using a 24-hour, seven-day operation with zero waste. It allows for no adjustment for preventive maintenance, unplanned downtime, shutdowns, or any other form of nonproductive capacity. Rather than building the estimated impact of these "normal" events into the cost standards, theoretical capacity cost estimates track the deployment of resources, regardless of the value created, desirability, or "commonness" of this use. When theoretical capacity is used, the capacity reporting system provides a total and comprehensive analysis of the actual deployment of the capability of the resources, process, or system.

Practical capacity is usually defined as the level of output generally attainable by a process; it is theoretical capacity adjusted downward for unavoidable nonproductive time, such as setups, maintenance, or breakdowns. While practical capacity is often more palatable to practicing managers, it is inferior to theoretical capacity because it *builds waste into* the cost standards. Embedding waste in standards is at odds with the philosophy of continuous improvement that defines modern business practice. Practical capacity may seem more reasonable, but employing it starts a company down the path of hiding and accepting waste.

Where theoretical and practical capacity start from the assessed value-creating capability of the firm's resources, the remaining three capacity baseline measures are driven by current company performance. Specifically, *normal capacity* is the average and expected utilized capacity of machine, process, or plant/unit over a defined period of time, while *budgeted capacity* is the planned utilization of the affected resources over the coming year. Often stated in earned man-hours, machine-hours, units of output, or percentage of normal capacity, budgeted capacity is currently the most common capacity baseline in companies using standard cost systems. Finally, *actual capacity* is the capacity deployed by the company for period production. A scorecard of what transpired during the period rather than what might have happened, actual capacity measurements are the least informative and least defensible basis for creating capacity cost estimates.

Given these various baselines, what measure makes the most sense? The answer to this question depends on several things. Specifically, the use that is going to be made of the resulting cost estimate or standard, as well as the assumed avoidability of specific types of capacity loss such as that due to planned downtime or existing management policies, drives the acceptability and desirability of a specific baseline measure. While many arguments can be and have been made about the relative worth of theoretical versus practical capacity baselines, these two measures remain the only defensible baselines if the underlying objective of capacity cost management, namely the elimination of nonvalue-added activities or waste from the productive process, is to be attained.

Theoretical capacity often is rejected out of hand by practitioners and academics alike as being impractical. In fact, early research in management accounting would suggest that theoretical capacity baselines, being by nature unattainable, would be demotivating.[4] To date, though, little research exists on the behavioral impact of "unattainable" standards in a continuous improvement setting. As such, the only proof that theoretical capacity may not be undesirable or impractical lies in the experiences of best practice firms. Companies such as Motorola, Texas Instruments, Hewlett-Packard, and Hills Pet Nutrition, a division of Colgate Palmolive, are effectively using theoretical capacity baseline measures within a continuous improvement philosophy of management. For these firms, it appears that theoretical capacity is a viable baseline, given their existing management policies and strategic objectives.

Accepting for the moment that theoretical capacity does exist and can be estimated accurately in some settings, the main argument for the use of theoretical capacity baseline measures lies in the search for *stable, reliable cost estimates*. Theoretical capacity is the only baseline capacity measure that yields a cost estimate that will remain the same regardless of how resources are deployed, what time frame is used for analysis, or which decisions are being considered. In a world driven by theoretical capacity concepts, the long-standing debate over incremental business and its impact disappears. If a company cannot meet the price barrier for its goods and services set by the market using theoretical capacity, it cannot compete. In this setting, incremental business represents a potential signal from the market that the customer-defined market value of the company's goods and services may be changing.

The arguments for and against theoretical capacity will likely continue ad infinitum. For a company designing a firm-specific capacity cost management system, the only relevant question is, what measure will create the desired behavioral, economic, and competitive impact? What baseline capacity measure will ensure that all forms of waste are identified and made candidates for elimination? What baseline capacity measure will be accepted by the culture of the firm, as reflected by its major stakeholders? The decision to move away from theoretical capacity has to be made carefully, for in the process the capacity cost management system stands to lose information content. Capacity cost management is a decision-making tool, an approach designed to support managers in making difficult decisions about what resources to attain, what resources to use, and what types of business to pursue. The effectiveness of the baseline measure of capacity in creating desired behavior and supporting essential business decisions is the only guideline that matters. For every firm this decision will be unique.[5]

☐ Capacity Deployment

Having established the baseline capacity of a process, the focus of the capacity cost management system design shifts to measuring the deployment of the capacity deemed to be available for use. There are generally believed to be five major categories of capacity deployment:[6] productive capacity, planned idle capacity, unplanned nonproductive capacity, excess capacity, and nonproductive capacity. *Productive capacity* is capacity that provides value to the customer. Productive capacity is used to actually produce a product or provide a service. According to existing

MAAP, the estimated cost of a unit of productive capacity should be based on the theoretical, assumed, maximum value-creating ability of the firm.[7] *Planned idle capacity* is nonproductive capacity that is currently not scheduled for use, having been set aside due to temporary lack of demand, preventive maintenance, or other management policy-driven reasons, such as planned shutdowns. *Unplanned nonproductive capacity* or unplanned idle time, on the other hand, is capacity planned for use that is temporarily out of action due to process variability, such as the lack of materials, machine or process breakdowns, or other delays or process defects.

Excess capacity is permanently idle capacity that is not marketable or usable under existing operating, marketing, or policy conditions. The final category, *nonproductive capacity*, is capacity that is neither in a productive state nor in one of the defined idle states. It includes setups, unplanned maintenance, and capacity consumed by making scrap or performing rework (for example, making or correcting errors). These categories combine to capture 100% of the deployment of potential capacity for a given time period (see Figure 2-3).

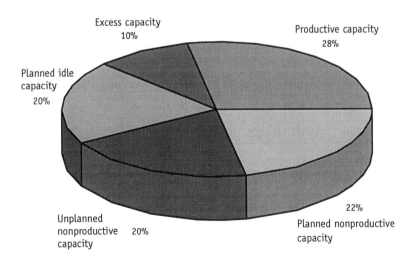

Figure 2-3. Capacity Deployment

The cost and potential implications of various levels of capacity deployment are established when the process or system is designed. The flexibility of the process, the total potential capability of the system, the embedded or structural waste, and the total estimated cost of using a unit of the provided capacity are driven by initial design decisions that establish the scope and nature of the resource commitments of the firm.

Given the fact that, once purchased, capacity becomes embedded in the structure and economics of the firm, assessing the value of specific capacity investments should factor in all levels of existing capacity and all potential options for attaining the needed throughput at minimal cost. This evaluation is most beneficial if done at the design or investment stage, where an analysis of whether the capacity that is planned to be put into place is the appropriate investment, including whether it meets existing firm risk profiles.

According to results of the field study, it appears that in creating a capacity cost management system it is important to track and report the current capacity deployment patterns and to provide this information in usable form prior to the decision to make further investments in plant, equipment, or processes. As suggested by Figure 2-4, a significant amount of *structural* capacity waste can be built into a system at its onset. Structural capacity waste, the sum of wasted resource capability made unavoidable by the design of the process and its constraints (bottlenecks), is a permanent drag on the profits of the firm.

Once the system is designed, it would appear that the only capacity element that can be managed is the deployment of the system's capability as defined by its bottleneck or constraining operation or activity. Idle capacity, as well as the other forms of productive and nonproductive capacity, captures only the use of currently available capacity, not the total potential of all the resources dedicated to the process, operation, or activity. Effective capacity cost management systems, then, apparently need to:

- Track the level of potential structural waste in any plant or process design;

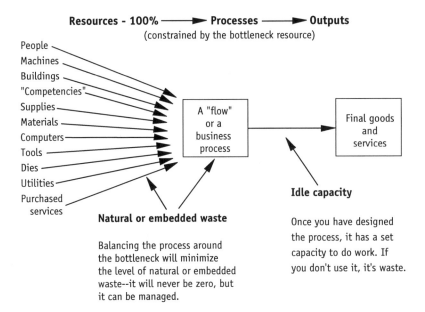

Resources - 100% ━━━▶ **Processes** ━━━▶ **Outputs**
(constrained by the bottleneck resource)

People
Machines
Buildings
"Competencies"
Supplies
Materials
Computers
Tools
Dies
Utilities
Purchased
services

A "flow"
or a
business
process

Final goods
and
services

Idle capacity

Natural or embedded waste

Balancing the process around
the bottleneck will minimize
the level of natural or embedded
waste--it will never be zero, but
it can be managed.

Once you have designed
the process, it has a set
capacity to do work. If
you don't use it, it's waste.

You have to measure waste if you're going to eliminate it.

Figure 2-4. Structural Vs. Idle Capacity Waste

- Support the search for alternative means to obtain the desired output, such as outsourcing;
- Ensure that, once resources have been committed to a process, they are used effectively in creating value for customers.

In the end, organizations making capacity decisions need to balance the impact of the decision on customer value measurements, such as defect levels, product delivery performance, and product prices. Capacity cost management is an intricate part of this decision process.

☐ Capacity Utilization Measures

The findings of this study indicate that deployment measures normally are built during the planning phase of operations. Once capacity is activated, the capacity cost management system (CCMS) turns its attention to tracking and reporting actual performance against these plans and the profit and cost implications of this performance. According to current practice and theory in operational capacity cost management (see Chapter 3), key factors in assessing capacity utilization include:

- *Throughput,* the rate at which a system generates revenues through sales;[8]
- *Activation,* the amount of time that a process is physically used during a period, whether or not the resulting output is needed to meet customer requirements;
- *Utilization,* the amount of time that the process is used to meet customer requirements or generates throughput;
- *Waste,* the nonproductive use of a company's resources;
- *Efficiency,* the total utilization of the process as a percent of the baseline capacity measure;
- *Standby capacity,* excess capacity used as a buffer to absorb unplanned shifts in the workload or other unavoidable forms of process variation;
- *Manageable capacity,* the amount of capacity that can be affected by a specific manager or management group, resulting in higher or lower total resource requirements or utilization;
- *Cost of capacity,* the total economic value of all the resources needed to keep a process at a specific stage of preparedness or deployment.

It is in the area of utilization that the cost and operational aspects of capacity cost management are brought together in a reporting format that focuses attention on the effectiveness and efficiency of resource deployment. Capacity utilization costs in the observed models are not limited to machine or asset depreciation charges. They include all the indirect resources, the overhead consumed to keep a process in a state of preparedness. Theoretical capacity applied to the physical assets of the firm provides the basis for the *relevant range* of the cost estimating exercise. Clearly, resources that cannot be deployed for 24 hours, seven days a week without renewal of their "purchase" are treated as semifixed, semivariable, or variable costs by the CCMS.

Accounting for Costs of Capacity, published in 1963 by the IMA (then the National Association of Accountants), provided an accounting-centered view of capacity costs and their definition. While many insightful comments and suggestions were made in this monograph, the authors' separation of capacity costs into *committed* and *managed* categories is a useful way to approach the cost estimation problem embedded in capacity costing. Committed capacity costs are those costs that are unavoidable in the short and intermediate term, while managed capacity costs are avoidable during this time period. The total cost of capacity, then, can be split into the following two components:

C_C: Estimated cost of capacity that will be experienced by the firm regardless of how it deploys its resources. C_C should be measured on a theoretical baseline and will incorporate most of the traditional "fixed" costs of operation.

C_M: The various levels and costs of resources consumed when the decision is made to hold the system in a state of preparedness or activation. Incorporating all the "non-fixed" or stepped costs, regardless of their degree of variability, C_M can be viewed as one complete cost formula for each of the potential or planned levels of activation. The baseline capacity measure here will be the predefined activation levels.

C_T: The total of C_C and C_M for the given level of activation.

The estimated cost of capacity for a process that is in a planned idle mode logically should be lower than that experienced during its productive periods.

Reflecting actual performance and its effectiveness, capacity utilization measures are the raw data for constructing management reports and engaging in various types of capacity planning activities. When matched with the appropriate cost-of-capacity estimate, utilization measures provide management with detailed information on the efficiency and effectiveness of current operations as well as the short-, intermediate-, and long-term potential for profit improvement through improved utilization. Tracking utilization without attaching the cost and profit implications of current performance reduces the impact of capacity reporting systems while severing a critical link between capacity management practices and financial results. Dollarized capacity estimates bring the economic message embedded in capacity reporting approaches to everyone's attention, in objective and understandable terms.

☐ Time Frame of Analysis

According to the data gathered during this study, three basic approaches can be taken to capacity management: operational, tactical, and strategic. As suggested by Table 2-1, these three views reflect the changing time frame and context of decisions that affect available capacity and its deployment. The three levels of capacity analysis reflect the life cycle of the firm:

- Short-term, operational time frames where decisions are focused on the flow of resources through existing plant and processes;
- Intermediate-term, tactical time frames where management decisions on capacity emphasize the changes in the processes that make up the value chain;

Table 2-1. Capacity Cost Management Phases

	Operational	Tactical	Strategic
Time frame of analysis	Short-term	Intermediate term	Long-term
Value chain emphasis	Velocity through existing processes	Removing NVA activities from processes	Structural change
Range of motion	Highly constrained	Moderate constraints	Minimal constraints
Management level involved	Lower to middle	All levels	Top management

- A long-term, strategic time frame that allows for questioning and changing all the physical, product-driven, and process-based constraints of the existing system. The structure of the value chain is the focus of decisions at this level.

At each of the three levels of capacity analysis and management, different issues arise. For operational capacity management, the emphasis is on managing the *velocity of materials*, the resources, through existing processes. Focused on current utilization levels compared to those that would be expected if only required activation was undertaken, operational capacity analysis is concerned with the short-term causes of process and demand variation and their impact on current profits and costs.

In the intermediate term, management turns its attention to making changes in the existing processes or their management. By eliminating nonvalue-added activities, streamlining processes, and searching out the least costly combination of existing resources and outside support, tactical decision making focuses on balancing existing process capability with emerging demand. In the tactical arena, critical areas are the flexibility of resources and processes and innovative ways to shift the nature of the flow or capacity of existing systems with minimal incremental investment.

Strategic capacity cost management is the engine driving the long-term profitability of a firm. It is at this level of analysis that new processes and systems are designed, the core structure and therefore committed costs of a process are locked in, and the potential competitive nature of the firm and its products is determined. Strategic alliances, building new plants, or shifting the product or marketing focus of the firm are all decisions that influence current and future capacity and its ability to create value for the customer.

For each time frame, it appears that a different set of issues and a different group of capacity tools and measurements apply. The remaining chapters in Part I deal exclusively with the cost, decision-making, and managerial issues confronting a company under these highly varying contexts.

□ Organizational Focus and Capacity Cost Management

The final dimension that seems to shape the design and use of capacity cost management systems is the unit of analysis, the focus of the organization. At least four potential levels must considered: the process level, the plant or subunit level, the company level, and the value-chain level.

The first three levels of analysis represent layers within the "skin" of the organization. The process level, which can range from one task to an assembly line, focuses on individual units of output and their velocity through the system. At the plant or subunit level, several different processes and unique types of outputs (product lines) are affected, while at the company level many different plants, processes, or subunits combine to create a complex organization that serves many different customers and markets.

The value-chain level of analysis captures those situations and opportunities that are outside the direct purview of the firm but that affect the total capability of the entire chain of companies needed to transform natural resources and basic competencies into final goods and services purchased by the consumer. Increasing empirical evidence shows that often a company can achieve significant improvements in its own capacity utilization by acting on other parts of the value chain. For instance, if a supplier's materials are creating unnecessary and undesirable variation in a process, the solution to this problem of nonproductive capacity may lie in helping suppliers improve their processes.

In putting the information provided by a comprehensive capacity cost management system to work to solve capacity problems, it appears that management needs to be able to explore the various levels of analysis (process through value chain) over all affected time periods and assumptions to ensure that solutions result in total improvement, not more or different kinds of waste. Companies using these systems increasingly are turning to relational database structures that feed into a variety of simulation programs to bring the power of capacity cost management to bear. Recent developments in areas such as fuzzy set theory and computer technologies all point toward a flexible, fluid, and evolving approach to capacity management—a truly movable feast.

The Capacity Conundrum

> Waste is worse than loss. The time is coming when every person who lays claim to ability will keep the question of waste before him constantly. The scope of thrift is limitless.—Thomas A. Edison

Defining the core issues and concepts embedded in measuring and managing capacity can seem at times like a monumental task, an unsolvable problem that defies every attempt at solution. This is a highly defensible position—any attempt made to define and measure capacity precisely is doomed to failure. Then why try?

The driving force behind the renewed interest in capacity cost management is the recognition by managers and the society they reflect that the ongoing, excessive waste of the productive capability of the world's scarce resources cannot continue.

The answer to the capacity management problem lies, then, not in finding *the* correct way to measure capacity but rather in understanding what events and decisions create wasted capacity and excess resource consumption. While capacity cannot be tightly defined, wasted capacity appears visible and measurable.

The combined results of this study suggest, therefore, that effective capacity cost management requires a recognition of and attention to the following issues:[9]

- In the short run, optimizing capital decisions and the effective and flexible use of investments that have already been made;
- Maximizing the value delivered to customers;

- Minimizing the requirement for future investment when possible;
- Supporting effective matching of a firm's resources with current and future market opportunities;
- Closing any gap between market demands and a firm's capabilities. At times, the firm may have excess capabilities; at others, shortages may exist. These capabilities may be physical, labor, technology, or capital based;
- Eliminating waste in the short, intermediate, and long run;
- Providing useful costing information on current process costs versus those contained in current or future investment proposals (for example, the opportunity cost of not investing in a new asset that could provide better capacity/cost results);
- Supporting the establishment of capacity utilization measurements that identify the cost of capacity and its impact on business cycles and overall company performance;
- Identifying the capacity required to meet strategic and operational objectives and to estimate currently available capacity;
- Detailing the opportunity cost of unused capacity and suggesting ways to account for that cost;
- Supporting change efforts and providing pre-decision information and analysis of the potential resource and cost implications of a planned change;
- Creating a common language for and understanding of capacity cost management.

In the pages that follow, the emphasis will return continually to the major themes presented here:

- Capacity is a systemic concept.
- Waste and throughput are primary capacity measurements, reflecting this systemic approach.
- No "solution" to the capacity measurement problem can be developed, given the fluid and highly interdependent nature of the productive process.
- Capacity measurements are based on assumptions that have to be revisited on an ongoing basis to ensure that unneces-

sary waste, excess capacity, or avoidable variations in the process are not allowed to creep in.

- As the time frame and unit of analysis change, the issues, challenges, and implications of capacity concepts radically change.

Capacity cost management issues emerge wherever resources are deployed to create value for customers. Gaining the most from a set of resources—minimizing the waste of these value-creating elements of the corporate puzzle—is capacity management. Capacity—the capability of an organization's resources, its ability to create value for its stakeholders—is an intricate part of the complex web of transactions, decisions, people, and processes that define modern business. Measuring and managing capacity, ever a movable feast, is at the heart of the business equation.

No gain is so certain as that which proceeds from the economical use of what you already have.—Latin proverb

☐ References and Notes

[1] J. Blackstone, *Capacity Management*, Cincinnati: APICS-SouthWestern Publishing, 1989, pp. 7–8.

[2] To improve the flow of this text, the term "product" will be used in place of product/service bundle. At all times, it is the total package of products and services provided by the firm that will be meant by the use of this term. Hence, the concepts apply to any company, whether in the manufacturing or service sector.

[3] This section is based on a publication by the two authors, Statement on Management Accounting 4Y, "Measuring the Cost of Capacity," published by the Institute of Management Accountants, specifically pages 3–5 of the document. This Statement will be referenced extensively throughout Part I of this monograph.

[4] The best known of the research efforts leading to the belief that cost standards had to be seen as attainable if dysfunctional consequences were to be minimized was done by A. C. Stedry (*Budget Control and Cost Behavior*, Englewood Cliffs, NJ: Prentice-Hall Inc., 1960). Since then, many different researchers, including K. Merchant and G. Hofstede, have documented the dysfunctional consequences of "tight" standards. Each of these research efforts has been built on a core assumption: that standards are static "yardsticks" used as the basis for evaluating individual and group performance. To date, no research has been done on the impact of theoretical standards in the continuous improvement

environment, where they serve as benchmarks rather than as performance measurement tools. The statements made in this section are premised on the suggested behavioral impact and nature of the continuous improvement approach to management, as defined by its proponents. This approach rewards improvement against, not attainment of, a preset "standard" of performance. Used as a metric of improvement or learning performance against standard is argued to be a significantly different concept and behavioral concern than suggested by traditional literature and research.

5   Before leaving this area, it is important to understand that there is no GAAP-defined reason for avoiding theoretical and practical capacity baselines. While a 1987 IRS ruling prohibits the use of practical or theoretical capacity baselines for tax reporting, there are no GAAP-defined constraints on this decision. In addition, since capacity cost management normally is seen as a management reporting system, GAAP requirements are a moot point.

6   These five "modes" of using available capacity have been previously defined and published in the CAM-I *Capacity Primer* and 0SMA 4Y (op. cit.). While some disagreement exists as to their comprehensiveness and how best to report these various elements of capacity deployment, the categories suggested here represent current best practice as defined by managerially accepted accounting practice.

7   This statement, while bold in nature, has been determined by the key experts and associations affecting and affected by management accounting policies as best practice.

8   As many readers will recognize, several of the key concepts surrounding utilization have been developed by proponents of the theory of constraints, such as E. Goldratt. Given that utilization is defined on the bottleneck operation or key constraining resource of a process, the applicability of these concepts is clear.

9   SMA 4Y, op. cit., pp. 4–5.

3

OPERATIONAL PERSPECTIVES

ON CAPACITY

A resource needs to have protective capacity in order to restore the damage caused by disturbances, not just at that resource, but at all the activities feeding it. What type of damage are we talking about in this case? Basically, the damage of exposing the constraints.[1]

Two issues dominate the operational approach to capacity management: understanding existing process constraints—the sundry causes of process variation that affect capacity utilization levels—and balancing the flow of materials or transactions through the value chain and its subprocesses. The underlying goal of these efforts is to increase the speed at which value is created within a constrained process. Focused on short-term issues and the management of existing processes, operational perspectives on capacity have a long history.

The operational perspective uses the following definitions of capacity management:

[Capacity management is]...the function of planning, establishing, measuring, monitoring and adjusting levels of capacity so that sufficient capacity is available to permit execution of manufacturing schedules....Capacity planning is the process of measuring the amount of work scheduled and then determining the necessary people, machines, and physical resources needed to accomplish it. Capacity control involves monitoring both work input and production output to ensure that capacity plans are being achieved, and taking corrective action if there are significant variations in input or output.[2]

Driven by a concern with meeting market demand for output, operational capacity models seek to ensure that product is available when and where the customer demands it. It is argued that gaining this control over the delivery of product by the manufacturing system depends on clear identification and effective management of actual and potential bottleneck resources.

Blackstone's 1989 monograph on capacity management provides an excellent summary of current operational models and concepts. The major points made in this seminal work include:

- Capacity is the rate at which work is withdrawn from the system, or

$$\text{Time available} \ \times \ \frac{\text{time worked}}{\text{time available}} \ \times \ \frac{\text{standard hours produced}}{\text{time worked}}$$

- Load is the volume of work in the system (see Figure 3-1).
- In measuring capacity, one averages some set of historical data.
- In calculating capacity, one sets capacity equal to the product of time available, efficiency, and utilization:

$$C = T \times E \times U$$

where C is the capacity available or required, T is the time available, E is the efficiency factor as a proportion, and U is the utilization factor as a proportion.

- Efficiency measures how closely predetermined standards are achieved.

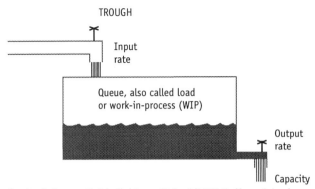

From *Capacity Management* by John Blackstone, p. 18. Copyright 1989. Used by permission of South-Western College Publishing, a division of International Thomson Publishing Inc., Cincinnati, Ohio 45227.

Figure 3-1. Load vs. Capacity

- Utilization is a measure of how intensely a resource is being used. To calculate machine utilization, the total time charged to creating output (setup and run time) is divided by the total clock hours scheduled to be available for a given period of time.

$$\frac{\text{Hours available} - \text{hours down}}{\text{Hours available}} \ \text{x } 100$$

- The theoretical maximum utilization is 1, or 100%. To achieve this maximum, the machine must never be out of service because of breakdowns, operator absenteeism, or lack of parts. Since breakdowns, absenteeism, and lack of work do occur occasionally even under the best management, it is unrealistic to have a utilization of 100%.
- Historical utilization should provide a reasonable estimate of machine utilization, provided that there has been no major shift in product mix, demand level, or the condition of the facility.

These views, applied within a constrained process, are the essence of the operational perspective, shaping the views and models that emerge from it as well as forming the basis for the remainder of this chapter.

Early Operational Models

Gantt's work in the early 1900s represented the first cohesive development of the operational approach to capacity management. Gantt's focus was on detailing the primary causes for idle time on existing machines as well as the cost of this idleness. The major causes of idleness that he identified included lack of orders, lack of labor, lack of raw material, lack of "worked" material, repairs, or poor planning (see Table 3-1).

The resulting cost of idleness was then classified into avoidable and unavoidable components, allowing the company to act to improve its performance. Although Gantt's model was developed early in the 20th century, it is reflected in most of the major new capacity models being implemented in companies today.

The value of Gantt's idleness charts lies in their efficient presentation of information combined with ease of use and communication of the resulting capacity performance information. Serving to highlight key capacity issues such as the root cause for planned and unplanned idleness, Gantt's model summarizes performance in both operational and financial terms. Gantt's idleness charts contain a tremendous amount of information for managers and arguably can be as useful in factories using departmental or cellular manufacturing approaches today as they were in the machine shops of Gantt's era.

☐ Church and Capacity Costing

As detailed in later chapters, the early giants in the capacity literature, namely Gantt and Alexander Hamilton Church, did not always agree on the optimal treatment of capacity or capacity costs. Church, who also began his career as an industrial engineer, felt that Gantt's models did not reflect organizational realities. This led the two to have a heated debate, published over numerous editions of *The American Machinist*, a popular journal of the time.

Table 3-1. Gantt Idleness Chart

Symbol	Dept. or Machine Class	% Capacity to Attain	% of Capacity Used on Day Turn 10 20 30 40 50 60 70 80 90	Details of Expense of Idleness Due to		
				Lack of Orders	Lack of Help	Lack of Raw Material
B	200 45" looms	80		F47 32 289 2 31	136 10	
C	687 - 54" & 58" looms	80		F267 80 85 4 76	1473 52	
D	136 - 65" & 68" looms	80		F142 62 432 83	441 94	
E	9 - 58" looms	70		F5 53 376 19	24 95	
F	111 - 68" & 72" looms	70		F194 68 1088 22	725 36	
G	1 - 72" loom	80		C 52 82		
H	1 - 58" loom	80		C 30 12	10 90	

Symbol	Details of Expense of Idleness Due to		
	Lack of Worked Material	Repairs	Poor Planning
B	- 19 40	20 92	6 39
C	A 15 54 194 14	493 89	136 42
D	A 1 28 3 55	41 32	6 30
E	4 65	14 30	38 99
F	A 84 319 57	288 53	271 15
G		1 95	
H		48	

Expense of Idleness

Symbol	Total	Unavoidable		Increase in Expense of Product %	Avoidable
		%	Amount		
B	3122 44	20	868 31	18.2	2254 12
C	3436 07	20	5646 65	18.2	2210 58
D	42 39 1069 83	20	7 71 1151 66	18.2	50 10 81 83
E	463 67	30	207 02	36.0	256 65
F	24 77 2888 35	30	8 92 3895 80	36.0	33 69 1007 45
G	54 78	20	9 92	18.2	44 86
H	41 50	20	3 10	18.2	38 40

From C. J. McNair and Richard Vangermeersch, SMA 4Y, "Measuring the Cost of Capacity," Montvale, NJ: Institute of Management Accountants, 1996, p. 31.

Interestingly, Church's view of capacity went through major changes as his career developed. "Early Church" models focused on separating the costs of good production from idle capacity costs for ongoing reporting but then adding idleness costs back into product costs at the end of the reporting cycle using a "supplemental rate" (see Figure 3-2). Focused on serving the needs of both internal and external reporting with the same set of numbers, Church argued that the supplemental rate method was a flexible, comprehensive approach to capacity cost management.

By 1931, Church began to question the use of the supplemental rate method, noting with increasing alarm that it tended to lead to suboptimal decisions and that it had taken on the nature of the full absorption costing model. The second model Church developed looks and feels like the later models developed by Goldratt under the theory of constraints. Specifically, Church's second model focused on applying all costs at the "point of the tool." In this later approach, still operational in focus, Church argued that the only costs that should be applied to product were those actually consumed by it. If the "tool," the

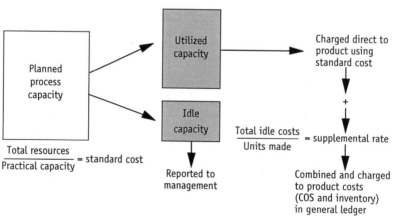

From C. J. McNair and Richard Vangermeersch, SMA 4Y, "Measuring the Cost of Capacity," Montvale, NJ, Institute of Management Accountants, 1996, p. 33.

Figure 3-2. Supplemental Rate Method

See what happens. Two jobs have passed safely by, each absorbing its share of the dripping dollars. Then an interval and two dollars plunk into the pool of waste!

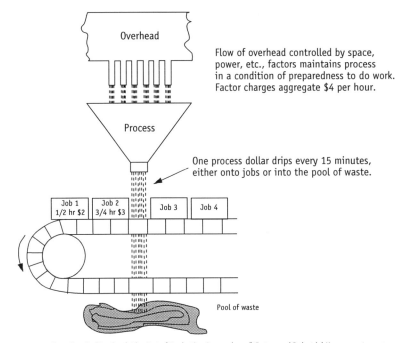

From A. Hamilton Church, "Overhead: The Cost of Production Preparedness," *Factory and Industrial Management,* January 1931, pp. 38-40, as reprinted in Richard Vangermeersch, ed., *The Contributions of Alexander Hamilton Church to Accounting and Management,* New York: Garland Publishing, Inc., 1986, p. 184.

Figure 3-3. The Pool of Waste

bottleneck in the operation, was idle, this cost fell into the pool of waste, unrecoverable from ongoing business (see Figure 3-3).

In this later model, then, Church took a systemic view of capacity, focusing his information and costing on the use of the bottleneck resource. Concerned with ensuring the effective utilization of the primary, constraining resource, Church's model was a precursor to velocity-driven operational models. Church differed from the operational perspective presented earlier, though, in his view that theoretical capacity was the only defensible baseline measure. Attaining theoretical capacity utilization was not the issue in Church's mind; keeping track of how and why capacity was used and wasted was key.

MRP and Capacity Management

For many reasons capacity reporting in any form entered a period of dormancy from 1933 until the late 1970s. When it reemerged, capacity concepts had undergone a radical change and were being driven by assumptions created in engineering models and operations science that built in buffers to create "realistic" standards. Standards, both for plant- and accounting-based capacity models, began to place their emphasis on the perceived behavioral impact of "unattainable" standards on plant employees.

The belief that standards had to be tight but attainable if dysfunctional behavior was to be minimized first emerged in the work of Stedry in 1960. Using a simple laboratory experiment, Stedry determined that unattainable standards lead to gamesmanship, bad attitudes, and a rejection of the standard itself. In this model, however, the role of the standard is evaluation—individuals are held accountable for making the standard. Creating a static, nondynamic approach to the development and use of standards, Stedry's study was mainly undisputed up until the emergence of the *continuous improvement paradigm*, which began to dominate management practice in the mid- to late 1980s.

MRP-based approaches to capacity are tied to the traditional static view of standards and capacity, rather than to the continuous improvement paradigm. Several operational models fall under this umbrella: rough-cut capacity planning, capacity requirements planning, input/output control, and operation sequencing.

☐ Rough-Cut Capacity Planning

Rough-cut capacity planning was developed to deal specifically with the fact that traditional MRP models were capacity insensitive, leading to the tendency to develop an overstated master production schedule unattainable under existing operating conditions. Rough-cut capacity planning, then, sought to validate the master schedule with respect to assumed or currently utilized capacity. As described by Berry, Vollmann, and Whybark,

> ...rough-cut capacity planning is an activity that involves an analysis of the master production schedule to determine the implied capacity requirements for critical manufacturing facilities....rough-cut procedures can be utilized quickly and inexpensively to examine capacity limitations and to evaluate tradeoffs for a variety of alternative solutions. [3]

A bill of labor or machine requirements forms the basis of rough-cut capacity analysis. Standard times for the various stages in the production process and the total demand or product mix expected to pass through critical resources are used to estimate the total demand placed on labor or machine time. Both run time and setup time are included in these time estimates, as follows:

$$\text{Operation time/piece} = \text{run time/piece} + \frac{\text{Setup time/lot}}{\text{Average lot size}}$$

Serving as an approximation of load on key resources, rough-cut capacity planning is based on the belief that a work center is not overloaded if its capacity available equals its capacity required. Rough-cut capacity models are deterministic in nature and hence, according to Blackstone, are prone to error in more stochastic settings. This fact led Blackstone to argue that capacity available must be greater than capacity required in order to avoid backlogs that would tend "to grow indefinitely." [4]

□ Capacity Requirements Planning and MRP

Capacity requirements planning (CRP) is defined by APICS as "...the function of establishing, measuring, and adjusting limits or levels of capacity...the process of determining how much labor and machine resources are required to accomplish the tasks of production. Open shop orders as well as planned orders in the MRP system are the primary input to CRP, which 'translates' these orders into hours of work by work center by time period." [5]

As noted by Blackstone, CRP "...is a detailed comparison on the material requirements plan and orders already in progress with available capacity, all defined within a closed-loop MRP system. CRP verifies that there is sufficient capacity to handle orders due to be released."[6]

CRP is applied using a tightly defined simulation model that takes planned orders from the MRP system and combines this information with critical lead-time offsets to determine the estimated time that a specific order will be processed at a work center. Integrated with information about progress on jobs already released to the process, CRP creates a machine load report for each work center. While simple in concept, CRP has, according to Blackstone, proved to be a tedious, time-consuming exercise in even the smallest shops. Blackstone presents some of the more detailed issues and examples of CRP in action. The book is recommended reading for anyone wishing more information in this area.

☐ Input/Output Control and Capacity

A third MRP-based operational model, input/output control, focuses on managing queues within the production process. Working from a logic captured in the diagram "Anatomy of a Late Order" by Blackstone (see Figure 3-4), input/output control focuses on identifying ways to reduce interoperational time and lead time by effective management of queue lengths.[7]

In input/output control models, the two aspects of queue control (the input rate and the output rate) are monitored using management by exception methods. Specifically, the model monitors actual input versus planned input and takes action if the cumulative deviation at these two data points exceeds a predefined threshold. Similarly, actual output is compared to planned output to ensure that the identified cumulative deviation is within tolerance. Management action is triggered only if thresholds are exceeded; otherwise no action is created within the system. As described by Wight, the basic principle of input/output control is "never put into a manufacturing facility or to a vendor's facility more than you believe he can produce."[8]

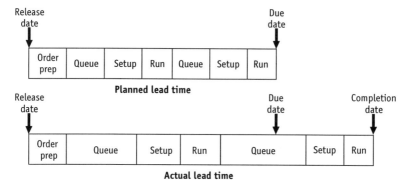

From *Capacity Management* by John Blackstone, p. 117. Copyright 1989. Used by permission of South-Western College Publishing, a division of International Thomson Publishing Inc., Cincinnati, Ohio 45227.

Figure 3-4. Anatomy of a Late Order

Short-term in nature, input/output control models are usually used in conjunction with CRP models. Focused on daily rather than the weekly time buckets common to CRP, input/output control allows for early release of orders if the actual loading on a machine center warrants it. As noted by Blackstone, consistent early releases are a signal that a company may be focused more on keeping a machine center busy than on ensuring that the right products are produced at the right time.

□ Capacity and Operations Sequencing

A final operational model building off of traditional MRP logic is operations scheduling. Interestingly, this model makes extensive use of Gantt charts, as reflected in Table 3-2, to create a deterministic simulation model of the production process and

Table 3-2. Bill of Material for a Widget (effective date 1/1/88)

Level	Part	Qty/Parent	Description
0	100	1	Finished widget
1	110	2	Subassembly
2	121	3	Component A
2	122	4	Component B

current loading factors. As summarized by Blackstone, performing a deterministic simulation requires the following data:

- A list of released orders and their present locations;
- A list of planned order releases from the MRP system;
- A list of tentative capacities available;
- Time standards from routing data;
- A list of events, called the event list, whose times are known (such as time of planned order release);
- A list of future events whose times are not at present known (such as start time for a job in queue awaiting the completion of a previous job). This list, called the waiting list, is organized by work center;
- A way of representing what has occurred in the simulation;
- A simulation clock.[9]

Using these data, a total processing time for each job as it goes into service is determined. Jobs then are placed in the queue using a FIFO (first in, first out) scheduling sequence. Combined with Gantt's idleness charts, this final model appears to provide a hands-on, visible tracking and management device for plant floor capacity control.

Bottlenecks and Other Conundrums

MRP-based operational capacity models focused on creating schedules for the entire plant that would accommodate planned production and foreseeable delays. The late 1970s saw the increasing questioning of existing assumptions and models in operations management, resulting in the development of systemic approaches to the plant capacity problem.

Two key models capture the essence of the systemic approach: just-in-time or cellular manufacturing and the theory of constraints. Where the former focuses on creating a balanced system that operates in a synchronized manner or "drumbeat," the latter places its emphasis on the management of the bottleneck resource. Each model will be explored in depth in the discussion that follows.

☐ Henry Ford and Modern Manufacturing

One of the most overlooked facts about just-in-time or cellular manufacturing is that it was originally conceived and implemented by Henry Ford in his River Rouge facility in Michigan. Henry Ford could not abide waste in any form, in manufacturing or in society in general. Constantly driven to identify and eliminate the sources of waste, Ford was one of the earliest systemic thinkers of the 20th century.

When faced with the challenge to build a global competitive position rapidly, Toyota turned to Henry Ford and his book *Today and Tomorrow*, published in 1926, to create its plants of the future. The resulting production model, cellular production, applied the logic of the assembly line to repetitive production settings. Essential elements of the just-in-time model include:

- Operations or work activities are broken down into equivalent time-based buckets that allow for balancing the flow through the process.
- Machines and operations are tightly sequenced, with minimal levels of movement and queue between steps in the production process.
- Kanbans are used to control the amount of work-in-process between process steps.
- If a defect or production problem occurs, the process is shut down until the error is remedied.
- Orders are "pulled" through the system based on actual customer demand. If no demand exists, production does not occur.

Cellular approaches to manufacturing embed the basic notions of capacity management into the operating conditions of the process. Proponents argue that matching the build sequence underlying the production process to that of the product itself ensures that units move quickly through the process and that all forms of waste (move, queue, defects, and rework) are minimized.[10]

Balance defines cellular manufacturing. Resources are balanced against work-flow demands, operations are time balanced to smooth out the flow, and all forms of variation that may have a negative impact on the underlying balance of the system itself are measured and targeted for elimination. Inventory is eliminated under cellular approaches, not as the goal but as the outcome of a well-managed process that does not require inventory buffers to operate efficiently.

The capacity of a cell is clearly defined on its slowest operation or bottleneck, but the goal is to balance the productive capability of the surrounding resources against this bottleneck to ensure that product moves smoothly along the flow. In cellular manufacturing, then, the role of *velocity* of materials through the process is visibly portrayed. When a variation-causing event occurs, such as defective material or defective work from a prior work station, the entire cell is idled. Idle time is easily measured and costed, as idleness affects the entire process if it affects any part of the flow. Providing the means for visible, effective management of the capacity of the production process, cellular manufacturing has rapidly become the method of choice in most factories today.

The power of cellular concepts extends beyond the plant floor, though, to any process that is repetitive in nature. Banks have adopted cellular flows for check processing and other back office operations, with significant improvement in productivity and reduction of costs and errors. The essence of cellular design—the smooth flow of materials and transactions through a process—leads to profit improvements.

One of the quirks surrounding the adoption of cellular manufacturing, however, is that if done properly, the method creates excess capacity. At Eaton Corporation's electronic counter group, this excess capacity created the need to find new business to fill existing equipment. Once waste was eliminated, resources were able to work to their optimal effectiveness; the result was that the company management was made unavoidably aware of the fact that it had waste all over the place.[11] In reality, cellular manufacturing doesn't create excess capacity as much as it reveals waste that was buried in traditional methods and processes for making product and delivering services. After adopting cellular designs, companies have found that inventories fall, the space

required to meet existing output requirements is radically reduced, and capacity, in the form of idle process time and empty
floor space, becomes available for other uses. Only through deploying these newly idled resources can a company really gain
the benefits of the cellular approach; idle capacity is just another form of waste, after all.[12]

☐ Of Bottlenecks and Other Constraints

At about the same time that cellular manufacturing methods
were becoming popular, Eli Goldratt created a competing model,
called the theory of constraints (TOC). Launched with the popular book *The Goal*, this model emphasizes the need to manage
effectively the flow of product through the bottleneck. What
sets this model apart from cellular approaches is the underlying
premise that having excess resources—an unbalanced plant—is
the optimal solution to the production problem.

The TOC model is based on the continuous improvement
paradigm. Several key principles underscore this approach.

- Throughput capacity is defined by the underlying constraints
  of a system, which may be physical (for example, a bottleneck)
  or invisible (for example, policy, measurement, or training).
- The goal is to increase throughput while simultaneously de-
  creasing investment (inventory) and operating expense, subject to meeting the needs of employees and customers.
- Capacity of the organization is infinite. To enable an organization to move closer to its goal, TOC focuses on removing
  the root problems that prevent improvement.
- The cost of idle capacity is not an opportunity cost unless
  customer orders exist that are not being filled.

Noreen, Smith, and Mackey detailed the key features of the
TOC model and how it interfaces with the management accounting system.[13] Emphasis is placed on the contribution made by an
order (its throughput) and the relationship this contribution has
to the order's impact on the constraining resource. Similar in

logic to a constrained resource cost-volume-profit analysis, TOC seeks to maximize the potential profitability of a process, as defined by contribution earned at the bottleneck (see Table 3-3). Emphasizing company profitability over keeping people or machines busy, the TOC approach highlights the key constraints inhibiting process performance.

By focusing attention on the primary process constraint or bottleneck, TOC seeks to prevent the waste caused when resources are activated without any real demand for the subsequent output. Within the TOC environment, available capacity is defined as

Time available x efficiency x availability x activation

As can be seen by this formula, capacity is valued only if it can be activated or applied to products or services that generate profit for the firm (throughput). TOC has several key assumptions.

- The utilization of a nonbottleneck resource is determined solely by the constraint, not by its own potential.
- Activating a resource is not the same as utilizing it.
- An hour saved at a nonbottleneck is a mirage.
- Capacity and priority need to be considered simultaneously, not sequentially (as is done in the MRP models).
- Plant capacity should not be balanced.

Table 3-3. TOC Contribution Report

Order Contribution Report for 06/21/93 through 06/21/93 Report date 06/21/93					
Order Number	Gross Sales	Variable Costs	Throughput	Constraint Hours	Throughput per Hour
Cutting tools					
41631	796	394	402	N/A	N/A
41910	156	40	116	.51	227
42424	306	41	265	1.50	177
42659	262	79	183	.66	278
42692	288	61	227	.34	668
43227	422	63	359	.50	718

From E. Noreen, D. Smith, and J. Mackey, *The Theory of Constraints and Its Implications for Management Accounting,* Montvale, NJ, Institute of Management Accountants, 1995.

In the TOC world, offloading the bottleneck or increasing its efficiency by breaking lots to fill a cycle of operation are just two of the ways that the capacity of the plant, as defined at the bottleneck, can be improved. Popular by any measure of the word, the TOC model provides a way to manage a nonconnected process flow with clear decision criteria and an ongoing recognition that the entire process and its value-creating ability are defined by the bottleneck.

Costing in an Operational Time Frame

Taking the operational perspective has a very specific implication for the cost modeling and analysis aspect of capacity cost management. The intense concern with the velocity of materials through the plant focuses everyone's attention on the denominator, the amount of work completed within a short time frame. If 5,000 hours of machine time are available, this is the baseline for determining what work can be accepted by the system. In the short-term, operational model, then, theoretical capacity is tightly defined and basically unalterable. The key factor to manage is the utilization of the system's potential to create value, not the expansion of that capability.

It is within this framework that the traditional definitions of capacity appear to be most easily applied. The total cost of capacity divided by the estimated theoretical capacity of the existing system's bottleneck resource or activity is the cost per unit of available capacity. The focus of the costing process turns, then, not to defining what the "cost of capacity" is but rather, how this purchased capability is deployed.

Purchased capacity can be used in several basic ways—value creation (actual production), idleness, or waste (including rework)—or it can be stored for downstream use (see Figure 3-5). Capacity that cannot be stored can be either used or wasted. In taking the operational perspective, then, the driving assumption is that the system itself cannot be changed; only the velocity

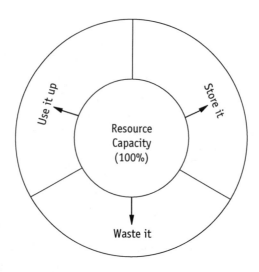

Figure 3-5. How We Use Our Resources

through that system, the amount of available resources deployed to value-creating activities, can be managed effectively.

Capacity cost management in this simple setting becomes a matter of reporting actual utilization and detailing the cost of unused resources, in the manner of Gantt's idleness charts. Focused on keeping score rather than analyzing potential capacity scenarios, the objective is to track current performance against theoretical or practical capacity and to analyze short-term incremental business against its capacity utilization effects. When idle capacity exists in the short term, it is likely to generate a search for business to fill that capacity. It is at this point, then, that the real reason for using a theoretical capacity baseline is best detailed.

☐ Direct Costing or Full Absorption Costing?

For many decades the debate surrounding direct costing versus full absorption costing has consumed the attention of academics and practitioners alike. On one side, the direct costers argue that any order that contributes positively to fixed costs and profit is good business. This is the core assumption of Goldratt's TOC models and the underlying premise in the operational models described above. Yet, as any manager or accountant can tell you, contribution pricing can lead to the demise of the firm, especially as fixed cost proportions grow as a percentage of a firm's total costs of doing business.

Full absorption logic is equally problematic, however. Suggesting that all current costs have to be covered in the price of each piece of business is a logical flaw. All costs of doing business have to be covered in the long term, but in the short term the only pertinent variable is volume—the velocity of materials through the system. In the short term, the system is structured and its costs are basically unresponsive to shifts in the way work is done or how much of it is completed. In this highly structured, unchangeable setting, volume, which is the denominator in the cost equation, is the only variable that can be managed.

Which leads one back to TOC but with a twist. If full absorption costing is used, then any piece of business has to cover its full costs. Yet the system incurs only incremental costs in taking this business. So what is the "correct" approach? Neither method is defensible. Instead, incremental business needs to be seen as using a portion of currently idled resources, a use that can be charged to a specific order at its theoretical baseline amount. If at the end of the period idle costs remain, they are charged off as a period expense. In this *competitive cost* framework, the goal is to understand what the current "best" of the company is and to ensure that the costs charged to a product, service, or customer reflect resources actually used by it. Idle capacity charges are the key to creating the stable short-term cost estimates that support analysis of any business opportunity.

Clearly the competitive cost still may not support taking some pieces of business that have a positive contribution, but it is at this point that the bridge to tactical and strategic capacity cost management issues offers insight and guidance. Specifically, if a company's current competitive cost is too high or the incremental price offered for its next piece of "capacity" is too low, the question that has to be asked is, what market signal is embedded in this transaction? Incremental business is, in reality, a signal from the market that a company's price points are decaying. If the incremental business isn't taken, the price point will still decay, and the company will have sacrificed incremental funds that could have been redeployed in a tactical or strategic way to reduce the total costs within the business system.

The key premise being suggested here is that there may be no such thing as incremental business if a theoretical capacity cost management framework is embraced. Incremental business is simply the cost improvement target that has to be reached through bottleneck management (short-term), process redesign (intermediate-term), or structural changes to the system (strategic, or long-term). Relatedly, capacity cost management in the short-term setting provides ongoing signals about the company's current competitive position, about the relationship between its resource utilization levels and profits, and about downstream pressures on the current cost and profit position. Short-term capacity cost estimates, due to their stability (if defined at the theoretical level), provide information that guides tactical and strategic decision making within the firm.

The guiding objective in this short-term framework is to ensure that the company remains strategically viable in the long term by constantly scanning and improving on its current activities and their value in the market. The essence of short-term capacity cost management, then, is reporting and analyzing current performance against current and future strategic plans, as well as ensuring that short-term capacity utilization is maximized (for example, bottlenecks are well managed). It is an objective that serves as information for future decisions rather than as a control over current performance. Capacity cost estimates and the competitive cost estimate are the basis for future action, not retroactive control.

Operational Models of Capacity: A Summary

The basic emphasis in all operational models of capacity is on controlling the flow of resources through existing processes and machine centers. Whether these models are discrete, reduction-ist approaches (MRP) or systemic in nature (cellular and TOC), they focus predominantly on the day-by-day, minute-by-minute control of the plant. Maximizing the velocity of materials through the plant, as driven by customer demand, appears to be the es-sential element of these models and the solutions they suggest.

In total, the operational models provide a set of robust tools for estimating, managing, and prioritizing the movement of or-ders through the plant. Where the MRP and TOC models build from more traditional plant designs, however, cellular approaches reconfigure the process to decrease the amount and impact of variation on the flow. Capacity in the operational perspective varies from a "units produced per period of time" approach, as suggested by Blackstone and the APICS model, to a more mar-ket-based, value-driven concept of capacity as the utilization of resources to meet demand. In the former case, unitized capacity measures build on standards that have the potential to build in waste. Unavoidably complex in nature, these detail-driven mod-els attempt to capture and define capacity in a deterministic way for the entire flow through the plant.

TOC and cellular-based operational models bring a different light to the capacity problem. Systemic in nature, they recognize that system performance is defined by constraints and cannot be modeled and solved in a deterministic way. Instead, the goal is to manage only one point in the system: the bottleneck. The two models diverge widely, though, in their tolerance for systemic waste. In a cellular design, operations are balanced to ensure minimal on-going waste of resources and maximum reliability and uniformity in the flow. Goldratt's world, on the other hand, takes the existing structure of the plant as given, focusing solely on short-term man-agement solutions to improve the available capacity and effective utilization of the bottleneck resource to create throughput.

The final, unanswerable question is, can capacity be tightly defined and measured? Can a complex process be modeled in a deterministic way, or does the interdependency lying just beyond human understanding spell defeat for any attempt to define and tightly measure and control the capacity of an entire range of linked machines and processes? For MRP-based approaches to work, the world has to be controllable, and variation measurable. In a systemic world, only flow and events that generate variation in the flow or velocity can be assessed and managed. In the end, it is one's assumptions about the world that will determine which model and logic are "right."

> Reason may fail you. If you are going to do anything with life, you have sometimes to move away from it, beyond all measurements. You must follow sometimes visions and dreams.—Bede Jarrett, *The House of Gold*

□ References and Notes

[1] E. Goldratt, *The Haystack Syndrome*, Croton-on-Hudson, NY: North River Press, 1990, p. 239.

[2] J. Blackstone, Jr., *Capacity Management*, Cincinnati, Ohio: APICS/South-Western Publishing Co., 1989.

[3] W. Berry, T. Vollmann, and D. C. Whybark, *Master Production Scheduling: Principles and Practice*, Falls Church, VA: American Production and Inventory Control Society, 1979, p. 15.

[4] Blackstone, op. cit.

[5] *APICS Dictionary*, 6th edition, Falls Church, VA: American Production and Inventory Control Society, 1987.

[6] Blackstone, op. cit., p. 87.

[7] Blackstone, op. cit., p. 117.

[8] O. Wight, "Input/Output Control: A Real Handle on Lead Time," APICS Capacity Management Reprints, Falls Church, VA: American Production and Inventory Control Society, 1984, pp. 107–129.

[9] Blackstone, op. cit., p. 141.

[10] Numerous sources for the cellular model exist. R. A. Hall's *Zero Inventories* is considered to be one of the best books in this area (Homewood, IL: Irwin Professional Publishing, 1983).

[11] The essence of the Eaton story is captured in the book *Crossroads: A JIT Success Story*, by R. Stasey and C. J. McNair, Homewood, IL: Irwin Business Books, 1991.

[12] Many of the ongoing comments about waste and its impact have their source in the book *The Profit Potential* by C. J. McNair (New York: Wiley Publishing, 1994).

[13] E. Noreen, D. Smith, and J. T. Mackey, *The Theory of Constraints and Its Implications for Management Accounting*, Montvale, NJ: Institute of Management Accountants, 1995.

4

THE TACTICAL PERSPECTIVE IN CAPACITY COST MANAGEMENT

Know thyself. Ulysses showed his wisdom in not trusting himself. A Yale undergraduate left on his door a placard for the janitor on which it was written, "Call me at 7 o'clock; it's absolutely necessary that I get up at seven. Make no mistake. Keep knocking until I answer." Under this he had written, "Try again at ten."—William Lyon Phelps, *Essays on Things.*

The operational perspective is much like the student's first request for awakening—urgent, yet often ignored. In moving to the tactical view of the organization and the role of capacity cost management in this setting, the key becomes knowing the organization, its capabilities, its true constraints, and its nature. A second-level warning system, the tactical perspective takes a longer and wider view of the challenges facing the organization than that embodied in the operational approach. As such, more of the "game" can be managed. Managers in a tactical framework can do more than just push more volume through a process; they can change the nature of the work being done by the system.

The tactical perspective is bounded by a six-month to three-year time frame and focuses on loosening the impact of current constraints on the processes that make up the company's value chain. In the intermediate or tactical time frame bottlenecks are not only managed, they are eliminated. In addition, the activities that make up processes can be managed once the framework for analysis and action is expanded. The models for analyzing capacity cost management in the intermediate term reflect this expanded time frame as they begin to focus on the "why" for the constraints and put in motion plans to eliminate these hurdles or minimize their impact on the system.

While broader in nature than the operational perspective, the tactical view does still function within limits. Specifically, the changes that can be made are restricted to minor changes to the work flow within a process, the structure of the process itself, and the type of work done to meet customer needs. Tactical decisions cannot change the structure or basic product matrix of the firm. Tactical decisions cannot radically redeploy company resources. These efforts are the domain of strategic decision making.

In the tactical mode, the focus is on improving performance by reducing the resources needed to complete existing work or increasing the amount of work that can be done by the process by eliminating bottlenecks and nonvalue-added activities. Tactical capacity cost management, therefore, allows management to focus on the entire cost equation: Both the numerator (cost) and the denominator (work done) can be changed substantially. The boundaries to these activities are the existing strategy, product mix, and physical resource structure of the firm.

The capacity cost models being developed to address tactical issues include normalized costing, activity-based costing, capacity variance analysis, the resource effectiveness model, the cost containment model, and the first-level analysis within the CAM-I and CUBES approaches. Each of these models has its unique strengths and weaknesses, focusing on different aspects to manage within the capacity domain. All reflect an increasing concern with effectiveness rather than efficiency as well as a recognition that the system as currently designed has limits to the value it can create. It is to these models that we now turn our attention.

Basic Tactical Models

What defines a tactical model? First, the time frame of analysis expands, allowing for multiperiod change efforts to improve existing performance. In some of the tactical models, this multiperiod focus is the basis for developing the cost estimates and capacity measurements. In others, the application of the model is multiperiod in nature. A second issue in tactical models is that only the core structure of the system, its physical resources, major processes, and product offerings, remain untouchable; the domain of action is quite large. Third, the number and type of costs (for example, resources) that can be acted on increase significantly; most costs are responsive within a tactical time frame. Fourth, the solutions available to management are bounded by a larger organizational strategy that defines the optimal course of action. Finally, the view taken expands beyond understanding basic transformation flows to considering the interaction of processes and their impact on the entire organizational and industry value chain. Taking very little as a given, tactical decision making is the arena where most managers operate.

While tactical models are expansive, some of the models described here bridge the short-term and intermediate-term periods. Contrary to pure operational approaches, these models, due to their reliance on historical records of financial and operational performance, require multiple data points. It can be argued that some of these models are actually very short term in focus, but creating them and using the information they provide requires a multiperiod perspective. Having stated this caveat, attention will now turn to the models placed in a tactical framework by this study.

☐   Normalized Costing

The first issue in taking a tactical perspective is that of time—the implicit time horizon of action is significantly expanded. This expansion is reflected in a revised formulation of the capacity cost estimate, as evidenced by current practice at Caterpillar, Inc. Called "normalized costing," this approach focuses on understanding how resources are being used currently, how much waste is built into current systems, and what total throughput, and hence cost performance, is attainable.

Normalized costing is a capacity cost measurement model that uses average performance over time, adjusted for abnormal events, in its calculations. As described by Caterpillar's financial management group, the essence of the normalized approach is focused on understanding machine-hour utilization patterns over a three- to five-year period, as well as the cost implications of this performance. Abnormal expenses are eliminated from the resulting operational cost pools, giving a "normal" or recurring cost of production for various areas of the plant. Augmented by cost analysis that estimates the degree of variability within a cost pool, the normalized estimate provides a reliable basis for decision making.

A practical capacity baseline is used at Caterpillar in assessing the potential of a specific cell or machine center. Management continues to debate switching to theoretical capacity, but to date the behavioral and interpretative problems inherent in the theoretical approach are felt to outweigh the potential benefits. The capacity cost measure developed under the normalized approach is a multiyear average that does not charge idle capacity to current production. Idleness costs are summarized in a separate account and become management's responsibility to eliminate or redeploy.

In looking at the basic nature of normalized costing, the decision to leave out abnormal events, combined with the ongoing analysis of utilized rather than total capacity costs, makes this system a highly defensible, logical alternative to traditional costing methods. It aids managers in determining the impact of idle and nonproductive capacity on total performance, while avoiding many of the initial implementation problems that follow on the heels of a decision to employ theoretical baselines in the capacity cost management system.

Caterpillar, Inc. finds the normalized costing approach to be a viable basis for constructing management accounting information. Incorporated within an elaborate, detailed, and highly flexible management information system, normalized costing is used for all management reports at Caterpillar. The fact that normalized costing incorporates three to five years of data to derive its estimates makes it an intermediate-term model by definition. In addition, though, the fact that its focus is on the future—on identifying current trends and their impact on profitability—makes this model a logical choice in any company that operates within a relatively stable setting with well-defined and well-managed processes. Utilizing reliable accounting estimates defined by and tied to actual production performance, the normalized model is a responsive system that allows for multilayered analysis and ongoing adjustments to changing business conditions.

In a stable, more traditional company structure, then, normalized costing provides significant information. Its weakness lies in its very strengths—it requires a relatively slow pace of change to deliver reliable estimates. In a constantly changing environment, the "normalcy" needed to develop these estimates is difficult to achieve. So to the extent that cost-based economic estimates are reliable in the intermediate term, normalized costing provides a good basis for creating capacity cost management systems.

☐ Activity-Based Cost Systems

Normalized costing is focused on productive processes. A relatively new accounting model, activity-based costing, develops economic estimates for other parts of the business, including the "hard" and "soft" activities performed in nonmanufacturing areas of the firm.

Activity-based costing (ABC) had its birth in research done by George Staubus in the mid-1970s, but the concept truly reached its peak with the work of Robin Cooper and Robert Kaplan at the Harvard Business School. As described by Cooper and Kaplan, "activity-based cost systems estimate the cost of resources used in organizational processes to produce outputs." While defining costs in a traditional, linear fashion, ABC still provides a solid beginning for a company on the road to understanding its value-creating ability.

In the activity-based world, idle or unused capacity is the key link between internal management information and the general ledger systems used for external reporting. The form this relationship takes is:

Activity availability = activity usage + unused capacity

According to this equation, unused capacity represents the difference between the cost of resources actually used to complete various activities and the cost of resources supplied or available to do that work. Unused or idle capacity is the gap between what could have been done and the work actually accomplished, stated in financial terms.

The information developed under the ABC approach can be presented in a format similar to that in Table 4-1. The sorting of costs between used and unused categories indicates that excess resources are being consumed. The exhibit also highlights the impact of unused activity capacity on operating profits. Combined with other forms of reporting, this model can be used to highlight the often-overlooked components of subunit or organizational capacity. ABC also flags activities by their level of assessed value-added, providing the basis for targeted removal or reduction of the costs caused by these activities.

The ABC approach gives a company the ability to track its capacity costs directly to those activities that consume them. It also supports improved management of the assets not directly tied to core activities because it increases organizational awareness of the impact of idleness and waste on overall performance. Providing information on both the quantity and cost of idle ca-

Table 4-1. Example of ABC Income Statement

		Used	Unused	
	SALES			20,000
Less:	EXPENSES OF RESOURCES SUPPLIED AS USED			
	Materials	7,600		
	Energy	600		
	Short-term labor	900		9,100
	CONTRIBUTION MARGIN			10,900
Less:	ACTIVITY EXPENSES: COMMITTED RESOURCES	*Used*	*Unused*	
	Permanent direct labor	1,400	200	
	Machine run-time	3,200		
	Purchasing	700	100	
	Receiving/inventory	450	50	
	Production runs	1,000	100	
	Customer administration	700	200	
	Engineering changes	800	(100)	
	Parts administration	750	150	
	TOTAL EXPENSES OF COMMITTED RESOURCES	9,000	700	9,700
	OPERATING PROFIT			1,200

Robin Cooper and Robert S. Kaplan, "Activity-Based Systems: Measuring the Cost of Resource Usage," *Accounting Horizons,* September 1992, p. 7.

pacity, the ABC model supports analysis of alternative solutions to capacity problems.

ABC helps managers predict the impact of changes in volume and mix, process changes and improvement, introduction of new technology, and product and process design changes on activity cost. Serving as a useful bridge between more conventional views of capacity cost management and the more sophisticated models currently under development at CAM-I and Sematech, ABC places its emphasis where it counts most: on identifying the type and amount of resources consumed in the productive process.

Hewlett-Packard Corporation (HP) is a company that has made extensive use of the ABC approach in designing its cost systems and basic performance measurements. Identifying why work is done and the resources work consumes provides Hewlett-Packard with the means to change the way it deploys its resources in the intermediate term, ensuring that it is constantly redirecting its efforts to those activities and processes valued by the customer. For this company, constraints come in many forms, both flow based (bottlenecks) and process based (nonvalue-added activities). Focused on eliminating waste throughout the organization, HP constantly strives to identify nonvalue-added activities and costs. Eliminating this form of waste increases the effective capacity of HP's processes while reducing the overall cost to deliver products and services to customers.

At HP and other firms, ABC has proved a significant improvement over traditional product-costing methods, and, when adjusted for waste, underutilized capacity, or nonvalue-added work, it appears to provide insight into the internal economics of the firm. Understanding the internal economics or invisible value-creating mechanisms of a firm ultimately can spell the difference between mediocre and stellar performance. The internal economics of the firm "power up" the basic capacity of resources (physical and nonphysical), providing a baseline for driving improvement efforts.

The shortcomings of ABC arise from its ongoing tie to the core paradigms and issues that define traditional costing. In ABC, a dollar is a dollar. What this means in basic terms is that a dollar of cost is equated to a dollar of potential value. Yet there is increasing evidence that management is a nonlinear process and that the value creation process is, relatedly, nonlinear in nature. Another concern with ABC is that it imposes variability on a set of resources (see Figure 4-1). When studying capacity, one concern is with the percentage utilization a company makes of a set of resources. An equally important concern is with the avoidability or responsiveness of the resource set to changing work patterns and customer demands.

In ABC, it is difficult to separate the underlying nature of the resources from the ABC cost estimate. The result is the potential for a false signal or belief that costs can be managed by reducing the number of activities that occur. In reality, as the number of occurrences or activities are reduced, the cost per activity increases. Why? Because most of the costs held captive by a process are fairly unresponsive or fixed in nature. Reducing the number of occurrences has very little impact on financial results unless the reduction kicks a step in the stepped cost function. Implicitly managing to the margin, ABC presents costs in a nonmarginal way. At the least, this aspect can lead to confusion in the management ranks. At the worst, it can lead to reduction in activities, both value-adding and nonvalue-adding, with no downstream improvement in performance.

By adjusting ABC for capacity utilization, the objective is to offset some of the effects generated by the imposed variability. Tallying the idle capacity in a process to a separate account appears to create the stability in the ABC cost estimate required to make it a more effective management tool.

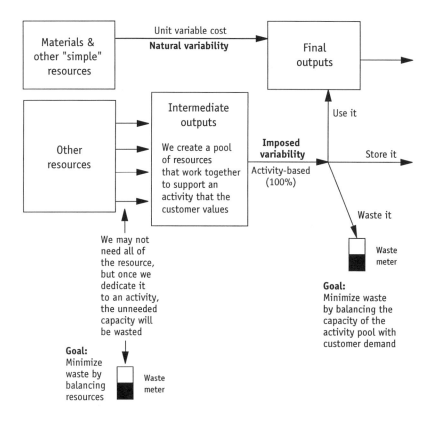

Figure 4-1. Activity-Based Costing: Natural vs. Imposed Variability

Implementing ABC is the first step in creating any effective cost management system. Because ABC models focus on units of work completed (for example, activities), the capacity for that work can be defined in reasonably objective, reliable, and visible ways. In the end, it is important in any cost system to make sure that the right costs are in the right bucket and that the utilization of that purchased capacity is tracked. In making these calculations, a firm is on the road to the true destination: understanding its *capability* or value-creating ability. Value creation, not cost, is the essential element in the economics of the firm. Value and cost are linked through effective resource utilization.

☐   Integrated ABC-TOC Model

In many respects, the integrated linear programming model that ties ABC to TOC represents a major contribution to the business literature. Developed by Robert Kee,[1] the integrated model estimates the optimal production model for a firm subject to the capacity of the individual activities constituting the firm's production structure.

The model treats unit-level costs and resources as continuous variables, while batch- and product-related costs are represented as discrete variables within a linear programming framework. As captured in Table 4-2, the resulting equations and model incorporate the interactions between the cost, physical resources, and capacity of production activities. Specifically, the opportunity cost of the resources is used to determine an optimal product mix, one that allows a company to select products with the highest contribution margin per unit and the highest profit per unit for a bottleneck activity. The opportunity cost arising from the use of resources tied to the bottleneck activity is reflected in the relative profitability computed for each product.

One of the most critical shifts in perspective embedded in Kee's model is the use of marginal revenue as the basis for making capacity-constrained decisions. If at least one bottleneck operation exists, this approach provides a superior solution to either a pure TOC or pure ABC model. In comparing these characteristics

Table 4-2. Comparative Analysis of ABC, TOC, and Integrated Models

	ABC Model	TOC Model	Expanded ABC Model
Product mix			
X₁	-0	50,000	30,000
X₂	-0	100,000	100,000
X₃	-0	25,000	30,000
X₄	20,000	-0	-0
Excess resources			
Assembly (labor hours)	100,000	-0	10,000
Finishing (labor hours)	100,000	55,000	55,000
Setup (hours)	-0	-0	-0
Purchasing (orders)	200	235	200
Engineering (drawings)	500	500	500
Profit			
Projected income	$3,180,000	$2,280,000	$4,620,000
Cost saving available from excess resources*	-0	2,307,000	-0
Available income	$3,180,000	$4,587,000	$4,620,000

* The cost savings from excess resources was computed by multiplying the excess capacity of each activity by its respective cost driver rate. The cost of excess resources is excluded from income under ABC and the expanded ABC models.

Robert Kee, "Integrating Activity-Based Costing with the Theory of Constraints to Enhance Production-Related Decisions," *Accounting Horizons,* December 1995, pp. 48-61.

to the problems identified with ABC, the integrated approach addresses many of the operational concerns embedded in the ABC model. What it cannot or does not fix are the behavioral implications of using costs in a variable way when the underlying resources cannot be managed or cannot respond in a variable manner.

The integration of ABC and TOC provides a solid baseline for tracking existing capacity utilization to the source or bottleneck of the process. In merging the activity and bottleneck concepts, Kee provides a means for understanding the economics of this basic trade-off and the impact of various operational decisions on the final profits of the firm. In this respect, the integrated model bridges the gap and fills some of the "holes" in each body of literature. Unfortunately, the elaborated model also suffers from many of the shortcomings embedded in a more traditional, relatively short-term model of the firm. In a world where bottlenecks shift at least daily and where value creation varies when the work making up the flow changes, it is difficult to apply any linear model and end up with results that ring true to an operational manager. Management is a nonlinear process, with trade-offs that defy mathematical measurement and manipulation but that must nonetheless be made.

Capacity cost management, if effective, gives managers insight into this nonlinear world. If the sole purpose of this set of tools is to detail existing usage patterns or to record the economic cost of current decisions and deployment patterns, capacity cost management fails in its basic mission: to improve the ability of the firm to meet its customers' needs and achieve a sustainable competitive advantage. Capacity cost management is about more than directing resources or tallying their utilization. It is about understanding the value-creation process, as defined by the customer, and constantly striving to make sure that most of the firm's resources are directed to the activities and outputs the customer values. In the end, the company that thrives knows how to get more than a dollar's worth of value out of a dollar of cost. It is this goal that defines the sustainable profits of the firm.

Capacity and Waste

One of the core issues faced by tactical capacity cost management systems is the identification and elimination of wasted resources. Building from a systems perspective, waste-based capacity management systems do not assume that a dollar of cost is equal to a dollar of value nor that all dollars spent are equal. Instead, waste-based capacity management systems capture and reflect the fact that value has to be a multiplicative function of cost or the firm cannot survive.

As suggested in Figure 4-2, the essence of waste-based capacity analysis is that the amount of waste versus utilized resources is identified and the causes for this waste are detailed. The first panel in Figure 4-2 illustrates an Ishikawa fishbone dia-

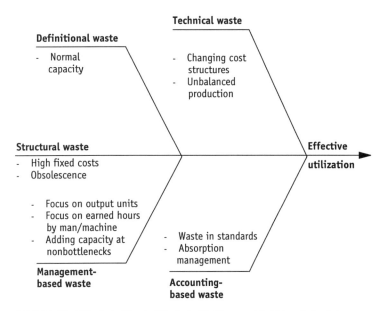

C. J. McNair, "The Hidden Costs of Capacity," *Handbook of Cost Management*, B. Brinker, ed., New York: Warren, Gorham, & Lamont, Inc., 1994.

Figure 4-2. Diagnosing Capacity Utilization

gram, a cause-effect approach to understanding capacity. In detailing the various subsystems or primary drivers in a process, this model sorts out all the various forms of waste from effective utilization, providing a means for taking action to eliminate this waste.[2]

The main focus of waste-based capacity cost management approaches is on understanding first what level of utilization is taking place, then changing the policies and assumptions that are leading to excessive levels of capacity waste. Looking at a simple example of a brewery that has several high-speed pack-out lines, the basic analysis underlying a waste-based capacity model can be developed (see Figure 4-3). Specifically, starting with theoretical capacity as defined on the bottleneck in the system, the filler head, the various ways in which potential capacity is assumed or managed away can be identified.[3]

The decision to use practical rather than theoretical capacity at this brewery results in the first drop-off of capacity utilization,

> **Example:** Total line 2 capacity is 2000 BPM at the theoretical level (filler-constrained). On a 24-hour clock this is a total bottles/day potential of 2,880,000 bottles of output, or 20,160,000 for 7 days.
> Current run levels are about 1022 bottles per minute of 16 hours of run time for 5.5 days of operation.

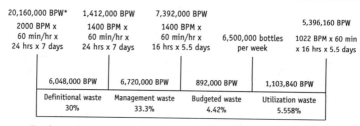

Total capacity waste: 14,763,840 BPW, or 73.23% of available capacity

* BPW is an abbreviation for bottles produced per week of operation.

Figure 4-3. Why the Definitions Matter

resulting in a 30% loss of potential throughput. Relatedly, management's decision to operate the plant 16 hours for 5.5 days, rather than 24 hours for 7 days (utilization of normal capacity baseline) leads to a 33% loss of output. From this "normal" level budgeted capacity is derived, in this case representing another loss. Finally, the process ends up running at only 1,022 bottles per minute, an efficiency loss due to glass-handling problems, the true process bottleneck. In the end, only 28% of the potential, purchased capacity was being used in this setting.

This basic analysis has been performed in many companies, with equally disturbing results. Most companies are using only 20 to 25% of their effective capacity. In almost every case, this high level of waste has been found to be embedded in traditional cost standards, hidden from view in a budgeted number that incorporates all prior sins and future errors in the search for an "attainable" budget target. The risks inherent in this traditional view of capacity are that new plants or major capacity additions may be made because the plant is running at "115%" of capacity.

The question that needs to be asked is, what type of capacity is this laudable performance being gauged by? If a company is running at 115% of budgeted capacity, it is still throwing away about 60% of its potential throughput. The danger in the traditional approach was witnessed at a midwestern company that had recently built a new plant when, in reality, changing the management policies at the existing facility would have provided enough capacity to meet current and downstream needs. Management at this company now reports and tracks operations at theoretical capacity as it continues to struggle to overcome the profit drain created by excess plant and equipment.

The variance approach would seem to be very short-term and operational in perspective, yet it provides the basis for future analysis and change in process management techniques that improves utilization. At a very basic level, simply multiplying the lost throughput times the profit earned per bottle of beer at Best Brew can get attention. Given the regulated nature of Best Brew's environment, average profits per bottle are $0.25. The lost capacity, then, translates to more than $3.5 million in lost profits *per week*.

While the demand for the output can be argued to vary, the right question to ask is, what capacity would be needed to serve peak demand if no waste was built into the process? Most of the $3.5 million is foregone profit driven by the current definition and management of "capacity" used by the plant. How much of this foregone amount can be reclaimed is up to marketing and management. Getting action on this front is more likely when the distressing reality of current utilization levels is reported and monetized.

Another way to think about the Best Brew data, then, is how much value the utilized 25% of the capacity is generating. A basic formula for this relationship would be:

Utilized capacity x value multiplier = current profitability

In Best Brew's case, the value multiplier would need to be at least 4 to result in a break-even position (0.25 x 4 = 1). To remain in business, the 25% of effectively deployed assets each have to generate $4 of revenue for the firm to stay in business.

Since this firm was profitable, the value multiplier was estimated to be about $5, roughly a 20% profit margin.

The waste-based capacity models, then, turn the corner from traditional, historically based views of capacity to suggest that the primary focus should be on what is *not* used, not on what is used. Rather than being satisfied with 115% capacity utilization (a theoretically impossible result), management should be concerned about having only a 25% effective utilization level. Seventy-five percent of this company's resources are wasted. If this company did not operate in a price-protected, cost-plus, regulated market, it would likely be facing profitability problems.

Overcoming the deadweight loss that wasted capacity or any wasted resource represents is a major challenge to any management team. Meeting this challenge to reduce waste begins with a capacity cost measurement that enables or makes visible the potential to create value from waste, not one that hides it behind assumptions and tradition.

□   Resource Effectiveness Model

A capacity cost measurement model that analyzes the economic impact of capacity management decisions on company performance is the resource effectiveness model. This model is concerned primarily with supporting planning and analysis of current and future capacity investments. It is used by Hills Pet Nutrition to support its short-, intermediate-, and long-term capacity planning decisions.

The resource effectiveness model tracks four key measures, as suggested in Figure 4-4: resource effectiveness, asset utilization, operating efficiency, and runtime efficiency. Standard runtime is examined as a percentage of total available time under different operating conditions to generate these capacity metrics. For instance, resource effectiveness compares standard runtime against pure theoretical capacity, while asset utilization measures adjust this equation for reductions in theoretical capacity due to management policies that reduce the plant's available time.

The results of this time-based analysis are easily translated into dollars through a process costing model defined on minutes of process time consumed. Combining operational and financial data, the resource effectiveness approach creates a powerful basis for sensitivity analysis and decision making that can be placed easily into capital investment models. If an organization combines the information in this model with real-time data collection and reporting on the plant floor, it can gain capacity information that spans all organizational levels and time frames.

The key element of the resource effectiveness approach that makes it so powerful is its reliance on time-based measurements

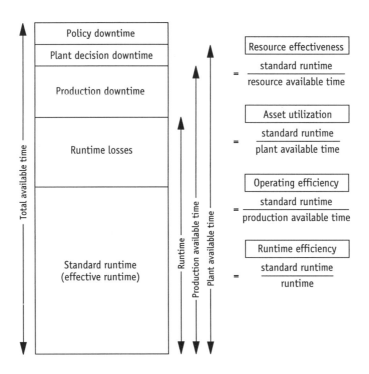

C. J. McNair and R. Vangermeersch, "Measuring the Cost of Capacity," SMA 4Y, Montvale, NJ: Institute of Management Accountants, 1996, p. 18.

Figure 4-4. Resource Effectiveness Model

for integrating operational and financial data. When time-based approaches can be used, they should be. Time is a stable, well-defined baseline measure for capacity, one that reduces all resources to their most basic nature. Supportive of throughput-based and related management techniques, time-based capacity cost management systems are easy to define and implement and provide reliable estimates of the profit-creating capability of a set of resources.

A second major feature of the resource effectiveness model is its intolerance for waste. Reflecting many of the same tenets as the approach developed at Best Brew, the techniques developed at Hills provide a solid baseline for identifying, eliminating, and avoiding excess and idle capacity across multiple time periods and decision frameworks. Used as a decision-support tool within a simulation-based reporting package, the resource effectiveness model allows Hills's management to better understand and manage cyclical demands on capacity with minimal disruption of the manufacturing process.

☐   Relational Databases and Capacity Reporting

Two models, the CAM-I and CUBES approaches, have been developed to help the semiconductor industry better understand current and potential impacts of capacity management practices on throughput and profitability. Relying on relational database structures to provide a set of comprehensive analytical tools, these models are designed to support the strategic decision process by helping managers understand and define the many states of capacity, measure these states, and then communicate them in a simple format.

The CAM-I capacity model is built from activities at the operational level that can be reported using several different formats. Developed by CAM-I in conjunction with Texas Instruments, the model is a collection of capacity data that includes the supply of capacity, the demand on that capacity by specific products, and the constraints within a process that limit the production of good units. The model is implemented through a series of templates that form the backbone of the capacity cost management database. The basic formula underlying the model is:

Rated capacity = idle capacity
+ nonproductive capacity
+ productive capacity

Idle capacity in this model is capacity not currently scheduled for use, whether due to the lack of demand, unavailability, or marketable but idle conditions. Nonproductive capacity, then, is neither idle nor productive and includes such items as setups, maintenance standby, scheduled downtime, unscheduled downtime, rework, and scrap. Variability is the primary cause of nonproductive capacity in the CAM-I framework. Finally, productive capacity under the CAM-I approach is the capacity that provides value to the customer—it results in the delivery of good products or services to the market (see Table 4-3).

Table 4-3. CAM-I Capacity Model

Rated Capacity	Summary Model	Industry Specific Model	Strategy Specific Model	Traditional Model
Rated capacity	Idle	Not marketable	Excess not usable	Theoretical
		Off limits	Management policy	
			Contractual	
			Legal	
		Marketable	Idle but usable	Practical
	Non-productive	Standby	Process balance	Scheduled
			Variability	
		Waste	Scrap Rework Yield loss	
		Maintenance	Scheduled Unscheduled	
		Setups	Time Volume Changeover	
	Productive	Process development		
		Product development		
		Good products		

CUBES, the capacity utilization bottleneck efficiency system, was developed by John Konopka at Sematech, a consortium of semiconductor manufacturers in the United States. It was driven by the same concerns as the CAM-I model and defined within the same industry; the similarities between the two models is striking. The CUBES model focuses on both capacity planning and identifying/implementing continuous improvement efforts in capacity utilization; communicating these results is a by-product, not the purpose, of the CUBES model.

The CUBES model combines the logic of cycle-time analysis and activity-based analysis to generate an integrated view of capacity cost management issues that moves beyond the process level to incorporate key opportunities for improvement across the entire industry value chain. Building from the rich database required to run semiconductor processes effectively, the model combines static capacity measures and models with a dynamic simulation that predicts capacity utilization under various assumptions and operating conditions, resulting in an analysis similar to that in Figure 4-5.

Both the CAM-I and CUBES models rely on relational database structures and intensive data manipulation to achieve their results. The CAM-I model, focused on time-based measurements, takes a different route through the capacity maze than the more activity-based and analytical CUBES model. Where the CAM-I model seeks to enhance understanding and control over the process, CUBES focuses on supporting continuous improvement efforts through dynamic simulations that incorporate many of the interdependencies that define the industry's value chain.

Both models can be adapted for use in other industries. Which model is chosen will depend on the core concerns of the company: analysis or control. CAM-I is more directly tied to responsibility accounting and communication within an organization, while CUBES seeks to support the management team in deciding how best to deploy existing and potential capacity. Both models require significant detail and data collection to drive their analysis as well as a relatively sophisticated management and information system capability.

□ The Cost Containment Model

The final tactical-level capacity model is focused on service settings, whether embedded within a manufacturing company or a freestanding service company.[4] Driven by the recognition that in many service settings baseline capacity can be very difficult to define, the model focuses instead on containing the costs created by specific activities. The objective of the cost containment model is to analyze and control future spending, not by enacting across-the-board cost-reduction mandates but rather by isolating the nonvalue-adding activities from those that add value. In addition, the cost containment model sets a spending limit on the activities performed within an area: shifting resources from nonvalue-adding to value-adding work is the only option for a service system facing increased demand for its output.

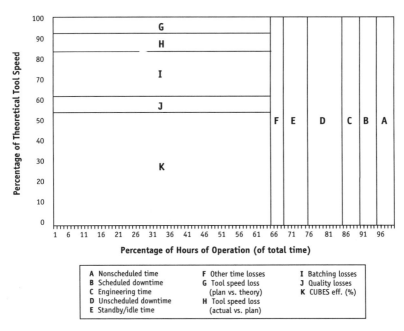

From John M. Konopka, "Capacity utilization bottleneck efficiency system--CUBES," *IEEE Transactions on Components, Packaging, and Manufacturing Technology*, September 18, 1995, pp. 484–491.

Figure 4-5. CUBES Analysis of Potential Capacity Utilization
CUBES (E10 Template) Efficiency Analysis Graph

Spending guidelines serve as the basis for implementing the cost containment approach. These guidelines can be based on internal analysis, best-in-class benchmarking, customer survey, or management judgment. As suggested by Figure 4-6, the analysis focuses on current spending against this benchmark or standard. An analysis of the value-adding, priority 1 activities in this

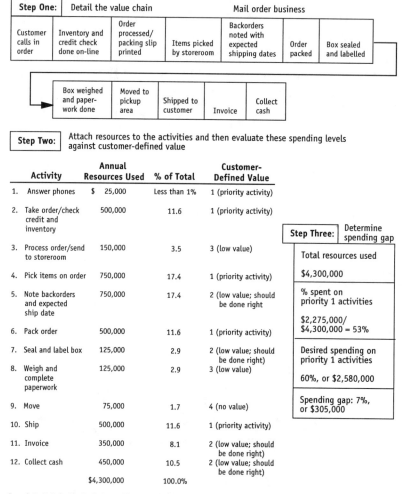

| Step One: | Detail the value chain | | | | | | Mail order business | |

| Customer calls in order | Inventory and credit check done on-line | Order processed/ packing slip printed | Items picked by storeroom | Backorders noted with expected shipping dates | Order packed | Box sealed and labelled |

| Box weighed and paper-work done | Moved to pickup area | Shipped to customer | Invoice | Collect cash |

Step Two: Attach resources to the activities and then evaluate these spending levels against customer-defined value

Activity	Annual Resources Used	% of Total	Customer-Defined Value
1. Answer phones	$ 25,000	Less than 1%	1 (priority activity)
2. Take order/check credit and inventory	500,000	11.6	1 (priority activity)
3. Process order/send to storeroom	150,000	3.5	3 (low value)
4. Pick items on order	750,000	17.4	1 (priority activity)
5. Note backorders and expected ship date	750,000	17.4	2 (low value; should be done right)
6. Pack order	500,000	11.6	1 (priority activity)
7. Seal and label box	125,000	2.9	2 (low value; should be done right)
8. Weigh and complete paperwork	125,000	2.9	3 (low value)
9. Move	75,000	1.7	4 (no value)
10. Ship	500,000	11.6	1 (priority activity)
11. Invoice	350,000	8.1	2 (low value; should be done right)
12. Collect cash	450,000	10.5	2 (low value; should be done right)
	$4,300,000	100.0%	

Step Three: Determine spending gap

Total resources used

$4,300,000

% spent on priority 1 activities

$2,275,000/ $4,300,000 = 53%

Desired spending on priority 1 activities

60%, or $2,580,000

Spending gap: 7%, or $305,000

From C. J. McNair, *The Profit Potential*, New York: Wiley & Sons, 1995.

Figure 4-6. Spending Effectiveness: Cost Containment in Action

shipping example suggests that the company is spending too few resources on value-adding work. To maintain the current total costs of serving a customer, the 7% shortfall in spending on value-added work must be offset by reductions in spending on nonvalue-adding activities. The most obvious place to look for these savings is in the level 3 and 4 activities not valued by the customer. In the example, these low-priority items account for $350,000 of the total cost of the process, which is sufficient to meet the $305,000 shortfall in spending on priority 1 activities as well as support a $45,000 reduction in overall costs.

The cost containment approach has been used by companies such as Apple Computer and Stratus Computer to control costs while ensuring that customer needs are met. At Apple, the logic has been applied to its customer service area, while at Stratus the cost containment approach is used throughout the budgeting process to ensure that the company follows a controlled growth strategy.

Containing service capacity costs is typically an ongoing process of negotiation, compromise, reflection, and analysis. Service outputs are hard to define, and the resources used to create superior service are often intangible, being tied to the human resources of the firm. In this complex, ambiguous setting, management has to be guided by its understanding of the value component in the completed work assessed against the estimated resources consumed by an activity. Driven by the demands of customers and the market, the cost containment approach provides a distinctly different slant on the capacity management problem.

Creating Action in a Tactical Setting

The models developed above are similar in their focus on existing processes and the boundaries of the organization. In many companies today, however, new approaches to these standard problems are being developed. For instance, supplier alliances are being used to augment capacity within a tactical time frame, allowing a company to step away from the black-and-white world of traditional capacity decision making. Relatedly, companies are turning to cellular and other just-in-time manufacturing and management approaches to increase effective capacity by redesigning the flow of work and materials through an organization. Finally, business process redesign is being used to remove work or nonvalue-added activities from an organization, resulting in a higher ratio of value-added cost to total cost. In each of these instances, the focus of the capacity analysis moves beyond the current processes, value chain, and markets to question the core assumptions used to manage the business.

It is in these areas that capacity cost management begins to be transformed from a tactical tool to a strategic one. The line between tactical and strategic decision making is fuzzy, and the movement from one to the other is often difficult to perceive. If the decision to augment capacity results in short-term outsourcing, the decision most likely falls into the tactical range. On the other hand, if the outsourcing option takes on a long-term, alliance-based approach, it rapidly becomes strategic in nature. Due to the shifting nature of these higher-level options to solving the capacity management problem, they will be more fully developed in the next chapter.

Having recognized that the process of bounding capacity analysis and the models that underlie it is itself an ambiguous process, it is clear that there is no one right definition of capacity, no one right approach, no one "true" cost of capacity, and no single model that suits every need within one company, let alone across industries and diverse settings. Capacity cost management is a journey, not a destination; one that leads toward increased value-added and reduced waste. The best measures and models to use in supporting this journey are those that create and sustain continuous improvement in the company and its core processes.

The primary challenge in creating a capacity cost management system, then, is to identify the elements of the capacity puzzle that can be acted on and to identify accurately the responsiveness of resources to changes in work patterns. In a highly constrained, high-fixed-cost setting, the cost containment logic may be the most defensible, while in a setting with high levels of variable cost a utilization- and waste elimination-based model may make more sense.

Understanding what parts of the capacity puzzle can be managed in the intermediate term, as well as the overall impact on profitability created by process and product problems, is the key to choosing a tactical capacity model. In a stable setting with well-defined costs, the normalized costing approach used by Caterpillar can provide a tremendous amount of information with only minimal incremental costs. On the other hand, in a highly ambiguous, complex, and poorly defined setting, the only real possibility is the total spending on a type or category of work. In this case, attention has to be focused on containing the amount of resources consumed by a cluster of activities or ensuring that most of the spending is directed toward value-enhancing and value-creating efforts.

In the end, tactical capacity decisions either affect the velocity of materials or transactions through a system by eliminating bottlenecks or redesigning low-value activities out of the process or change the value-creation profile of the organization within its structural and product constraints. Taking the existing product and plant structures of the firm as a given, tactical decision making focuses on increasing the effective utilization of company resources within its current strategy. Tactical capacity analysis is a puzzle with a defined set of pieces that can be put together in a limited, constrained number of ways, albeit creatively. The final and major test of capacity cost management lies in its ability to support strategic analysis and improve the competitive position of the firm. This final set of issues and models is addressed in the chapter that follows.

> All effort is in the last analysis sustained by faith that it is worth making.—Ordway Tead, *The Art of Leadership*

☐ References and Notes

[1] R. Kee, "Integrating Activity-Based Costing with the Theory of Constraints to Enhance Production-Related Decision Making," *Accounting Horizons*, December 1995, pp. 48–61.

[2] The source of this section is "The Hidden Costs of Capacity," by C. J. McNair, published in the *Handbook of Cost Management*, 1994 edition, B. Brinker, ed., New York: Warren, Gorham & Lamont, Inc.

[3] The approach and relative utilization figures presented in this section are based on actual data developed during the course of a field study of a major brewery. The relationships identified subsequently have been applied to and verified in a wide variety of settings.

[4] This model was developed at Stratus Computer and is explained in more depth in the book *The Profit Potential*, by C. J. McNair, New York: Wiley & Sons, 1995.

5

VALUE VS. COST: STRATEGIC CAPACITY COST MANAGEMENT

Our ideas are only intellectual instruments which we use to break into phenomena; we must change them when they have served their purpose, as we change a blunt lancet that we have used long enough.—Claude Bernard, 1865.

Capacity cost management has as many faces as there are forms of assets and strategies that shape their use. In both operational and tactical capacity cost models, the emphasis is on the *deployment* of existing resources. The cost of capacity in these short- and intermediate-term approaches can be measured with a reasonable level of accuracy because the resources that make up the defined capability to do work can be identified. Moving into the long-term area, the focus of capacity cost management changes significantly. No longer concerned with the use of existing assets and processes, management turns its attention toward shaping the future. In the long term all aspects of the capacity puzzle can be controlled, all costs become variable. The products and services the purchased capacity provides can be and usually are changed, leading to a totally new set of demands on the firm's resources.

The focus of this, the final "practice" chapter, is to look at capacity from the outside in, as a market- and customer-driven package of productive potential to create value, not as a constraint on current performance. The last course in the movable feast, strategic capacity cost management provides the basis for creating the corporate future and defining the processes and activities that will form the foundation for a sustainable competitive advantage.

Bridging the Strategic Gap

Strategic capacity cost management builds from knowledge gained at the operational and tactical levels. Three specific capacity models developed earlier are designed to bridge the gap between ongoing capacity management and strategy: CUBES, the resource effectiveness model (REM), and the CAM-I model. While these models are deployment focused, they all provide insight into the long-term implications of current asset and process capabilities.

☐ The CUBES Model

The CUBES model is predominantly tactical in nature, but its line and plant simulations can be used to determine overall resource requirements under a variety of demand conditions as well as potential cycle times and delivery windows, given a solid knowledge of which products and services are to be provided. Working from a series of sensitivity variables, including demand, mix, reliability, process capability, and engineering usage, the CUBES static capacity model is transformed into a dynamic analytical tool.

The shortcoming of CUBES in the strategic arena is its tie to current plant and processes in defining, analyzing, and planning capacity management. The CUBES model is a constrained optimization: strategic capacity cost management is constraint bursting in nature. Creating a solid database of potential outcomes of using existing resources is, however, a required first step in determining whether new forms of capacity are likely to be needed in the foreseeable future. This is the type of information ably provided by the CUBES approach.

☐ **Resource Effectiveness: Understanding Today and Tomorrow**

The resource effectiveness model (REM) was developed by Hills Pet Food to prevent errors in future strategic capacity decisions. Truly a bridge between current and future needs, this model's primary concern is ensuring that all the potential of existing resources is fully deployed. Building from theoretical capacity baselines, REM provides the dynamic simulation capabilities of CUBES with minimal complexity in its definition and maintenance.

As with CUBES, the focus of REM is more on understanding current capability and ensuring that no excess capacity is added to the system than on rethinking the entire capacity puzzle. By constantly measuring and drawing management's attention to plant decisions and policy downtime, the model keeps everyone's eyes on total available capacity rather than on that part of the resources that has been used in the past (practical or lower levels of utilization).

At Hills, no capacity decision is made without running a series of simulations through REM to see if different routings, scheduling modules, or management policies can be used to free up the needed production time. Designed for the low-variety, high-volume process manufacturing setting that defines the Hills operation, REM forces everyone to remember that new capacity represents new constraints and new costs that won't easily go away should volumes or product mix change. REM is strategic, then, in that it is always looking forward, always querying the system for ways to avoid new capacity purchases, which create long-term, unavoidable costs for the company.

☐ The CAM-I View
of Strategic Capacity Cost Management

Of the three bridge models, the CAM-I model provides the clearest linkage between tactical and strategic views of capacity. Placing capacity decisions in the same realm of strategic import as market segment and product selection decisions, this model focuses on creating a communications link between operations and management, a link that can be used to assess the current capacity status, to show trends, and to plan changes in capacity. In addition, the model can provide the information and justification manufacturing needs to secure investment for new business initiatives.[1]

The range of strategic capacity decisions that the CAM-I model supports includes the total quantity of capacity, the type of capacity, the location of capacity, the attainment of new capacity, and the segmentation of capacity. Focused on manufacturing productive capacity, the primary emphasis of this model is on the following issues:

- Whether internal and external demand variation should be handled with increased inventory, increased capacity, or longer lead times to customers;
- Make versus buy decisions;
- Buy versus lease of assets decisions;
- Whether to buy large chunks of capacity rather than small chunks;
- Selecting commodity versus customer-designed capacity.

Noting that strategic capacity cost management issues continue after the acquisition decision, the CAM-I model is also concerned with supporting management in determining how much capacity to use for development, how to allocate capacity to existing products, how much to diversify products, processes, and capacity in one factory, and when to abandon current capacity.

The CAM-I approach argues that a company can build its basic corporate strategy around a product or process perspective. In the former case, the products are developed, then the processes and capacity necessary to make them are acquired. The product idea can occur well ahead of the decision to purchase the capability to make the product efficiently and effectively. Product decisions lead to strategic capacity decisions, which then shape the tactical and operational policies that guide the deployment of this capacity under this approach.

An example of a process-driven strategy is reflected in REM. The emphasis in this setting is on making sure that the products currently made and planned to be made fit within current and planned process capabilities. In a process setting, the emphasis in capacity decisions is on flexibility, while in product-line decisions it is on matching production capability with product features. In industries with high fixed costs, capacity is a primary barrier to entry for competitors. Keeping in the forefront of process capability forms the basis for current and future capacity cost management decisions in these firms.

In all three of these bridge models, the emphasis is on the deployment of resources. All three are inside-out views of the capacity cost management puzzle, representing company-centered decision making focused on cost and waste avoidance rather than on value creation. To create a sustainable competitive advantage, all resources have to be deployed effectively, but effective deployment does not guarantee that a competitive advantage will be gained. Ensuring that the company's strategic capacity decisions meet this second, tougher criterion requires a change in the focus and nature of capacity cost management.

Capacity and Value Creation

Creating a sustainable competitive advantage begins with understanding what current and potential future customers value. Value-driven capacity management starts from the outside, the market. It strives to ensure that the company's product/service bundles match customer needs and, once matched, that these value profiles drive the shape and nature of internal decisions.

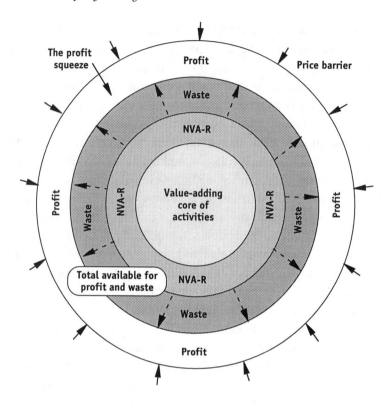

Figure 5-1. The Basic Economics of Business

Value-based capacity models (VBCM)[2] are shaped by the basic economics of the market presented earlier in Figure 2-1 and repeated here in Figure 5-1. The focus of VBCM, though, moves away from concerns with managing the internal dynamics of value-added, nonvalue-added, and wasteful activities to understanding what defines the value-added core. What product/process/service features does the customer value? Why? How much value is placed on the output of one activity or process versus another? How effectively are current resources deployed against the customer's defined value attributes? In creating new capacity, products, processes, or services, how can this value equation be improved?

VBCM is shaped by the external market and its assessment of value, not the internal dynamics of the firm or its current management philosophies. VBCM is a nonlinear, systemic model that adds value-creating ability to the list of key strategic capacity issues such as the flexibility of existing resources; their degree of responsiveness, in costs and productivity, to shifts in product/process strategies; their variety-absorbing capabilities; and the reliability of the process and its outputs.

At the heart of VBCM is the development of customer value profiles, as suggested in Figure 5-2. The logic underlying value profiling is well developed in the market research literature. Using a data collection approach based on a trade-off, such as asking a customer to allocate one dollar of purchase price to the various product and service attributes currently available or potentially desired, the value profile defines the value-added core (VAC) of the firm.

The rankings in Figure 5-2 reflect the value assessment of an imaging device within a radiology department of a hospital. The value rankings for a market segment range from product attributes to service attributes and include quality, cost, delivery, reputation, and organizational issues. These value rankings are the

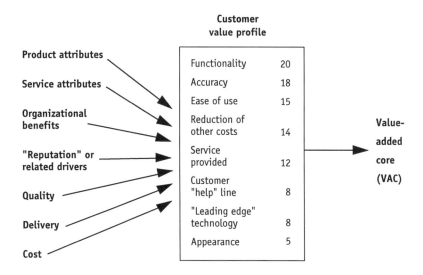

Figure 5-2. Deploying the "logic of the market" begins with understanding what the customer values, why, and how much

clearest signal of what trade-offs the customer is making in choosing a specific product/service bundle.

As long as the potential product/service bundle can be described to the customer, a value assessment can be created. At the oven range plant for a major white goods producer, the value profile was obtained during the design phase for a new line of kitchen ranges. In the imaging example the rankings were made for a current product that was being redeployed with a new service bundle.

The value profile provides several key pieces of information for a company in making its strategic capacity decisions.

- What product attributes are valued?
- What is the relative value of various aspects of the product/ service bundle?
- If resources are to be acquired or redeployed, what are the optimal areas to focus on?
- What current activities are being performed that the customer in reality doesn't value or reimburse the firm for?
- How much can be spent on each key element of the product/ service bundle as a percentage of total expenditures?

The key difference between VBCM and traditional capacity modeling, then, is that the company does not define what aspects of its processes and activities are value adding—the customer does. Reaching outside the firm for strategic direction, the emphasis of this model is on the continuous redeployment of resources to those activities, products, and services that customers value. Capacity acquisitions that do not meet this objective can be justified only if they reduce the cost of existing work, freeing up more resources for value-creating work.

Taking a customer value profile and transforming it into a strategy for current and future capacity, product, and process decisions starts with understanding the gap between current spending patterns and what is needed to meet customer requirements. Traditional cost models provide little usable information for this *gap analysis*; activity-based costing is a prerequisite for analyzing current spending against customer value profiles. The driving force in this form of activity-based cost analysis, however, is not products but rather the value profile. What resources are used to create and ensure product functionality? What is the cost for providing desired services? How is the cost to provide leading edge technology incurred?

Creating a value-based activity costing model results in a new cost hierarchy, one that focuses on:

- Value-creating activities/processes;
- Activities and processes that are expected and that create negative value assessments if not present (hygiene factors);
- Business sustaining or nonvalue-added but required activities;
- Value-degrading activities;
- Needless or wasteful activities.

Having performed the sorting of current activities into these five basic categories, the company can assess its spending patterns against those items valued by the customer. The resulting gap analysis is the first step in creating a strategic, market-driven approach to capacity management.

Several interesting pieces of information can be discerned once the gap analysis is completed. First, the company's overall *value creation multiplier* can be estimated by summarizing current resource utilization patterns on three dimensions: utilized for value-creating or hygiene activities, stored for future use, or wasted (total resource cost for the period less utilization and storage estimates).

The resulting estimation of utilized or effectively deployed cost is divided by current company profits before interest, taxes, and unusual items, resulting in the value creation multiplier.

In both the range plant and the medical imaging example, the effective utilization of resources, defined and measured in this strict sense, was approximately 25% of total expenditures. To break even under this scenario a company would have to generate $4 of total value for every $1 of resources purchased.[3] Generating a profit would require an even higher value multiplier.

Having established the company's overall value creation multiplier, attention then can be directed toward those actions that can improve performance. Driven by the value profile, strategic decisions about current and future product/service bundles and the structures used to deliver them can be made. The nonlinearity of a VBCM begins to be important at this stage. Specifically, the value rankings of the customer provide the means to prioritize spending and identify where to focus efforts to eliminate activities and costs.

At this point in the analysis, many elements of the value-cost puzzle that makes up VBCM can be dealt with:

- Identification and development of plans to eliminate or reduce nonvalue-adding activities and product/service attributes;
- Reprioritization and redirection of spending and investment plans to prioritize those areas valued by the customer;
- Enhancement of service profiles to increase the value of the company's product/service bundles;
- Education/interaction with the customer to create an awareness of potentially overlooked value attributes of the product/service bundle that the firm currently offers;
- Identification of areas within the industry value chain where leverage and strategic alliances can help improve the value/cost ratio;
- Focused product, process, service, and company redesign to better meet "true" customer preferences;
- Market segmentation or identification of new customers whose value profiles more closely match that provided by the firm.

In an early stage of development, VBCM focuses on redefining the basis of capacity management away from meeting internal needs to maximizing the deployment of resources in areas valued by the customer. The model ultimately will assign value multipliers to the various processes and activities performed within a firm, creating an "options" framework for current and future capacity investment and deployment decisions.

As with many of the new management models being developed on an almost daily basis in the management literature, VBCM represents a bundling of models and techniques that already exist. The key to its effectiveness in changing the investment or strategic orientation of the firm is that these "old" models are deployed in a new way. Reflecting the lessons embedded in the continuous improvement paradigm and the systemic models that underlie it, VBCM is just one of a new wave of capacity and cost models, such as CUBES and CAM-I, that promise to pave the way to a new vision of effectiveness in capacity management.

In the end, creating a sustainable competitive advantage comes from understanding how a company creates value and what power a dollar of spending has in improving a company's value-creating abilities. A focus on creating value begins with taking a holistic view of the organization, one that recognizes that the profit potential of a set of resources is not a constant but rather the key activity in the manager's tool kit. The tighter the fit between the value profile and cost profile of the firm, the greater the value creation, hence profits that can be earned over time. Reaching this profit potential is not the outcome of squeezing more work out of a company's employees or pushing more product through existing plant. Powering up the "costs," the purchased productive capacity of the firm, is the key to gaining a sustainable competitive advantage.

The Strategic Capacity Puzzle

Models are interesting ways to view and analyze capacity in any time frame, but in the end the essence of the strategic capacity cost management puzzle comes down to understanding not only how the company is performing currently against customer expectations but also how the firm can be positioned to take advantage of new products, technologies, and business designs (see Figure 5-3). Strategic views of capacity have to incorporate all these factors, resulting in a set of action plans that define the future.

Where the bridge capacity cost models and the emerging VBCM approaches focus on creating a migration path for capacity

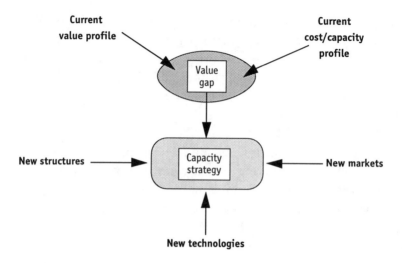

Figure 5-3. Forces Shaping Strategic Capacity Cost Management

deployment, another set of options exists for a company that seeks to change its capacity profile. Specifically, a company can decide to:

- Build a new plant;
- Design and build a new product or set of product/service bundles;
- Exit existing markets;
- Implement a major redefinition/redesign of its business processes;
- Pursue strategic alliances to increase the scope and availability of capacity;
- Engage in joint ventures to expand into new markets;
- Integrate forward or backward in the industry value chain.

Each of these options brings with it a unique set of capacity issues and concerns about current and future cost profiles.

☐ Major Capacity Additions

One of the most common traditional issues in strategic capacity cost management is the decision to add a new plant or a new line to an existing plant. Guided by the assessed utilization of the existing facilities, these decisions more often than not have led to increased rather than decreased operating costs. Whenever capacity has been defined at less than theoretical capacity, in fact, a ratchet effect (see Figure 5-4) has been created where higher levels of waste are embedded in the total cost profile of the company.

The building of a new plant creates a permanent layer of cost that is difficult to eliminate in the long run, let alone change in the short and intermediate term. In fact, much of the renewed interest in capacity cost management emerged as a result of applying the "new" (or renewed) theory of capacity costing to existing plants and facilities. In a field test of the basic variance capacity model presented earlier, it was discovered that most companies were actually using less than 25% of their effective capacity (range from 15% to 40%; mean 25%). As at Hills Pet Nutrition, this less than encouraging utilization analysis is often done *after* more capacity has been added rather than before.

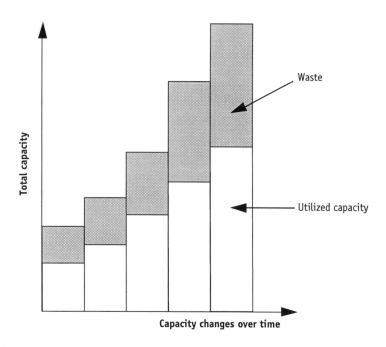

Figure 5-4. Wasted Capacity: A Ratchet Effect

The ratchet effect of capacity waste is one of the major issues shaping a redefinition of the "need" to add a new plant to a company's existing facilities. In setting after setting, it is becoming clear that adding new capacity is the most expensive solution available to meeting short- and long-term capacity shortfalls. Changing management policies, including the hours of operation and the nature of the production process itself, provides a much more cost-effective and flexible solution to the problem. Increasing plant space adds a permanent layer of fixed cost to the company that cannot be easily avoided, changed, or reduced. Acting as an anchor on profits, new plants and facilities can drain the firm's value-creating ability faster than almost any other decision or action the firm takes. A new plant means new constraints, not new opportunities.

Before adding new capacity, then, companies are beginning to consider the following set of questions:

- Are we operating even close to theoretical capacity?
- If not, could an additional shift be added to the existing work force?
- Could changes be made to bottleneck management to ease constraints?
- Could processes or products be redesigned to reduce the demand on the plant?
- Can an outside vendor be used to relieve current capacity constraints?
- Are there products that are low-profit items but high-capacity users that can be eliminated with minimal strategic impact?

These questions, plus a renewed focus on understanding the root cause of all forms of capacity waste, are the basis for the CUBES, CAM-I, and resource effectiveness simulation models. Focused on preventing the acquisition of a new plant before this costly decision is undertaken, companies are turning to capacity cost management models to ensure that new plants and facilities will lead to reduced costs and increased competitiveness rather than increased costs and reduced competitiveness.

☐   Redesigning Product/Service Bundles

When capacity is viewed as the capability to create value for the customers, a new approach to strategic capacity management emerges. Specifically, companies are beginning to redesign their product/service bundles to reap more of the benefits embedded in their industry structures. For instance, the medical imaging group mentioned earlier is a leader in its technology. This position affects the market, however; there they are considered the high-cost provider of what is seen as a commodity product. Having created a product and a physical plant designed to produce that product, the company had few options available on the product side of the capacity puzzle.

In this setting, the capacity that needed to be analyzed strategically was the product/service bundle as understood by the customer and delivered by the company. Using a value-chain approach, the company decided to reanalyze the role of its product in the entire "episode of care" in the hospital setting. After visiting two sites, one that was dissatisfied with the technology due to its "high" cost and another that was enamored of the product because of its "low" cost, management discovered that the way the customer envisioned the product defined its value. At site one, the digital imaging product was used in the same way as traditional x-ray technology. No changes were made to the way the procedures were performed or the episode of care was delivered.

At the second site, though, the technology was used to enable process changes that increased the time spent with patients. More time with patients resulted in higher service levels, higher perceived quality of care, and increased satisfaction of the x-ray technicians with their jobs. This bit of information led to the recognition that the capacity that needed to be managed was the deployment of the digital imaging device in the hospital, not the physical plant used to make the machine. In other words, the strategic analysis determined that internal resources should be shifted from making and selling machines to providing business process redesign services to the hospitals to increase the value created for the ultimate customer—the patient—and referring physicians.

Is this an example of strategic capacity management? Most definitely. Specifically, the recognition that capacity has both a soft and hard side and that value creation relies on the deployment of this capacity to those activities and processes valued by the customer drove the decisions and overall business strategy of this firm. Capacity means more than machines. In this setting, capacity in the plant wasn't what was essential to improving company performance; the utilization of its human capacity was. Redefining the product/service bundle effectively shifted resources from nonvalue-adding efforts, all tied to the traditional view that the company sold machines, to value-creating activities generated by the enhancement of the product/service bundle.

☐ Exiting Markets

Strategic capacity decisions are often tied to dynamic shifts in the markets the company serves. One of the major forms of waste in a company is permanently idled capacity due to exiting a market. It hits a firm right where it hurts—at the bottom line. The CAM-I model makes a major issue of identifying and eliminating permanently idled capacity, but in the real world taking the step to write off or sell existing assets is one of the most difficult decisions to make.

At no place in the organization is this stress felt more than at the plant level in a multiplant, multicountry setting. During a visit to a large plant owned and operated by a telecommunications business, the discussion turned to the impact of recent corporate decisions on the performance of the plant. Specifically, an entire line of robots had been idled when a decision had been made to move a product offshore for production. The frustration of the plant manager, whose overhead and capacity utilization measures were far below target, was evidenced when he asked for ways to "put baggies on the machines and their costs."

The harsh lesson learned when decisions are made to outsource existing products or to exit markets is that assets, while easily purchased, are hard to get rid of downstream. In many cases, the assets are inflexible. The very features that made these assets desirable in the first place often serve as their undoing in the long term. For instance, the robots in this plant were purchased because their capabilities so closely matched those needed to make the subsequently outsourced product. The problem was that these capabilities made the machines basically useless for other applications—the "build platform" was either too small or too large for the other products made by the company. The inflexibility of this "flexible" capacity led to major downstream constraints and excess cost for this firm.

In exiting a market, the capacity issue becomes one of avoidability of the costs in the affected plant. If costs can be avoided or if the capacity is flexible enough to be redeployed to other uses, the cost implications of this strategic capacity decision are minimal. More often than not, the decision to exit a market results in permanently excess capacity that needs to be liquidated.

The support costs of the organization, though, cannot be reduced as easily as the physical assets of the firm. As ABC models proliferate, it is becoming increasingly clear that the soft costs of capacity are seldom reduced when the hard costs are eliminated by the decision to exit a market. In the end, the following questions need to be addressed when focusing on the strategic implications of exiting a market.

- What costs can be eliminated if the market is exited?
- How long will it take to eliminate the costs?
- How will idled resources be redeployed?
- For resources that are permanently idled and cannot be easily redeployed, how is this new layer of waste going to affect the long-term health of the firm?
- Are there ways to rent out idled capacity or otherwise find new uses for the existing facilities?
- What support costs will or will not be affected by the decision?

Costs are sticky on the downside, leading to the need to assess carefully the entire life cycle of a product within the process that is being designed to support it. In some Japanese companies such as Toyota, plant capacity decisions are intricately tied to the product life cycle. When a new product is launched, the requisite, optimal capacity for that product is already planned. Process improvements are factored into the decision regarding how much capacity to create, leading to the ongoing reduction of waste as the basis for meeting increased product demand. Upon exiting a market, the capacity has been totally consumed, used up with minimal waste in making the entire bundle of products originally envisioned for the plant.

Not all plant or market exits can be planned, but they can be avoided if careful analysis is made before new resources are acquired to ensure that the new resources are truly needed. Strategic capacity management tied to the life-cycle costs of the firm is a long-term analysis that begins before products are launched. Since capacity costs ratchet up much easier than they ramp down, exit decisions can fail to provide the promised benefits. Perhaps a lesser of two evils, strategic decisions to exit markets still represent a major source of permanently idled, hence wasted, capacity.

☐ Other Options—Adding Capacity Without Adding Plant

When approaching capacity in a strategic sense, the goal is to add assets when needed, and only when needed. Many companies are, in fact, turning to new ways to increase their productive capacity, ways that totally eliminate the risk of downstream disposal problems while providing optimal flexibility to respond to changing markets. Whether achieved through process redesign, strategic alliances, joint ventures, or integration forward or backward into the industry value chain, these innovative approaches to adding capacity without adding plant are reshaping business practice.

Business process redesign is being used to reduce the amount and cost of nonvalue-added work within an organization, freeing up resources to do other work. Companies such as Johnson & Johnson are using process redesign to increase the capacity of their finance group to provide decision support. Finding ways to perform transaction processing with fewer and fewer resources while improving the level of service provided, J & J has turned to shared services structures to provide needed benefits. Strategically redeploying finance resources to value-adding work, the CFO organization at J & J is redefining its processes and creating new forms of "capacity" for its internal and external customers.

Strategic alliances are giving companies the ability to expand their services or reduce the cost of existing product/service bundles, with minimal short-term costs. For instance, Lucent Technologies is partnering with Babson College to provide a degree-based finance leadership development program. Faced with the need to develop rapidly the capacity to deliver this program, Lucent made the decision that it was more cost effective and value creating to form a strategic alliance with a university than to develop a high-quality finance program on its own. In addition to gaining the needed services, Lucent was able to transform its internal activities into a degree program that has helped it attract high-quality candidates while avoiding additional costs to educate one individual at a time in a traditional university setting. Lucent has obtained the "capacity" to deliver this program without purchasing any of the physical and human assets ordinarily required.

Other companies, such as Polaroid and Caterpillar, rely heavily on joint ventures to increase their capacity while expanding into new markets. In a joint venture, minimal resources are put at risk to attain new manufacturing capability. In addition, the access to the new market is improved. Providing technical expertise, minimal physical assets, and engineering support, Caterpillar and Polaroid rely on their joint venture partners to share in the costs of providing product while minimizing the amount of investment required to penetrate new markets.

Finally, companies are using the knowledge gained from strategic cost analysis to change the way they compete in their industry. Utilizing value-chain logic, companies are shifting their resources to capture more of the value potential in an industry. One of the best-known examples of this approach is the result of work done by John Shank with Champion Paper. Positioned as a producer of high-grade, designer paper for a small but potentially profitable market, Champion began searching for ways to increase the profitability of its operations. Rather than changing the way it managed its physical assets, the firm changed its definition of its raw materials. Where in the past the company had purchased trees, turned them to pulp, then dyed the pulp to the desired color, it was realized that by moving down in the value chain it could eliminate upstream costs while continuing to provide the same product bundle to its customers. The answer lay in the scrap market: scrap paper was to be substituted for virgin fibers. Eliminating its reliance on upstream papermaking operations, Champion was able to reap a competitive advantage by changing its raw-material requirements.

As evidenced by these examples and hundreds not detailed here, capacity in the long term means more than assets, more than processes; it is the value-creating ability of the firm, however that is attained. Strategic capacity cost management reaches far beyond the boundaries of existing plant and equipment, beyond the current product/service bundle, to incorporate the myriad of flexible, innovative ways companies are expanding their capability to create value while minimizing the resources these efforts consume. Wherever resources are, should be, or can be deployed, capacity issues exist. At the heart of the business equation, capacity cost management is the key to creating the corporate future.

Concluding Remarks

Managing capacity is truly a movable feast, one that brings a company and its management into close proximity with every major business issue possible. Whether focused on maximizing the velocity of materials through the plant in the short term or redeploying resources to improve the value-creating ability of the firm, capacity cost management is the key to gaining and maintaining a competitive advantage.

The models, examples, and historical analysis developed in this monograph span almost 100 years of practice and theory in capacity cost management. What is striking in the end is that almost every idea, every model, every approach was envisioned by the early thinkers. Church would not be surprised by anything written in these pages but would rather be amazed at the fact that, 75 years after he originally wrote most of these ideas down, they are still being discussed as "new." It would seem that truly the more things change, the more they remain the same.

Only in the area of strategic capacity management can it be argued that the term "new" may be applied to the models, techniques, and practices that are emerging. As companies turn to horizontal or process management structures, as organizations begin to take on the appearance of networks embedded in larger networks, and as computers and other telecommunications technologies pave the way for the virtual corporation, the concept of capacity in the traditional sense may fade. Will better utilization of a machine or a plant always matter? The answer clearly is yes.

But will better capacity utilization mean superior company performance? The answer to that question is more doubtful in the future than ever before. Reducing excess resources, eliminating waste, and striving for continuous improvement remain as essential today as ever, but the definition of value, and where that value is created, are forever being changed.

In the end, it is the company that understands its value-creating abilities, as defined by the customer, that will prosper. Using these external signals of value to guide its capacity decisions, firms likely will find that capacity in the "soft" sense (people/process capability) will assume ever greater importance over capacity in the "hard" sense (machine utilization). But capacity cost management will remain, with the feast consumed in a different location but available nonetheless. Definable only

when it is least interesting, capacity remains the sphinx of the
business world.

> The thought of the unknowable and the infinite becomes
> truly salutary only when it is the unexpected recompense of
> the intelligence that has given itself loyally and unreserv-
> edly to the study of the knowable and the finite. There is a
> notable difference between the mystery which comes be-
> fore our ignorance and the mystery which comes after what
> we have learned.—Maurice Maeterlinck, quoted in *Charac-
> ters and Events,* Vol. I, by John Dewey.

☐ References and Notes

[1] The CAM-I model discussion in this section is based on the monograph
Capacity: A Manager's Primer, by T. Klammer, Arlington, TX: CAM-I, 1996.

[2] The VBCM approach is a new model created by C. J. McNair in
conjunction with several major corporations. It uses an options pricing
framework to analyze current capacity "investment" decisions within a
firm and to shape future capacity management approaches. The focus of
this model extends beyond capacity but has its roots in the research
summarized in this monograph.

[3] It is interesting to note, in both the Best Brew example detailed in Chapter
4 and the research completed for this chapter, that approximately 25%
of all resources are deployed to value creation. It is difficult to say at this
early stage of this new research stream whether this pattern will continue
or to what degree improvements in the design and measurement of the
costs in the system will shift these results. For now, it simply remains as
an interesting finding.

6

CAPACITY: AN ONGOING SAGA

Once learning solidifies, all is over with it.—Alfred North
Whitehead, *Dialogues of Alfred North Whitehead.*

In exploring the past, present, and future of capacity cost management, the diversity of models, views, and assumptions emerges
as the dominant feature of this complex area of study. On one
hand, capacity can be defined as simply the denominator in the
basic cost equation, the estimate of work that can be done by a
set of resources. On the other hand, capacity can represent the
organization's total value-creating ability, an ambiguous yet critical concept tied only loosely to the cost of the resources consumed. The definition of capacity, the scope and time frame of
analysis, and the objectives served by its deployment all serve to
shape the beliefs and practices that make up the field of capacity
cost management.

The first part of this monograph has explored the practice-
based issues surrounding capacity cost management. Wide ranging in focus and concern, this discussion has underscored the
fact that there is no one right view of capacity, no "capacity for all
seasons." Understanding capacity cost management is a journey,
a saga of discovery and rediscovery, not a destination. In the pages

that follow, the issues presented to this point will be summarized, providing the basis for making the transition to Part II: The History of Capacity Cost Management.

The Many Faces
of Capacity Cost Management

Three major categories of models define the field of capacity cost management: operational, tactical, and strategic. These categories of capacity models differ in terms of their overall focus, level of constraint, primary points of action, and responsiveness of the underlying cost function. While all focus on maximizing the use of available resources, how this optimization process is envisioned and defined varies greatly from one approach to another. Serving as more than a sorting mechanism, these categories reflect major shifts in the assumptions shaping capacity management practices. In revisiting the time frames and models, attention now turns to the key differences in assumptions and actions that can be taken.

☐ Capacity in the Short Term

The first major decision made in developing capacity cost management practice is defining its overall focus. Is the model to be concerned with short-term management issues, or is the development of a long-term strategy most critical to the firm? In making this choice, management is consciously (or unconsciously) framing the type of questions and answers the capacity cost management system can provide. At its heart, the choice of a time frame is driven by the core issues and challenges facing the firm. Is the key to survival the optimization of short-term performance? If so, then the capacity of concern is that at the *point of the tool.* When focusing on short-term performance, management is faced with multiple constraints, limited options, and low variability and responsiveness in its cost structure.

Taking the status quo as the basis for capacity decisions, a company caught up in short-term issues has one key factor that can be changed: *waste*. The product mix is driven by the market, prices are set by external forces, available capacity is limited to the resources already at hand, and the ability to make changes is negligible in the highly constrained and structured short-term world. Capacity cost management in this setting becomes a simple process of optimizing the velocity of materials through existing processes while minimizing the amount and cost of wasted resources caused by production.

In the short term, the cost structure of the company is basically unchangeable and unresponsive to management decisions. The only part of the cost equation that can be changed when the numerator or dollar value of required and consumed resources is fixed is the volume of work completed by these resources. Resources are either used effectively, stored, or wasted in this simple setting. The resulting profitability of the firm and its underlying processes, then, is driven by the level of capacity utilization alone.

Given the limited, tightly constrained range of motion that defines the short-term capacity cost management problem, it is crucial that the definition of capacity be as stringent as possible and that the reporting system provide accurate, unambiguous estimates of the level of effective deployment. In the short term, capacity can be defined fairly accurately. In the short term, the relative amounts of utilized, stored, and wasted resources can be reasonably estimated. The role of capacity cost management in this setting, then, is to provide the information needed to drive continuous improvement in the utilization of the firm's resources.

The capacity models being deployed in companies facing short-term capacity challenges reflect these basic concerns. At a major domestic refrigerator manufacturer, every major station in the assembly process has a posted waste notification and summary of performance. If a unit is scrapped at any point, the impact of this quality failure on profits and meeting production goals is known immediately by everyone involved. In one brewery of a major beer manufacturer, the waste of liquid and of bottled goods is monitored and posted throughout the production process. In both cases, the goal of management is to make everyone aware of the impact of waste on throughput and profits.

On a more general level, cellular manufacturing and the TOC models are embodiments of the core issues in short-term capacity management. Cellular designs, which seek to improve the throughput of a process while minimizing the waste caused by excess resources, move, queue, and defects, define best practice in manufacturing today. In removing the sources of variation and waste from the production process, cellular designs do more than manage the bottleneck; they improve performance against two key elements in the short-term: waste and velocity through the process.

The TOC model, developed for a more complex, traditional production flow, provides some of the benefits of the cellular model. As suggested in Chapter 2, however, TOC embeds excess capacity within the process. This embedding of waste is at times conscious, being driven by the assumption that an unbalanced plant is the optimal design. At other times, the excess capacity is the result of past decisions that cannot be reversed or oversights by a management focused solely on the bottleneck. Yet even with this suboptimization, capacity utilization remains as the driving force behind the TOC model. TOC is capacity management.

The ongoing efforts of MRP adherents to add capacity dimensions to their models represent the one troubling aspect in the short-term capacity area. MRP is a dominant production scheduling and management tool, adopted by companies en masse during the 1980s as a solution to all ills. MRP does add discipline and structure to the chaotic flow of products through a complex factory, but its use begs the question of plant floor design. MRP models can be augmented to be sensitive to capacity constraints, but the fact remains that traditional, functionally focused plant floor designs are difficult to manage, let alone optimize in terms of their capacity deployment. Faced with solving complex algorithms and driven to define capacity precisely

across a wide variety of settings, the MRP models are the culmination of years of effort and exploration shaped by the Scientific Management movement.

Whether focused on detailed analysis and scheduling or defined on the management of the process and its bottlenecks,
short-term capacity management is a land of limited opportunities. Improvements in throughput and the level of waste it creates
can certainly be made, but they are the only significant points at
which management can take action to improve performance.

The responsiveness of the underlying cost structure of the
firm to these changes is minimal; in the short term very few
costs are truly variable. Committed costs dominate, driven by
both the structure and established management policies. The
managed costs element of the total capacity cost puzzle is limited to a small number of variable items such as avoidable labor
and utilities costs. As any practicing manager knows, the amount
of cost that really goes away when changes are made in the short
term is negligible. Improvements in short-term performance are
based on increasing the utilization of resources, not reducing
the number of types of resources consumed.

In summary, then, a number of key issues shape capacity
cost management practices in the short term.

- Utilization is defined and value is created at the "point of
  the tool."
- Velocity of materials through existing processes is the primary driver of performance.
- Waste is the key element that can be changed on the economic front.
- Constraints on action and degree of change are significant.
- Responsiveness of the cost structure to change is quite low.
- Due to the combination of these forces, capacity can be tightly
  defined and estimated with reasonable accuracy.
- Theoretical capacity, as defined by the current structure and
  management policies of the plant, is the most logical capacity baseline if waste is to be reduced and velocity of product
  through the plant maximized.

Improvements can be made in the short term, and the effectiveness of capacity cost management practices within this time frame can have a major impact on profitability. In understanding the short term, then, the key is to understand what can and cannot be changed and to ensure that ongoing efforts to improve the utilization of resources and processes are supported. While effective capacity management in the short term is a necessary but not sufficient condition for survival, neglecting the short term can lead to long-term failure.

☐ Mid-Range Notions of Capacity Cost Management

In the mid or intermediate term, the number of variables in the capacity puzzle that management can control increases significantly. Intermediate-term approaches to capacity concentrate on the flow itself—the structure, focus, and management of the processes that create value for customers. In this time frame, *cost* becomes a concept to be managed because a company can make significant shifts in the type of activities and the resources the activities consume.

It is hardly surprising, then, that the majority of true capacity cost management models exist in this intermediate term. For cost to have meaning and relevance within the decision process, enough time must be available to make changes to the way work is done. Changing the nature of work is the key to affecting the type, amount, and total cost of resources consumed by an activity, process, or product/service bundle. Changing the nature of work affects both the numerator (costs) and denominator (capacity) of the basic cost equation.

The empirical results from the completed field studies suggest that, although companies are using at least seven separate models to manage intermediate-term capacity costs, significant similarities exist in their focus and use. What features do normalized costing, activity-based costing, the integrated TOC-ABC model, the continuous improvement models (variance and Ishikawa), the resource effectiveness model, CAM-I, and

CUBES have in common? Specifically, they all:

- Develop measures that incorporate the entire cost equation, both numerator and denominator;
- Focus on improving resource effectiveness;
- Utilize multiple periods of data to track improvement efforts;
- Separate idle capacity costs from utilized capacity, analyzing the various root causes for this idleness;
- Recognize, track, and measure nonproductive capacity, idle capacity, and excess capacity;
- Assign responsibility for excess and idle capacity to the management group that has the most immediate influence over it;
- Seek to identify ways to improve the flow of products and services through the organization in total by changing or redesigning the underlying business processes;
- Deal with managing both the physical capacity of the plant and the softer service/support activities and processes;
- Take only the strategy and major structures/asset base of the firm as a given in defining capacity management and improvement efforts;
- Recognize the increasing difficulty in precisely defining and measuring theoretical capacity;
- Are concerned predominantly with supporting tactical management decisions, not the ongoing management of the shop floor;
- Emphasize planning, not control.

In the intermediate term, then, the focus of the capacity cost management models turns toward changing the cost structure of the firm by acting on the processes and activities that create this cost.

While not all costs are avoidable in the intermediate term, many are. For instance, management policies regarding how many shifts a plant will run as well as how breaks, shift changes, lunches, and planned time will be handled can be changed radically in the intermediate term, which can have a major impact on the utilization of existing facilities. In the intermediate term, the flow through a plant can be redesigned away from traditional structures that focus on making parts in batches to a flow design that emphasizes the product itself (cellular manufacturing). The impact of setup and maintenance, two major causes of nonproductive idle capacity, can be minimized or eliminated in the intermediate term through the implementation of quick changeover routines, total preventive maintenance programs, and modularization of basic product components.

As the activities that cause cost and hence consume capacity are identified and analyzed in the intermediate term, a company begins to understand better where waste is occurring and why it continues. Contrary to the short-term approach, this knowledge does not serve as a constraint but rather presents an opportunity for improvement. Increasing the velocity of product through the plant in the intermediate term means more than simply improving the management of bottleneck resources; the bottlenecks can be eliminated.

The key to capacity cost management in the intermediate term, then, is understanding the difference between the hard constraints embedded in the physical plant and existing product/market strategy of the firm and the soft constraints on action created by management assumptions. Mid-term capacity cost management models are assumption busters. Only assumptions prevent a firm from reaching toward theoretical capacity. Only assumptions drive the decision to hold excess plant when the addition of a shift or change in shift management policies could yield the same results. Only assumptions create high batch costs and the related low-value uses of available capacity.

The "we've always done it this way" lament is a clear signal that assumptions are inhibiting performance and creating excess capacity and cost. History, the tried and true ways of doing work, prevents a company from reaching its profit potential in the intermediate term and creates permanent layers of waste that are very hard to overcome in the short run.

The primary objective of intermediate-term capacity cost management models is making visible the assumptions that guide the management of capacity and drive its ultimate cost. Whether focused on understanding current performance against historical trends (normalized costing) or sorting out the root causes for excess and idle capacity (resource effectiveness, CUBES and CAM-I), these models create actions that have a major impact on the focus and structure of capacity costs.

□   Creating the Future
     Through Capacity Cost Management

While there are many different tactical or intermediate-term models for understanding and managing capacity costs, there is a dearth of models that truly address long-term, strategic concerns in this area. As detailed in Chapter 5, only four models exist in this area, three of which also serve tactical decision making and hence are tied to the historical trends and management policies of the firm (resource effectiveness, CUBES, and CAM-I). The fourth model, which takes a market-based, outside-in view of the capacity cost management issue, is in the very early stages of development.

While little formal modeling has been done in the strategic area of capacity cost management, the work that has been completed exhibits several core features.

- Value creation is the overriding concern.
- The entire structure, product/market strategy, and management of the organization is open to change.
- Optimizing the performance of the entire value chain is the goal.
- All costs are considered variable and responsive to changes in policies and structures.
- All assumptions are challenged.
- Customer requirements or the market shape the strategic responses of the firm.
- Capacity is redefined as the value-creating capability of the firm and is tied only loosely to the underlying costs and resources that create this value.

In addition to the four models that deal with strategic concerns, a wide range of management decisions and approaches are played out in the long term. Strategic alliances, the addition or closing of major facilities, entering or exiting product and national markets, and redesigning core product/service bundles are just a few of the ways management affects the value delivered to customers with new or existing resources.

Whether driven by current tactical models and management approaches or shaped by the changing demands of the market, strategic capacity cost management provides the greatest latitude for action, the greatest risk if improperly done, and the highest potential for quantum improvements in overall performance. Success in the long term means more than survival; it requires that a company create a sustainable competitive advantage through either product or process capabilities. Whether this advantage is gained through traditional approaches that focus on garnering economies of scale through efficient matching of plant and product features or on emerging organizational designs that emphasize flexibility and responsiveness to changing product/service demand profiles, the goal is the same: to create long-term value and profits through the effective management of all the resources of the firm.

Understanding the Present through the Past

The present state in any field of human endeavor is shaped by its history. The field of capacity cost management is no exception to this rule. In fact, it could be argued that understanding history is more important in the area of capacity than in any other field of management endeavor. The ebb and flow of capacity modeling, the radical shifts in perspective and practice that define the history of capacity cost management, encapsulate the development of modern business practice. Intricately tied to the macroeconomic trends that have defined 20th-century management, the historical development of capacity cost practices represents a truly unique opportunity for debating and creating the future.

The historical development of capacity reporting practices was briefly presented in Chapter 1, using a figure that is shown again here (see Figure 6-1). Having explored the wide range of extant capacity management models, the premise that these practices are driven by both macroeconomic trends and the degree of debate or uncertainty surrounding the notion of cost appears to have more merit. Clearly, for each new or different view of what a cost is, there is a new form of capacity and capacity management. Only when cost becomes problematic do capacity concerns surface.

In addition to macroeconomic and costing trends, though, it appears that the assumptions and objectives driving the management process also shape the development of capacity cost models. If management believes that it is operating at 115% capacity, then it is likely to add additional plant to existing resources. The baseline definition of capacity leads to different conclusions and different levels of visibility of capacity-based waste.

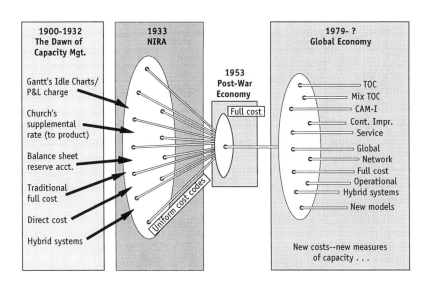

Figure 6-1. The Historical Development of Capacity Cost Management

In Part II, the focus of the discussion turns toward understanding trends in capacity cost management that have led up to modern practices. Specifically, in Chapter 7 the early discussions spanning 1900–1919 are presented, followed by the Golden Era in capacity reporting (1920–1932) in Chapter 8. Chapter 9 turns to the period from 1933–1952, when capacity dropped from view in the face of tumult in the markets, economy, and world at large. Chapter 10 details the decline of management accounting that occurred during the 1953–1978 period, ending with a review of progress in capacity reporting since 1979, in Chapter 11.

As the story develops, the fascinating and troubling interplay between government policy and business practices takes center stage. In addition, the sophistication of early models and theory in the capacity literature emerges as a striking contrast to the naivete of the full cost era in management accounting. Only in understanding the history of capacity reporting can the present be understood and the future shaped.

> History repeats itself, and that's one of the things that's wrong with history.—Clarence Darrow.

PART II

HISTORICAL TRENDS
IN CAPACITY COST MANAGEMENT

7

THE AGE OF DISCOVERY
1900–1919

> The work of organization includes the taking stock of the
> resources at one's command and planning the fullest use of
> them all.[1]

The opening era of capacity reporting was one of learning, exploration, and the development of formal models that were heavily anchored in the logic of engineering. It was also a period of debate, driven by the relentless search of Taylor[2] and others to find the *one best way* to do work. While diverse opinions about how to define and pursue these "best practices" were voiced by the writers of the period, one common thread runs through them: idle capacity is waste. Resting firmly on the bedrock of the competitive market and its unbending rules of performance, the debates of this period made no attempt to sidestep the very real impact idle capacity had on the profitability of a firm and its long-term viability.

The early 1900s were a period of discovery on all major social and economic fronts (see Table 7-1). It was the era of automation. Machines were rapidly taking the place of labor in factories, as mass production methods were developed and perfected. Henry Ford developed the first assembly lines during this period, pursuing optimal efficiency and effectiveness through process and mechanical improvements. The River Rouge facility stands today as a monument to his genius.

The early 1900s were also a period of discovery on other fronts. In 1903 the Wright brothers flew the first airplane at Kitty Hawk. This event would pave the way for a redefinition of travel in the world, laying the groundwork for moving materials and people faster and farther than the railroads. America's common goal during this period was *progress*, defined on doing things better, faster, and cheaper. To that end all society was focused.[3]

The age of discovery was built on a common belief that the application of scientific principles, brought to culmination in industrial engineering models and practices, would lead to commercial success and economic prosperity for all. Relatedly, on the economic front there was no end to the market for the goods

Table 7-1. Timetable of Macroeconomic Events, 1900–1919

1901   Alexander Hamilton Church, the leading proponent of engineering-based costing in this century, argued for ideal capacity approach with a supplemental rate treatment for shop charges due to idleness.

1906   John Whitmore, a U. S. accountant, puts Church's machine-rate method into accounting jargon.

1909   Church continues to stress the need to classify the costs of idleness so the production engineer can do something about it.

William Lybrand, founder of Lybrand, Ross Brothers, and Montgomery and a leading expert on cost accounting within the public accounting field, compares the direct-labor basis to the machine-rate basis for charging expense burden. He coins the term "normal conditions estimated" in this work.

1911   The Tuck Conference (Dartmouth College) on Scientific Management takes place, resulting in a strong statement of the benefits of this approach and suggesting adoption by all businesses.

1912   Frederick Taylor is charged with promoting unfair labor practices, resulting in a lengthy trial/testimony before a special House committee. Charges are dropped after Wilson is elected to the presidency. It appears likely that these proceedings were brought to secure the labor vote for Wilson in this hotly contested election.

1913   Lybrand's partner, Robert H. Montgomery, in his first edition of *Auditing: Theory and Practice*, recommends that "when the system is accurate and dependable, care must be taken to ascertain that the results shown thereby are used as the basis for inventory."

1914   The Great War (now called World War I) breaks out throughout Europe and leads to a boom in U. S. industry.

1915   Frederick Taylor dies.

         H. L. Gantt, perhaps the most famous industrial engineer in the world after F. W. Taylor, makes a strong case for the ideal capacity method with the charge for idleness as a separate amount on the P&L account (now the income statement).

         Church responds that it is unlikely that manufacturers would agree to that.

         Gantt retorts that this disinclination should not stop what is right.

         Church responds that not all idleness is of the same ilk, and to charge it all to the P&L would be inaccurate.

         William E. M. McHenry tries to bring Gantt's and Church's views together, writing "that it is wrong in principle and absurd in practice to add to the true cost of doing a thing the wholly misleading cost of not doing that thing or any other thing."

         Gantt also attempts a truce with Church, although he sneers at the accountant as "the servant of the financier."

1916   Bernard Baruch begins his long involvement in government with the Council of National Defense.

1917   Church begins to waiver on his treatment of the cost of idle time, suggesting that it be treated either as a supplementary rate or a direct charge to the P&L. Church clearly defines idle time as "waste."

         The United States declares war against the Axis powers.

         The War Industries Board is created with Baruch as the Commissioner of Raw Materials.

         An interdepartmental conference on "Uniform Contracts and Cost Accounting Definitions" is held and includes such important accounting experts as J. Lee Nicholson, W. S. Gee, R. H. Montgomery, and J. E. Sterrett. While the machine-rate method is stressed, direct labor approaches seem favored because they enhance the auditability of cost-plus contracts.

         The U. S. government funds a study on arranging and standardizing governmental and industrial cost accounting methods.

         R. H. Montgomery is appointed chief of the Section on Organizations and Methods in the Office of the General Staff. He works for General Hugh S. Johnson.

1918   Baruch is appointed chairman of the War Industries Board. Johnson represents the army on this board.

         The Great War ends.

1919   Henry Gantt dies.

produced in America's factories. In this setting of growing demand for product, the objective of capacity reporting was simple: to identify opportunities for improvement. This objective placed capacity reporting in the best position possible—as a signal of future profitability, not of current mismanagement.

The Pioneers of Capacity Cost Management

The first discussions of capacity utilization and the "best" way to measure it occurred in the opening days of the century. In 1901, Alexander Hamilton Church introduced this topic as part of his efforts to define engineering-based costing. Church returned to this topic on an ongoing basis (see Bibliography), becoming the most prolific writer on costing issues between 1900 and 1932.[4]

Church's concern with capacity grew from his ongoing fascination with the costs caused by the increasing automation of factories in the United States and Britain. Seeking to determine the amount of production a set of resources and their associated "burden" were capable of supporting, Church emphasized the need to track idle capacity as the key to untapped profits. His logic for this attention to the value created *at the point of the tool* is best captured in his own words: "Unless an expenditure subserves, in some way, the efficient operation of the tool on the work, it is wasted expenditure."[5] To Church, the only expense that could be justified was one that increased the value-creating ability of a tool.

Yet Church was at heart a pragmatist. While he abhorred the charging of idle capacity costs to current production, he found that practicing managers felt driven to assign the "total cost" of doing work within a given period to some job or output unit. In developing capacity reporting models and methods, then, Church's goal was to present information about idle capacity in a format that would fit within the accounting model, yet that would reflect his deepest concerns: "Idle capacity equals wasted opportunities. But neglect or inability to employ opportunity to the full should not be visited on the work actually performed. In other words, the cost of idle machines should be separated from the process-cost of work."[6]

The culmination of Church's creativity was the *supplemental machine rate*. The supplemental cost pool would be used to accumulate all of the costs caused by idle capacity and related nonproductive or inefficient events related to machine utilization. The costs contained in this supplemental pool were to be allocated to jobs completed in the period under question, yielding a total cost number for inventory and income reporting. For internal reporting, though, the supplemental approach provided the information needed to help management determine the extent of idle capacity and its impact on profitability.

The key to understanding Church is recognizing his fervor for tracing costs to their causes. While not stated in these words specifically, again and again Church returns to the need to "let our methods follow the natural lines of the actual complexity of the setting."[7] It is this overarching concern with accurately matching costs to the processes that use them that explains Church's preoccupation with idleness charges: "… the greater the percentage of idle hours the less accurate will be the results of using simple costing methods." To Church, idle costs represented irregularity or variation in the true underlying relationship between resources (inputs) and the products created from them (outputs).

In Church's mind, idle costs also represented waste. It is this notion that stands Church in best stead in today's world. While his focus on individual machines as the cost object in a cost system has less relevance in a world of cellular manufacturing and process orientation, Church's ongoing desire to identify waste and to cost the impact of waste on current and future performance is, if anything, more relevant today than it was in 1920. A final quotation summarizes Church's views about waste and the need to measure it clearly so as to be able to deal with it: "In my idea waste is waste and when you have separated it out, face it squarely and admit that it is none the less waste if you arbitrarily spread it over jobs. I allow that this is sometimes an uncomfortable thing to do."[8]

In summary, Church made the following key assumptions in crafting his theory of capacity cost reporting:[9]

- The primary focus of any costing system for manufacturing is at the "point of the tool." Machines, not departments, jobs, or units of output, are the primary cost object.
- Idle capacity represents wasted opportunities to create product and hence generate income and profits.
- Expense burden is not a cost of production but rather the cost of the capacity to produce.
- The cost of the actual work completed on a specific job or product can be directly and precisely estimated. It is a constant level of cost that is the basis for estimation for bidding and pricing.
- Any swing in the total cost of operations and the cost of actual work is due to waste or idle capacity.
- Charging idle capacity directly to the profit and loss statement is not the best treatment available for a variety of reasons. (As noted later, in his last work Church recanted this position.)

All in all, Church spent more time thinking and writing about capacity and idle capacity issues than any management expert before or since. Unfortunately, in his own time Church found himself engaged in debates with adherents of the Scientific Management school, debates that he lost as much because of the power and authority his opponents were able to bring to bear on the issue as because of the power of their arguments alone. It is to one of these debates that the discussion will now turn.

☐ The First Great Capacity Debate

To state that the key articles of the Golden Era had a common knowledge base and a common theme (that is, the application of scientific reasoning to manufacturing issues) is not to say that these early writers on capacity agreed on all key points. In fact, it was a period of intense debate about the definition of capacity, the "proper" definition and treatment of the cost driven by idle capacity, and the roles and authority of the engineer/manager versus the "cost keeper."

While there were many participants in these debates, the key arguments took place between A. H. Church and H. L. Gantt. Gantt was one of the best known of the "Taylorites" and as such held a significant position of influence in his time. While Gantt was by training and experience an industrial engineer best known for the management charts that bear his name, he took a firm stand on the role and nature of costs, a stand that put him in direct contention with Church.

The articles detailing the debate between Church and Gantt on the "best" treatment of idle capacity charges were published in the *American Machinist* from June 17, 1915, to October 31, 1915. Gantt's article, "The Relation Between Production and Costs," was the opening piece in this debate. In it, Gantt developed his primary arguments for the treatment of idle capacity costs:

> It has been common practice to make the product of a factory running at a portion of its capacity bear the whole expense of the factory. This has been long recognized by many to be illogical... the amount of expense to be borne by the product should bear the same ratio to the total normal operating expense as the product in question bears to the normal product....The expense of maintaining the idle portion of the plant ready to run...is really a deduction from profits, and shows that we may have a serious loss on account of having too much plant, as well as on account of not operating our plant economically.[10]

The position taken by Gantt was that of an engineer-manager. Using a simple percentage relationship as the basis for assigning costs to productive versus idle capacity, Gantt's focus was on eliminating idleness costs from the "standard cost" of production. Logically, then, Gantt's views reflected Scientific Management's ongoing concern with the development of reliable standard costs as the baseline for managing and controlling operations.

Church was asked to discuss Gantt's article and its suggestions in the July 29, 1915, edition of the *American Machinist*.

Church's arguments turned on two major points: (1) Gantt's overly simplistic treatment of idle capacity costs as a percentage of "normal" costs and (2) the unwillingness of managers to charge these costs directly to the income statement:

> [regarding unused productive capacity]...To charge this at once to profit and loss is an easy thing to do, but generally speaking, I find a great disinclination on the part of practical manufacturers to do it....For estimating purposes the actual production cost is taken, but for accounting purposes the total cost is taken. This seems a safer plan than the drastic step of charging undistributed burden to profit and loss.[11]

Church, then, was walking the fine line between management and accounting. To this end, he attempted to find creative ways to distribute the costs of idle capacity that would bring attention to these costs while responding to the ongoing pressure from management to report operations in the most favorable or profitable light possible.

Returning to the details of the Gantt-Church debate of 1915, it is clear that Church had spent many hours defining the nature of idle capacity costs and how best to incorporate them in a company's financial reports. Equally clear is his belief that Gantt needed to rethink his position, as suggested by the following comments:

> I fear he [Gantt] is on rather dangerous ground....No percentage method of distributing burden can give effect to the varying call of individual machines on the expense represented by the burden, and it will easily be understood that if some machines absorb more expense than others, as they do, then the question of just which machines were idle and which were working on jobs is the very core of the expense-distribution question.[12]

The tone set by Church's reply, with its simplistic application of the concepts in Gantt's work, fueled the debate, which became increasingly heated over the next several issues of the

American Machinist. The essence of the debate after the initial round moved away from the "proper" treatment of idle capacity costs to a more personal level, as Gantt began to take the position that cost accountants had no role to play in defining cost practices. To Gantt, accountants were simply the recorders of costs while engineers defined management practice. Rather than rise to the bait about the relative roles of accountancy and engineering in a company, however, Church continued to focus his attack on Gantt's simplistic view of capacity costs as well as on Gantt's stated belief that he had found "the" answer to the capacity reporting problem.

Underlying Church's position was the firm belief that cost accounting is the area where engineering and accounting sciences meet and that as such, it bears the responsibility for mediating and measuring their differences. At the heart of this responsibility, in Church's mind, lay the development of methods for charging burden that accurately captured the underlying complexity of the business. To Church cost accounting was more than historical record-keeping: it was the essence of measuring and managing the resources, the capacity to create value, of the firm.

□ The Gantt-Church Debate: Final Comments

Within the round of debates between Church and Gantt one finds the detailing of the major issues that define capacity and its effective measurement and management. The issues covered by this debate included:

- Definitions of capacity and the cost of capacity;
- Preferred treatment for idle capacity costs from a financial accounting versus management accounting perspective;
- Identification of core responsibility for eliminating idle capacity;
- Idle capacity defined as a form of waste;
- Capacity as the capability to produce goods;
- Idle capacity and its relationship to prices;
- Behavioral impacts of charging idle capacity cost to products that did not cause it;

- The role of the accountant versus the engineer in organizations.

Church spent a significant amount of time laying out why capacity measurements mattered and detailing the definition and treatment of idle capacity charges. His fatal flaw resided in his belief that practicing managers would use actual or standard costs for estimating and total or full costs for financial reporting. One cost was all that management wanted, and full absorption product cost was their preferred choice. Breaking the cycle or logic of cost as a precise, definable, and reliable concept was a challenge in the early 1900s, one that remains today.

The Birth of Capacity Reporting

Clearly, Church and Gantt were not the only two persons concerned with capacity measurement and management during the 1900–1919 period. Cole, Edtterson, Kent, Scovell, Whitmore, and others devoted considerable time and energy to this topic. The following discussion summarizes the key points made by each of these early writers.

☐ William Morse Cole

In a somewhat lengthy and admittedly tortuous book[13] about the construction and interpretation of accounts, William Morse Cole devoted approximately 16 pages of more than 400 to the concept of idle time. While short in coverage, Cole's text made some interesting observations:

- A discount has to be made for the idle time that competition prevents charging to the customer (p. 286).
- Competitive market prices cannot be based on the cost as shown by the books, that is, the total or full cost number (p. 286).
- The most effective stimulus for reducing waste is to show that it costs something....if the idle costs are not so treated, then accounting fails the organization (p. 285).

• The proper treatment of idle capacity costs depends in part on the conditions of competition facing the firm (p. 283).

Cole's view was simple: idle capacity is a waste that cannot be passed on to a customer under competitive market conditions. It is a logical position, one that bears repeating and exploration today. While Cole's approach to costing might have been overly detailed, he had a firm grasp on the relationship between markets and prices that is in line with the best thinking today in such areas as target costing.

□ J. Edtterson

Edtterson's work is found in the primary source for the capacity debate in the Age of Discovery: *American Machinist.* Edtterson's position once again can be summarized in one statement: "Whatever system is installed, therefore, must be such as to enable the plant superintendent to attack the operations."[14] The key to deciding which information to report and how to report it should, in Edtterson's view, be driven by the need to understand operations better, not to cost a specific job or unit of output.

Edtterson shifted the capacity discussion onto a plane that would reverberate 70 years later in Goldratt and Cox's book, *The Goal.* To Edtterson the issue was not cost of output but rather a company's ability to improve the operation of its plant and eliminate unnecessary expense. Edtterson appears to be one of the earliest management writers to suggest that the role of cost accounting and idle capacity reporting was not to cost product but rather to provide the basis for improving operations.

□ Federal Reserve Bulletin

The reason for including this publication in the articles of this period is its detailing of various items used in its estimates on the "Percentage of Plant Capacity in Operation." Capacity utilization was a key data point for assessing economic conditions in the United States even at this early time, and the *Federal Reserve Bulletin* used it as one of its leading indicators of manufacturing health. The bulletin underscores the attention paid to capacity issues from the earliest days of mass production.

☐ H. L. Gantt and Idleness

Gantt's interest in and discussion of idle capacity went beyond the issues developed during the debate with Church to include analysis of the executive's role in influencing these costs. The key article in this second set of articles by Gantt was his 1919 piece titled "Influence of Executives," in which Gantt effectively argued that it is the responsibility of executives to reduce the cost of idle resources. Building on his earlier work, he went on to suggest that these costs should be kept separate from the costs of ongoing production, likening the alternative approach (e.g., full or total costs) to a socialistic model of management:

> It is just such studies as this, made in numerous plants, that have convinced us that a study of idleness is much more effective in increasing the output of the plant than a study of efficiency as it has been studied…. It is on this account that I say that a recognition of the cost of idleness and the allocation of this expense to those who are responsible for it, is the most important economic fact that has been brought to the attention of the business world for many years…. The adoption of such a policy is in the hands of the executives…. Our executives are of large enough caliber that they will see that it is the strongest force they can use to oppose socialism and combat bolshevism.[15]

Not one to mince words, Gantt makes a clear statement of why he felt driven to charge idle time costs to the income statement: Doing so assigns responsibility for this cost to the executives who can best act on it. Gantt goes beyond this point, though, to suggest that full costing undermines the capitalistic structure by rewarding both productive and unproductive use of resources equally: Both are recoverable in a full-cost plus pricing model.

There can be little doubt that Gantt's position in this later article, written in 1919, reflected the impact of World War I on the United States, including the short-lived attempt to create a uniform cost accounting model that was, at its heart, a full cost plus approach. The Great Depression would in the end, however, result in widespread use of full costing and disappearance of idle capacity reporting (see Chapter 9). If one believes Gantt, the full cost movement was a clear step away from the capitalistic structure underlying the U.S. economy of the early 1900s.

☐ William Kent and His Views

William Kent's writing consists of a series of charts that detail the causes of idleness and hence the possibility of managing it. For instance, he separated permanently idle machinery from temporarily idle capacity, noting that the former should be sold to generate cash and free the space for other use. On the other hand, in his view unplanned, temporary idle costs should be charged directly to the profit and loss statement because this treatment would generate the activity necessary to eliminate this cause of waste. The CAM-I model described in Part I clearly is consistent with Kent's views.

In taking this position, Kent constantly referred back to the need to employ the "exception principle" in management reporting, using the logic of the difference between planned activity levels and actual results as the basis for management decision making and action. To Kent, then, variance analysis was the best way to marry management and financial reporting. Finally, Kent suggested that the key to communicating this variance information was through the effective use of charts and graphs rather than the use of "dreary tables of figures." As such, Kent placed idle capacity reporting within the arena of responsibility accounting, sidestepping the more myopic focus on costing issues common in capacity literature.

☐ Clinton Scovell and the Concept of Unearned Burden

Scovell's primary contribution to the idle capacity discussion was his view that in reality idle capacity represents unearned burden and is therefore not a cost applicable to ongoing production. In making this distinction between earned and unearned burden, Scovell put a slightly different spin on Church's supplemental rate, suggesting that unearned burden or idle capacity costs should *not* be charged to manufacturing cost. Yet Scovell hedged this position when it came to detailing the relationship between market prices and this "unearned burden," suggesting that these costs had to be recovered in some way when prices were set.

In combining these two features, then, we find Scovell holding positions contrary to both Church's and Gantt's. This is an interesting fact, given that the two are believed to have been at odds during most of this period. Scovell's position or hedge is best captured in his own words:

> ...[the] expense known as unearned burden is not properly a part of manufacturing cost, although it must be recognized in the determination of a proper selling price....The unearned burden, or balance still remaining in the departmental accounts, should be closed to Loss and Gain for the period, since these charges represent the cost due to idle capacity for manufacturing. [16]

Scovell, it seems, was trying to define a technique to bridge the gap between costing for management decision making and that used for external reporting. Contrary to Church, he did not seem to believe that the interests of management would be served by distorting production costs with unearned burden, however that cost was allocated to output. In walking the fine line between financial and management reporting, Scovell placed his emphasis on recovery of unearned burden rather than its direct attachment to units of production.

☐ Uniform Contracts and
    Cost Accounting Definitions and Methods

Of the pieces presented as part of the Age of Discovery, only this document, *Uniform Contracts and Cost Accounting Definitions and*

Methods, bears any resemblance to positions taken after 1933. A precursor to the National Industrial Recovery Act (NIRA), this document set out to define a uniform approach to costing that would serve as the basis for bidding and price setting for government contracts. Interesting issues presented in the document include one of the few references to direct labor hours as the *"most accurate method"* for distributing overhead found in the literature of the early 1900s,[17] the complete support of "cost-plus" pricing methods that would fix the profit as a percentage of total cost, the restriction of all workers assigned to government work to an eight-hour day, and the spreading of idle costs into the general overhead assigned to a job.

While this document held sway for only a brief period (1917–1919), it is the original definitive and formal statement of support for full costing and the use of direct labor as the basis for allocation of overhead. Given the predominance of these two practices in cost accounting systems over the past 80 years, it seems likely that this document had a significant and long-lasting impact on the development of cost accounting practices.

Of even more interest is the fact that it was developed by many of the same persons who crafted the NIRA. In both cases, Franklin Delano Roosevelt played a significant role, first as assistant secretary of the Navy during World War I and later as president and the driving force behind the NIRA and other New Deal legislation.

For the Age of Discovery in capacity reporting, the uniform costing model has interest in the reactions it generated from business experts of the time, such as Gantt, who felt this approach represented a step away from the free market economy and an abandonment of the logic of costs as the basis for management. The uniform costing model, with its substitution of cost for value in the creation of a market price, represented the first major effort by opponents of laissez-faire capitalism to reshape the economic structure of the United States. Unfortunately, it was not to be the last of such efforts.

□ John Whitmore

The final writer of the 1900–1919 era, at least in an alphabetical sense, was John Whitmore.[18] Key to Whitmore's position was his belief that "the object of the accounts is always the same, to eliminate waste from the operations." Continuing on with this logic, as applied to idle capacity, he noted: "Accidents and blunders occur and the cost, as in some instances the cost of unused factory capacity, may be so great that it would be absurd to state it as part of the cost of the product."

Consistent with his single-minded focus on waste, Whitmore suggested that the cost of wasted material or scrap should include the factory capacity used to produce it. In search of a completely specified costing model that would provide solid, repeatable cost estimates free of the impact of waste, Whitmore provided a useful jumping-off point for developing capacity models that would focus not on what was done but on what wasn't done with a set of available resources.

Whitmore felt that the inclusion of idle capacity costs in production cost estimates would lead to fluctuations in the "cost" of a product and confusion for management in understanding the nature and cause of these changes. Concerned with the behavioral impact of a cost system, Whitmore noted:

> It [full cost estimates] fails to take into account influences which have their effect upon human effort: The sense of opportunity, the sense of necessity, and the exact knowledge of what ought to be done. It is one thing to set at work these influences, to show exactly what factory capacity is underutilized and what the resulting loss is, that the accounting for factory capacity is set up.[19]

Whitmore agreed with Church's machine-rate method for charging overhead to product but not with the decision to charge idle costs to units produced via a supplemental charge. To Whitmore, the behavioral impact of reporting idle capacity as an opportunity cost that would eat away at the profits and future of a company was the key to preventing this form of waste.

Although his writings came early in the management literature, Whitmore appears today to have been a forward thinker who seems to have understood the dynamics of cost systems within organizations better than many of his contemporaries and the accounting writers who followed.

Final Comments

The first 20 years of the 20th century laid the groundwork for the development of a sophisticated model of capacity reporting. In reviewing the earliest recorded work on idle capacity and its treatment, one is cast back into a period of relative stability, prosperity, and progress on all fronts. In this ideal setting, debates about the "proper" treatment of idle capacity, recognized by all to be *waste* in every sense, could take place. In fact, in reviewing the work of this period, there appears to be very little agreement in the positions taken by the various writers (see Table 7-2), yet strong agreement in their underlying assumptions.

In the face of these disagreements one message was clear: The goal of management was to maximize the use of all resources, whether man or machine. Idle capacity, one clear signal of underuse of resources, was a management problem to be solved with sound decision making that reflected the competitive position of the firm. Summarizing the 1900–1919 period, several points emerge.

- It was a period of debate, not conclusions.
- There was a strong movement toward complex, diverse costing systems that reflected the processes and nature of each firm.
- Sophisticated reasoning was evident, both in terms of the cost of idle time and the impact of idleness on the long-term viability of a plant.
- The discussions were management rather than accounting centered.
- There was a strong reliance on practical knowledge and common sense.

- In general, it was felt that passing the cost of idle capacity or waste to good units produced was illogical.

All in all, then, the Age of Discovery was a period of realism and reflection. While accountants and engineers struggled to

Table 7-2. Summary of Positions on Idle Capacity Reporting

Writer	Summary of Position
Alexander H. Church	Charges indirect costs and all idle costs to a supplementary overhead account, which is then to be applied to products based on their use of direct labor.
William Morse Cole	Is most concerned with eliminating waste in both the factory and back office. Argues that charging idleness costs directly to the P&L is the best way to ensure elimination of this form of waste.
J. Edtterson	Is concerned with assigning responsibility for costs to those who control them. Suggests charging only direct costs to the factory superintendent. Idle costs, by default (indirect costs affected) are to be attached to management.
Henry Gantt	Avid in belief that idle costs should be directly charged to P&L in period they occur. Focused on the unabsorbed burden, he suggests using the percentage of idle to total time as the basis for charging the idle costs out.
William Kent	Kent's focus is on product costing methods. He argues that idle costs should be directly charged to the P&L because this will generate the most attention to this cost and hence lead to its elimination.
William E. M. McHenry	While understanding the problems Church has with Gantt's percentage approach to the treatment of idle costs, McHenry sides with Gantt in practice, noting that it is absurd to charge a product with costs it doesn't cause. So idle costs are charged to P&L once again.
H. Clinton Scovell	Concerned with total manufacturing costs and the accurate tying of these costs to product, he supports the view that idle charges should be directly expensed to the P&L.
John Whitmore	Whitmore is a strong advocate of Church's machine-hour rate methods, suggesting that they serve as the best basis for dealing with idle capacity costs. He departs from Church, though, in the handling of idle capacity costs, suggesting that they should be charged directly to the P&L because of the impact they will have on the behavior of management in the firm.
FINAL SCORE	1 for charging idle costs to product (Church later recants!) 7 for charging these costs directly to the P&L

have the last word, all were focused clearly on the need to support management in its quest for competitive success. In looking at this period, one is struck by the sophistication of the arguments made and the vision of the writers. While early in the century, it was not a period that was "young" in thought.

> Expense burden represents, not the cost of production, but the cost of capacity to produce....idle time represents wasted capacity to produce.[20]

□ References and Notes

[1] J. Whitmore, "Factory Accounting Applied to Machine Shops," Part VI, *Journal of Accountancy*, January 1907, p. 213.

[2] Frederick Winslow Taylor was the father of the Scientific Management school that has dominated management literature for most of the 20th century. Focused on developing standards for all forms of work using time and motion studies, Taylor's impact on the modern business world cannot be overstated.

[3] A comprehensive discussion of the role of the concept of progress in defining the period from 1750–1900 in the United States can be found in R. Nisbet, *History of the Idea of Progress*, New York: Basic Books, 1980. Also see R. Vangermeersch, *Alexander Hamilton Church: A Man of Ideas for All Seasons*, New York: Garland Publishing, Inc., 1988.

[4] A comprehensive compilation of Church's key articles and excerpts from his books can be found in *The Contributions of Alexander Hamilton Church to Accounting and Management*, R. Vangermeersch, editor, New York: Garland Publishing, Inc., 1986.

[5] Ibid., p. 123.

[6] A. H. Church, "Costing on Method C," from his book *Manufacturing Costs and Accounts*, New York: McGraw-Hill, 1917, p. 71.

[7] A. H. Church, "The Proper Distribution of Expense Burden," *Engineering Magazine*, 1908.

[8] A. H. Church, "Distribution of the Expense Burden," *American Machinist*, May 25, 1911, p. 999.

[9] This precise figure is detailed in Church's book, *Production Factors in Cost Accounting and Works Management*, New York: *Engineering Magazine*, 1910, pp. 113–125.

[10] H. L. Gantt, "The Relation Between Production and Costs," *American Machinist*, June 17, 1915, pp. 1055–56, 1061–62.

[11] A. H. Church, discussion of "Mr. Gantt's Theory of Expense Burden," in *American Machinist*, July 29, 1915, pp. 209–210.

[12] Ibid, p. 210.

[13] W. M. Cole, *Accounts: Their Construction and Interpretation,* Boston: Houghton Mifflin Company, 1915.

[14] J. Edtterson, "Direct and Indirect Costs," *American Machinist,* March 7, 1912, p. 34.

[15] H. L. Gantt, "Influence of Executive," *Annals of the American Academy of Politcal and Social Sciences,* September 1919, pp. 260, 262, 263.

[16] H. C. Scovell, *Cost Accounting and Burden Application,* New York: Appleton, 1916, pp. 176, 194.

[17] *Uniform Contracts and Cost Accounting Definitions and Methods,* p. 12.

[18] The articles included in this overview are those written from August 1906 through January 1907 in the *Journal of Accountancy.*

[19] J. Whitmore, "Factory Accounting Applied to Machine Shops," Part. IV, *Journal of Accountancy,* November 1906, p. 27.

[20] A. H. Church, 1911, op. cit., p. 992.

8
THE GOLDEN ERA OF CAPACITY REPORTING: 1920–1932

> There is one point, however, which does not seem to have been clearly grasped by some, and that is that what I propose as the real cost of an article is not what it apparently has cost in the past, but what it should cost if the proper manufacturing methods were used and the shop were run at full capacity. This might be called the *ideal cost,* and toward its attainment all efforts should be directed....[1]

The Golden Era of capacity reporting (1920–1932) was, without a doubt, its most glorious moment. Debates focused on idle capacity costs resulted in an agreement on best practice for this expense: Idle capacity would be treated as management-based waste that would be charged directly against operating income rather than buried in product costs. Whether cost accountant or engineer, the writers of this period reflected Gantt's position that hiding idle capacity in product cost was a formula for competitive failure.

The logic and models developed during the Age of Discovery came into full bloom during the Golden Era. Witnessing the birth of the National Association of Cost Accountants (NACA), the creation of the first managerially accepted accounting principles (MAAPs), and the application of value-based economic models to business, the Golden Era was truly a unique period in business history. This uniqueness is even more striking when compared to the subsequent regression in thought and technique brought on by the Great Depression and FDR's New Deal legislation. An age when almost anything that could be envisioned could be done, the Golden Era remains as a beacon of what might have been and what can be.

The period from 1920 to 1932 was also one of economic freedom. This freedom did have a cost attached to it, as the booms and busts that inevitably occurred on the heels of the ending of World War I affected the economies of every major industrial country in the world. The United States was not immune to these events. As described by Chandler, from the Roaring Twenties to the Great Crash of the stock market on October 24 and 29, 1929, the American economy and the businesses that it comprised faced a feast or famine world: "The sharp recession following World War I had a shattering impact on many of the new industrial and marketing companies....The sudden and continuing drop in demand from the summer of 1920 until the spring of 1922 was...the first period of hard times that the modern business enterprise had to face."[2] In this era, the corporate giants that still occupy the global competitive landscape today matured from entrepreneurial to managerial enterprises.[3]

The booming economy of the mid-1920s was played out through business. On every front, American businesses were growing and thriving. With this growth and the development of the decentralized corporation came a heady feeling of optimism that led to excessive, high-risk investments in the securities market. Few people even today are unaware of the devastation wreaked on the American economy as paper fortunes, built on little or no real capital, disappeared in a cloud of black smoke on October 29, 1929.

Such excesses of prosperity and poverty left their mark on the authors who wrote during this period. As the following discussion unfolds, it becomes obvious that the ever-threatening specter of the Great Depression as well as the economic and political drama unfolding in Europe (see Table 8-1) cast their eerie light on the optimism and objectivity of the NACA capacity debates of the 1920s. It was a period of calm before a storm that would span 17 years and affect every continent on earth.

Debating the Future

> [Nearly all of the speakers]…have emphasized the fact that if cost accounting is to be of the greatest service and be given proper recognition in the business world, it must cease to record only historical facts, and must predetermine proper standards of cost and production.…the engineer and cost accountant must work together.[4]

Table 8-1. Timetable of Macroeconomic Events, 1920–1932

1920	W. M. Lybrand writes about such topics as ideal and practical standards and stresses that an increase in overhead costs is not necessarily a bad event.
1921–22	A short but sharp recession occurs that wipes out most of the price increases of the World War I period.
1921	The National Association of Cost Accountants (NACA), founded in 1919 by J. Lee Nicholson, W. S. Gee, William H. Lybrand, and others, has a session at its annual meeting on "The Distribution of Overhead Under Abnormal Conditions."
	R. H. Montgomery, in his third edition of *Principles of Auditing,* stresses the importance of good management principles and techniques in the determination of the cost of inventory.
1922	Mussolini leads the Fascists into Rome.
1929	On October 24 and October 29, the "Great Crash" occurs on the New York Stock Exchange. It triggers a mass default of banks across the country, as paper fortunes disappear as quickly as they were made. The country sinks into a deep and apparently unresolvable depression.
1930	A. H. Church, in his last book, surrenders on the supplemental method and calls for a charge off of all idle capacity costs to the P & L.
1931	Congress forms the War Policies Commission, at which Johnson and Baruch had R. H. Montgomery appointed as executive secretary.
1932	Franklin Delano Roosevelt is elected president of the United States, defeating Herbert Hoover. Key to the campaign is Roosevelt's pledge to put everyone back to work through the auspices of the "New Deal," which focuses its attack on laissez-faire capitalism as the basis for all the economy's ills.

As the Golden Era of capacity reporting unfolded, many of the giants of the Scientific Management period were entering into their "golden years." Gantt, pivotal to the developments of the Age of Discovery, died in 1919, although his influence lived on through his work and that of L. P. Alford, who wrote a biographical sketch of Gantt's work in 1934. Church, once locked in active debate with Gantt and considered a leader in the field of cost accounting, faded from view, dying in poverty and obscurity in 1936 after publishing his last major works on capacity and the treatment of burden expenses between 1930 and 1931. The Golden Era, then, was an era of transition and juxtaposition of old and new that served as a fertile ground for developing an economically sound model of cost.

☐ H. L. Gantt: Alford's Recollections and Collections of "Ganttisms"

The prior chapter found Gantt locked in debate with Church over the "proper" treatment of unabsorbed overhead costs. Gantt was in pursuit of a stable cost, what he later came to call a "true product cost." His position on the treatment of idle expense or unabsorbed burden costs grew from the belief that the market would reimburse a company only for the "true" cost of the product:

> Some of us got busy to find out what was the real trouble, and we found that they had been charging—all of the cost accountants had been charging—to the cost of an article all the expenses incurred during the progress of manufacture of that article, and asking for a profit on top of that. Secondly, costs varied up and down according to seasonal expenses. So after studying that matter out, we came to the conclusion that that theory was entirely wrong; that if the cost of an article included only those expenses needed to produce it, this cost would not fluctuate so much with variations in business; it would be very nearly stationary. [5]

Ever present in Gantt's mind was the central role played by the market in defining optimal business practices. His view was simple: Low costs would lead to high profits. In Gantt's view, then, it was imperative to keep the market in mind when developing costing practices. Idle capacity was waste, not part of product cost.

Gantt is best remembered today for the development of Gantt charts, which track variation from standard, signaling when a process has moved outside of acceptable levels of operation. With his interest in idle costs, then, it is hardly surprising that Gantt also developed an "idleness expense chart" (see Table 8-2). This chart would show up in a wide number of books during and after the Golden Era, including Jordan and Harris's classic, *Cost Accounting: Principles and Practice*, published in 1920. As the reproduction of Gantt's idleness expense chart shows, a bar graph view of capacity utilization, including a detailed breakout of *idleness by cause*, the associated expense of this idleness in terms of *avoidable* and *unavoidable* idle costs, and finally, a column for remarks, made up a tightly defined and measured capacity reporting system.

Gantt's obsession with idleness expense and its treatment led him to question constantly how the cost accounting profession was handling these costs: "The view of costs so largely held, namely, that the product of a factory, however small, must bear the expense, however large, is responsible for much of the confusion about costs and hence leads to unsound business policies."[6] The business policy Gantt had in mind was the full cost plus pricing approach that seemed even during this period to play a strong role in the cost accountant's work.

In his 1919 testimony, Gantt used an example of a company that had decided to buy one of its major products from a competitor because it was offering a price lower than the cost of making the product (26 cents to buy; 30 cents to make). Troubled by this decision, Gantt asked the owner for a breakdown of the 30 cents of cost. The reply he received was, "13 cents material, 5 cents labor, and 12 cents overhead."

Gantt, upon hearing these numbers, asked a second question. "What percentage of the overhead is real, and how much is due to idleness expense?" The answer received was that of the 12 cents of overhead charged to this product, 7 cents was idleness expense, and only 5 cents was identifiable product cost. In

Table 8-2. Idleness Expense Chart

Symbol	Dept. or Machine Class	% Capacity to Attain	% of Capacity Used on Day Turn (10 20 30 40 50 60 70 80 90)	Lack of Orders	Lack of Help	Lack of Raw Material
			Details of Expense of Idleness Due to			
B	200 45" looms	80		F47 32 289 2 31	136 10	
C	687 - 54" & 58" looms	80		F267 80 85 4 76	1473 52	
D	136 - 65" & 68" looms	80		F142 62 432 83	441 94	
E	9 - 58" looms	70		F5 53 376 19	24 95	
F	111 - 68" & 72" looms	70		F194 68 1088 22	725 36	
G	1 - 72" loom	80		C 52 82		
H	1 - 58" loom	80		C 30 12	10 90	

Symbol	Lack of Worked Material	Repairs	Poor Planning	Total	Unavoidable %	Amount	Increase in Expense of Product %	Avoidable
	Details of Expense of Idleness Due to				*Expense of Idleness*			
B	19 40	20 92	6 39	3122 44	20	868 31	18.2	2254 12
C	A 15 54 194 14	493 89	136 42	3436 07	20	5646 65	18.2	2210 58
D	A 1 28 3 55	41 32	6 30	42 39 1069 83	20	7 71 1151 66	18.2	50 10 81 83
E	4 65	14 30	38 99	463 67	30	207 02	36.0	256 65
F	A 84 319 57	288 53	271 15	24 77 2888 35	30	8 92 3895 80	36.0	33 69 1007 45
G		1 95		54 78	20	9 92	18.2	44 86
H		48		41 50	20	3 10	18.2	38 40

From C. J. McNair and Richard Vangermeersch, SMA 4Y, "Measuring the Cost of Capacity." Montvale, NJ: Institute of Management Accountants, 1996, p. 31.

Gantt's mind, then, the true cost of this product was 23 cents (18 cents prime plus 5 cents overhead). Just as clear to Gantt was the fact that the company should not outsource the production of this item but rather meet the competitor's price in the marketplace.[7] In summary, Gantt's position on the treatment of idleness expense in product costing was:

- A product should be charged only with its "true" costs of production.
- The competitive market will reimburse a company only for the true cost of a product.
- The tie between cost and market price is, at best, tenuous.
- Idleness expenses should be charged to the profit and loss statement.

Rejecting the full cost model and its repercussions, Gantt pursued with single-minded fervor the development of "true" product costs freed from the crushing weight of waste. It was a position echoed in the halls of the NACA during the debates of 1921, 1924, 1926, and 1933.

☐ The 1921 NACA Debate

By 1920, only one year after its formation, the NACA began holding annual meetings that served as forums for debate and the exchange of ideas. In 1921 the theme of the debate at the Association's annual meeting was "The Distribution of Overhead Under Abnormal Conditions." Abnormal conditions meant, of course, a period of either excessive demand or excessive supply—the boom or bust periods in the economy.

While the debate was meant to focus on both under- and over-capacity settings, in 1921–22 companies found themselves mired in a short but sharp recession triggered by the end of World War I. The majority of the capacity debate, therefore, centered on the treatment of unabsorbed burden, or idleness expense, rather than its converse. C. B. Williams chaired these sessions and was the author of the article in the 1921 NACA Yearbook that summarized this debate.

In making a profit and loss statement...we should deduct the normal cost...from the sales to show gross manufacturing profit. From this would then be deducted the unabsorbed overhead and other expenses, showing a result which might possibly be a loss. We should thus know what the profit was on the business which had been obtained and what the loss was because the plant was partially idle.[8]

To fully understand Williams's summary statements, it is useful to go further into the debate itself. First on the list of issues was the discussion of what a "normal" cost was and why it should be used. Hasbrouck Haynes, owner of the Haynes Corporation, provided insights here:

The advantages of using a constant, normal, or average overhead, are largely psychological....[It] does permit the management to go ahead and figure their list prices and future profits without the upsetting factor of this excessively high overhead staring them in the face in such a way as to disturb their equilibrium and cause their reasoning faculties to become warped, because of the apparently panicky or impossible conditions confronting them.[9]

In Haynes's view, then, the motivation behind developing a normalized overhead charge was psychological—it would drive the right behavior. Separation of idleness expenses from earned overhead would not change the long-term profitability of the company, but it would prevent the "warping of reasoning faculties."[10] To Haynes the behavioral impact of full cost versus "normal" costing methods was the essential element in choosing one over the other.[11]

Of course, this was a debate, and Haynes's view, reflective of Gantt's model for handling unabsorbed burden (idleness charges) as period expenses, was not the only one voiced, as the following comment by C. R. Stevenson suggests:

...we are going to get a mighty dangerous idea in our minds. I believe if we are going to base overheads on standards, what I call normal rates...we have got to have clearly in mind that unearned burden which is going into our profit and loss, and being incurred as a loss in a period like this, has to be made up in our periods of activity.[12]

It appears that there was considerable disagreement over the role of standard versus actual costs in the emerging cost systems of the 1920s. The strong language used by Stevenson suggests that the movement away from actual costs as the basis for cost accounting practices was viewed as dangerous by many; a company's ultimate profitability was tied to actual costs, not standards.

A second major point of contention during this debate was the accounting treatment of the unabsorbed burden that the "normal costing" model would inevitably produce in a time of reduced demand. While most of the managers and cost accountants were firm in their belief that unabsorbed burden should be reported as a direct charge to income in the year of the loss, a minority wanted to place this charge in a reserve account on the balance sheet, as indicated by this comment from John M. Scanlon:

> Nearly all of our cost systems have been too rigid and have treated each month or year as if it were a separate and distinct period. This has probably been brought about by having the cost accounts controlled by the general books....[13]
>
> By setting up a Reserve for Idle Time during good years, costs will be equalized, since in periods of production the overhead charges absorbed will be more than normal, and during periods of depression they will be less than normal.[14]

In reading through this entire discussion, the emotional response to Scanlon's remarks practically jumps out from the printed page, dusty as it is with age:

> I do not believe anyone will agree that an unabsorbed burden can with safety be carried over as an asset into the new year. It is a pretty poor asset.[15]

> In reference to unabsorbed overhead, we have unabsorbed overhead due to lack of work, due to idleness on account of machines laid up for repair, and due to being short of men....

I agree with Mr. Jordan that the only safe and sound policy is to absorb into our profit and loss statement at the end of every year the overhead which has not been absorbed into the costs. Any company that is not following such a policy is not conservative, and its reasoning is unsound.[16]

Scanlon lost in his bid to place unearned burden on the balance sheet as a reserve account. The majority of those present deemed such an idea both nonconservative in its approach and illogical in its results.

In fact, the majority of persons present at the 1921 debate were very clear in their opinion as to the "best" treatment of idle costs:

> Viewing the question from the standpoint of correct accounting, I cannot see that this unearned or overearned burden is any part of manufacturing cost....[17]

> I believe that the members of this Association, and accountants and business men in general, are pretty well convinced that the old method of charging all of the overhead expense incurred during a given period into the cost of the product turned out during that period is erroneous, in that it results in figures which do not represent the true cost of goods manufactured, and gives the executive incorrect information regarding the operations of his factory.[18]

Idleness costs were not to be added to the "true" cost of making a product. These costs did not belong in product costs or in any other form on the balance sheet. Idle costs were a charge against management that would appear below gross margin.

The 1921 debate on the treatment of unabsorbed burden or idleness expense resulted in the preliminary statement of a MAAP, a managerially accepted accounting practice[19] for these items, as reflected in the concluding statements made at the end of the meeting by J. P. Jordan.

> ...we agreed, with only one dissenting vote, which came along after the meeting was over, that the normal capacity basis should be expressed along something like the following line.

"The normal capacity basis" is the total possible time (that means any kind of work, machine or other), less reasonable allowance for break-downs, repairs, inefficiency, reasonable lack of operators, and all other regular normal delays outside of lack of orders to run on.[20]

...It was the consensus of opinion that in the regular financial accounting of the company all over- and under-absorbed burden should be carried to profit and loss at the end of the year.[21]

This group of practicing managers and accountants came to tacit agreement on a MAAP for reporting idleness expense that included a definition of "normal" capacity based on the capability of the plant, not the average production in prior periods. (This "normal" utilization level was, for all intents and purposes, what is commonly called *practical* capacity today.) In addition, the attendees agreed to place the unabsorbed burden due to idle capacity directly into the profit and loss statement.

To close this discussion, one more statement, by C. B. Williams, needs to be introduced, as it bears on the developments of the Full Cost Era in Chapter 9:

We have Lenines [sic] and Trotskys in every vocation and we have them in cost accounting. Through misguided judgment, they seek to destroy everything that has been done in the past. I am sure that the great body of business men and cost accountants will give little heed to their propaganda, because they realize that the way to make progress is to improve what you have, rather than to tear down without offering a workable substitute.[22]

In the above quotation Williams was referring to the growing pressure to adopt a "total cost" or full cost model for absorbing overhead. Striking in his comments is his tying of the full costing model to the development of socialism and communism as counter forces to the capitalistic model. Williams, typical of the majority of attendees at this meeting and reflecting earlier comments by Gantt, was clear in his belief that the only sound way to handle idleness expense in a competitive marketplace was to remove it from product costs.

☐ The Debates Continue

In almost every year from 1921 to 1932, the NACA Yearbook carried at least one major article on the ongoing debate on capacity reporting practices. These articles most often were structured as a series focused on a specific capacity question, forming a "debate in writing." In 1924, the debate centered once again on the best treatment of idle costs in setting predetermined overhead rates and the inevitable variation between actual costs and absorbed standard costs, as reflected in W. H. Alden's comments:

> ...the entire amount taken out of manufacturing burden is chargeable direct to P & L and appears on the monthly profit and loss statement as an expense of the business caused by failure to keep the shop completely occupied....
>
> It should be understood that the treatment of idle facility expense in the manner referred to does not in the long run decrease profits; its effect is merely to indicate losses at the time when they occur....
>
> The proper accounting for the expense of idle facilities also gives increased value to expense figures given to foremen and department heads....[23]

In other words, Alden suggested that the key issue in the capacity reporting debate was the need to support action and decision making in the firm. The goal was to separate idle cost by its causes and then use responsibility accounting logic to attach these costs to the individual(s) who could change them.

In 1926, the results of the third major debate on capacity reporting practices appeared in the NACA Yearbook under the heading "The Question Box." The focus of this debate (see Table 8-3) was on the definition and preferred choice of capacity for management reporting. Practical in nature, this discussion grappled with the differences between variable and fixed elements

Table 8-3. Points Debated at the 1926 NACA Meeting

1. What are the best ways of accounting for the fixed charges on similar facilities acquired at different prices? Examples: (a) Two or more identical machines bought at different times and different prices. (b) Old model and new model machines for doing the same work. (c) Similar machines differing in size but frequently used interchangeably.

2. Is it sound policy never to take orders below "normal cost"? If so, what, besides direct labor and material consumed on the order, should be reckoned into "normal cost"—particularly all of the normal burden? Or if not all, what part and that part determined on what principle or plan?

3. Is cost accounting generally more useful to business by determining costs of product (the finished article ready to sell) or costs of functions or factory services (e.g., steam costs, yard costs, or sometimes a department cost)?

4. Should the cost department be part of the shop management (works department), or a subdivision of the accounting department?

5. Is the cost accountant often prevented from getting results because operating men do not understand accounting?

6. When should direct labor be combined with burden to make a composite rate? Are there any circumstances seeming to indicate such combination as convenient which may lead to unsuspected trouble?

7. When should experimental work be charged as selling expense? When as part of manufacturing burden? When, if ever, capitalized?

8. When should outlays for new tools be capitalized? Charged to the job on which first used? Charged to burden?

9. Should work in process be carried in the cost ledger separately as labor in process, material in process, burden in process? Why or why not?

10. When should depreciation (or total burden) be taken as a rate for unit of product (per barrel, per ton, per piece) rather than per month or per year?

11. When should group bonus be used?

12. Should setup time be included in piece rate or be kept separate—particularly for the increase in factory efficiency?

13. When is it best to make a labor or payroll distribution daily, rather than by a weekly or longer payroll period?

14. What kinds of shop management details are handled best by a committee rather than by someone in authority giving orders?

15. Should normal burden be set: (a) by the best long-sustained experience of the plant, including ups and downs of sales demand; (b) by the best well-sustained operating efficiency; (c) by the best short spurt of operating excellence; (d) by some engineering or time study standard better than any operating experience?

16. What have you done this last year which has been most worthwhile: (a) to simplify or economize cost work, (b) to make cost results more vivid or effective for operating men—managers, superintendents, or foremen?

After all was said and done—number 15 was chosen by the attending group as the most critical issue of all. This choice, more than any others, underlines the critical role played by capacity reporting issues during the Golden Era.

of burden as well as the relative impact of using theoretical versus practical capacity definitions on management behavior and decisions.

The focal point of the 1926 discussion was a simple example, developed by the chairman of the meeting, Clinton H. Scovell, that laid out the cost implications of different levels of production or capacity baseline measures:[24]

	Production	*Burden per Unit*
(a)	700	$ 1.43
(b)	860	$ 1.16
(c)	930	$ 1.08
(d)	1,000	$ 1.00

These levels were used as reference points by participants in the debate, as shown in this comment by F. L. Sweetser:

> The best basis for pointing the way to cost reduction by your organization is the (d) basis....it will give something to shoot at that is worth while, and, gentlemen, we are facing at this time a competitive period when we want to know how low we can afford to go on selling prices. I think it is very important for the management to know where that danger line is.[25]

In choosing the lowest cost or theoretical capacity basis, Sweetser focused not on the "costing" or accounting puzzle but rather on the influence these numbers would have on management decision making. His quest for the lowest cost was echoed by another participant in this debate, Harry Bullis:

> I believe that normal burden should be set by the most economical operating performance—the point of most efficient operation, where increasing economies cease and diminishing economies begin. This performance is the "exactly right gait" for the plant, and occurs when personnel, equipment, and materials are correlated in such a manner that operating costs are reduced to the minimum and profits for the entire organization increased to the maximum.[26]

Following on Gantt's logic, the goal underlying these comments was to reduce costs to the point where demand would increase to fill existing capacity.

While the majority of cost accountants and practitioners continued to pursue methods for capacity reporting that would place idleness costs on the income statement as a free-standing line item, not everyone agreed with this approach. Charles VanZandt, in fact, argued that idle capacity costs should be placed in product costs.[27] As was the case in the 1921 debate, though, VanZandt's "outlier" position was rapidly attacked by those present.

> I think Mr. VanZandt's theory is absolutely untenable, because I do not believe we can project our figures accurately enough to keep some differential out of profit and loss.
>
> ... what we want to know, is where we are falling down, and we want to know it very definitely so we can work with the organization.[28]

> ...I think I will take the liberty of saying that that difficulty, which you describe so vividly and so accurately, is a difficulty in the education of the owners, and I think in today's discussion we must confine ourselves to the point of view of cost accountants and operators who do not have *that particular mental disability* [emphasis added]....[29]

It appears that even to suggest spreading idleness expense to current production was to trigger ridicule and response. Only the uninitiated would suggest that accounting methods should be distorted to make it easier for owners to digest the information on prior results. Putting variances due to idleness anywhere but in a free-standing account was simply illogical, as a final quotation from this debate illustrates:

> I had in mind that cost accounting has entirely got away from an idea that prevailed fifteen or twenty years ago, when we waited until the end of a production period to find out what the burden was and what the production had been, and then divided one by the other so that we would *spread all the cost over all the product* [emphasis added]. Of course, that is going back

to first principles, and I suppose everybody in this room will agree that for all practical purposes we have discarded that.[30]

In the end, the group reached agreement to use "practical" capacity, defined within a balanced production system, as the basis for developing burden rates and charging these costs to either product or idleness expense on the income statement. Practical capacity, the (c) line in the table shown earlier, was seen as at once attainable, motivational, and stable enough to support the development of true product costs.

By 1926, then, the MAAP approach to capacity reporting detailed in 1921 was accepted practice. Not only was it accepted, any alternative position was seen as illogical and indefensible. Any person wishing to spread these excess costs to inventory was described as feeble-minded, a label that occurred over and over again in the debates of the 1920s. The ultimate goal—informing and supporting decision making—took precedence. In reflecting back on these discussions, it is difficult to believe that only seven years after the 1926 debate full costing would reemerge as the method of choice.

☐ Church Recants: The Cost of Preparedness

One of the most important articles of the Golden Era was Church's 1931 piece, "Overhead—The Cost of Preparedness." In this article, Church recanted his use of a supplemental rate to charge idle capacity costs to current production, moving far beyond the realm of costing to focus on the potential profits embodied in the notion of capacity: Overhead costs are necessary to prepare a company to do work.

Direct quotations do a far better job of capturing Church's position than any restatement of his views could do:

> Under the popular methods of overhead distribution there is, in fact, no real relation between burden and cost—it is an arbitrary and misleading mathematical trick....No clear picture is forthcoming as to the effectiveness of overhead expenditures or their impingement on processes.

Overhead is the cost of preparedness to do process work. Whether working or idle this cost is the same…a standardized cost, or time, or rate is a minimum. It represents the minimum effort in whatever units it may be reckoned, by which some objective can be obtained.

Whatever falls into the pool of waste—and it will be seen that not only process dollars but other items do so fall—is not part of the true cost of product….The only way to deal with this loss is to charge it off to the loss-and-gain account….It is wasted preparedness.

…[idle capacity cost] is a loss that should not have happened. To attempt to include it in costs is only to deceive oneself and narrow the real margin of profit on the jobs that happen to be going through, to falsify the information on which sales prices are calculated….Immediately any process stops, not merely does absence of profit appear, but actual out-of-pocket losses begin.[31]

Church went on to develop four basic efficiencies of production: (1) the efficiency of preparedness, (2) the efficiency of utilization (see Figure 8-1), (3) the efficiency of processing time, and (4) the efficiency of direct labor.[32]

What is striking in this very short but conceptually very deep article is the logic of the market that underlies it. It was, after all, 1931 when this article was written. The Great Depression was in full bloom, creating a culture of hopelessness and a growing mistrust of the market model. While he had not yet taken office, Roosevelt's attack on the laissez-faire capitalism model was taking shape.

With Church's final statement, then, the curtain dropped on the Golden Era of capacity reporting. The logic of the market, which made the "correct" treatment of idle capacity costs so evident to everyone, was abandoned for a model that placed increased power and reliance on government intervention. In this fading light, the future of capacity reporting and the economic logic that should have shaped it collapsed, leaving in its wake the mathematical tricks Church so decried.

See what happens. Two jobs have passed safely by, each absorbing its share of the dripping dollars. Then an interval and two dollars plunk into the pool of waste!

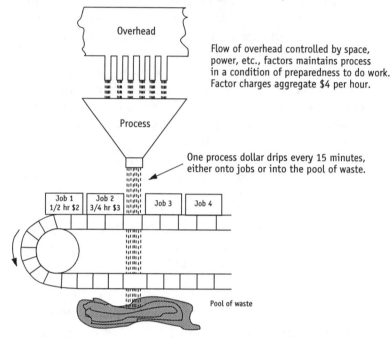

From A. Hamilton Church, "Overhead: The Cost of Production Preparedness," *Factory and Industrial Management,* January 1931, pp. 38-40, as reprinted in *Journal of Cost Management,* Summer 1995, p. 70.

Figure 8-1. The Cost of Preparedness

The Golden Era: Its Ebbs and Flows

The public has an interest in prices based on cost; prices which will cover the overhead, including a "fair return" on the investment for a representative firm. If prices lose touch with this standard in an upward direction it is exploitation. And if they lose touch with it in a downward direction that is demoralization, and is bound to create a reaction.[33]

Throughout the Golden Era of capacity reporting, one fact was understood and accepted: The will of the market was the final judge and jury for every business.

While a significant amount of time could be spent summarizing and discussing the major points made by each of the writers and thinkers of the Golden Era (see Bibliography), it is more interesting to focus on the message contained in these works and how that message began to shift after the stock market collapse in 1929.

☐ A MAAP for Capacity Costing

The Golden Era was unique in that a MAAP for the treatment of idle capacity costs emerged that did *not* reflect a full costing or accounting-centered approach. In reviewing all the pieces developed during this period, then, the following points of agreement emerged:

- Normal capacity is defined as theoretical capacity less "reasonable" allowances for downtime, repairs, and related "unavoidable" events.
- Capacity is defined on the bottleneck resource or activity within a process.
- The process and its ability to create value (its preparedness) are the essential elements in the concept of capacity.
- Idle capacity costs represent wasted productive capability, a waste that cannot be recouped in future periods (if it could be, there would have been more support for balance sheet treatment of this expense).
- Idle capacity costs should not be included in product costs in any way.
- Idle capacity costs, in the form of unabsorbed burden, are to be charged directly to the company's profit and loss statement in the year they occur. Charging idle costs to the income statement directly is the only way to ensure that these costs remain visible and manageable.
- The causes of idle time and idle capacity costs should be carefully tracked and analyzed to eliminate or minimize these costs.
- It is management's responsibility to minimize idle capacity costs.
- If a company attempts to pass idle capacity costs through to customers (full absorption costing), it will get caught up in a "death spiral."

- This treatment would support the development of "true" product cost figures that would prove to be stable baselines for pricing and for management of the firm. It is also the most conservative treatment of this expense.

Impressive in their comprehensiveness, the capacity reporting practices developed during the Golden Era were based on a careful analysis of the nature of these costs and who could influence them.

□ A Movable Feast

On the macro level, the MAAP described above gained great acceptance during the Golden Era, but the strides made during this period extended beyond a static discussion of best practice at the plant level of analysis. In fact, as we trace our way from 1920 to 1932, four distinct levels of idle capacity costs emerge:

- Idleness of one specific machine,
- Idleness at the bottleneck in a process or "little shop,"
- Idleness for the plant or company in total,
- Idleness from a social accounting perspective.

Clark, Church, Crockett, Scovell, and others were concerned not only with idle capacity costs on a local scale but with the impact of this form of waste on the health of the economy at large. The relentless pressure of competition and the market's intolerance for excess cost and waste constantly reemerge as justification for taking an ever-expanding view of capacity.

The discussions of this period, then, focused on capacity as a *movable feast* of opportunity—opportunity to profit. No one appeared to shy away from the tough realities of the market or to promote the development of standards that did not bear some resemblance to the true economic costs of a product. Capacity was the ability to make money, harnessed in the machines, people, and processes that defined the maturing managerial firm. It was an ability that had to be gainfully employed if it were to support ongoing economic prosperity.

In the Golden Era, all the costs of doing business, including idle capacity costs, were dealt with honestly and openly. The iron law of the marketplace was understood and accepted; there was nowhere to hide inefficiency and poor management. At every stage of the production process and every link in the value chain moving product from raw materials through final goods in the customers' hands, the goal was to minimize wasted resources (time, costs, or preparedness). Management accounting was to serve this unending search for improvement in the processes used to create value for customers. Financial reporting would simply have to wait its turn in the quest for dominance. It was to be a short wait.

☐ Warning Signs on the Horizon

While this period officially ended in 1932, one more debate, published in April 1933, is a fitting end to the discussion of this turbulent period. There were two principal players in the 1932 New Haven debate: R. J. Bernard and G. Preshaw. Bernard was the controller of Sargent and Company. The subtitle of Bernard's article notes: "Negative side wins on proposition that unabsorbed overhead should be charged to profit and loss in the year in which it is occurred." The "negative side" Bernard argues is that unabsorbed burden should be charged to the products actually produced in a period, not to profit and loss.

Following Bernard's arguments leads one back to a different era, when business was clearly and inextricably tied to human frailties:

> I should like to make it clear at the outset that what I desire to point out are the human weaknesses to be found in connection with the application of unabsorbed overhead, when the adopted custom is to write it off indiscriminately and often ill-advisedly into profit and loss, instead of passing it through into cost of sales as goods are sold and applying to inventory that part of the variance which is represented by the goods on hand.

Actual cost should contemplate not only the standard cost of the product, but also the relative factor of unabsorbed overhead. Standard cost and unabsorbed overhead are coincident and interrelated and, therefore, should be charged to cost simultaneously. In so far as actual cost is concerned, the standard cost is an element of cost in the same degree that unabsorbed overhead is an important element of cost. The distinction lies in the fact that standard cost measures the expectancy or promise of performance whereas actual cost is the performance.

It is clear, therefore, that in accordance with the fundamental principles of sound accounting, the perfectly natural and appropriate thing to do with the unabsorbed burden is to apportion it to the product by means of the supplementary rate, thereby including in the inventories that part of the variance which is represented by the goods on hand.[34]

In the very shadow of Church's abandonment of the supplemental overhead rate that he had created, Bernard used this rate as the basis for "sound" accounting treatment of unabsorbed overhead costs. What is striking in this lengthy statement of Bernard's position is its reliance on "common sense," "human weakness," and "true conditions" as catch phrases to solidify and add power to his argument. These were the very words used by earlier writers in this era to support the charging of idle capacity costs to the income statement. It appears that "sound accounting" had changed in meaning and intent by 1932. Unbelievable as it may seem, the Golden Era ended with the upset victory of full costing over the logic of the market.

Only Bernard's article appeared in the April issue of the *American Accountant*. Preshaw's position, the one that had lost out in this debate, didn't appear until June of that same year. Preshaw, who was a cost accountant rather than a controller, was concerned with value creation and a firm believer in the notion of a "true cost," as the following comments suggest.

The cost accountant, when he evaluates an inventory, is in effect the buyer, and as such we must accord him the right to question the propriety of increasing the value, or cost, to him by including such elements of cost as are unrelated to the value of the goods offered him.

...All of which leads to a consideration of what are actually the elements of cost, and upon what concept we are permitted to say that this element enhances and adds to the value of our product, and that element does not; or to measure the degree to which a specific item of expense may properly be regarded as having increased its value and above which it must, therefore, be excluded....Formerly, and under the most elementary teaching, we were to regard a unit cost as the sum of all expense divided by the sum of all the products. The error in this conception lies in the presumption of fact that the unrestricted occurrence of an expense adds to or enhances the value of a product.

Unabsorbed burden, by a set of specious arguments can not be simply waived into inventory, without first making a satisfactory answer to the question: In what measure has this amount added to the value of the product?...Value can only be created as a result of productive effort, measured in the light of properly constructed standards. To inflate current assets by amounts representative of no such effort, or, if you please, amounts representing excess or extravagant expense, errors of judgment, unskillful use of materials or equipment, is merely to give value to a dead, lifeless, valueless thing.[35]

Preshaw was destined to lose this argument. Yet his desire to place value creation at the forefront of the product costing process is at the heart of the current drive to reshape the landscape of business. Customer-defined value was to prove, 60 years after Preshaw's comments, to be the key to competitive survival.

In 1932, the logic of the market and the role of value in establishing a linkage between a company's use of resources and customers' demands for the same, lost out to an accounting-centered position. How could Preshaw lose? Did this loss come from the mere fact that he, as a cost accountant, was deemed a "less authority" on accounting matters than Bernard, a card-carrying

CPA and company controller? Did the loss emanate, instead, from the increasing pressures of the Great Depression and the need to use accounting numbers to rationalize business results? Or did Preshaw lose because his logic was flawed? Was the full costing model presented by Bernard and vividly apparent in common practice even today, really superior—was it sound, scientific accounting? Within these questions lies the essence of the great capacity reporting debate, a controversy that once again rages in the pages of the management literature.

A. H. Church wrote in 1930:

> At the time in question, nearly twenty years ago today, the idea of separating wasted capacity (idle time) from true cost of jobs was entirely new and unfamiliar. No other method than that of percentages, and, to a small degree, hourly burdens, was in use, and, in introducing the new views, or overhead, it was desirable not to depart too far from established usage, which of course called for the prorating of all current expenditure over current jobs. By the device of the waste ratio, or as it was termed the "supplementary rate," this complete prorating was still possible, although the author was careful to point out that it was not essential, and that the *waste ratio* was not and could not be part of true cost.
>
> As it turned out, no element of the new method was more severely criticized than the "supplementary rate." It was (somewhat to the author's surprise) generally recognized that it was no part of true cost and that, therefore, *wasted capacity should be charged off to profit and loss. Today, this idea is so generally accepted that there is perhaps no danger in the contrary course.*[36]

☐ References and Notes

[1]   H. L. Gantt, "The Relationship Between Production and Costs," *Transactions,* Vol. 37, American Society of Mechanical Engineers, 1915, as reprinted in *Journal of Cost Management,* Spring 1994, p. 10.

[2]   A. D. Chandler, Jr., *The Visible Hand: The Managerial Revolution in American Business*, Boston: Harvard University Press, 1977, pp. 455–456.

3 General Motors, E. I. duPont, Ford Motor Company, General Electric, Westinghouse, Union Carbide, Monsanto, and Sears Roebuck, already successful in their marketplaces, were among the first organizations in the world to adopt sophisticated management techniques and organizational structures.

4 H. G. Crockett, "The Distribution of Overhead Under Abnormal Conditions," NACA Yearbook, 1921, p.

5 L. P. Alford, *Henry Laurence Gantt, Leader in Industry,* New York and London: Harper & Brothers, 1934, p. 180.

6 Ibid., p. 174.

7 H. L. Gantt, "Influence of Executives," *The Annals of the American Academy of Political and Social Sciences,* September 1919, pp. 257–263.

8 C. B. Williams, "The Distribution of Overhead Under Abnormal Conditions," NACA Yearbook, 1921, p. 206.

9 H. Haynes, "The Distribution of Overhead Under Abnormal Conditions," NACA Yearbook, 1921, p. 208.

10 Ibid.

11 A key terminology issue has to be clarified at this point. During the Golden Era, the term "normal" used in any costing application was the same as the term "practical" today. To overlook this issue or shift in definitions creates significant distortion in the logic of the times. It seems interesting, in fact, that after the Golden Era, the words "practical" and "normal" came to mean different things, a variation in capacity cost management terminology that would lead to downstream embedding of waste.

12 C. R. Stevenson, "Discussion," NACA Yearbook, 1921, p. 237.

13 J. M. Scanlon, "The Distribution of Overhead Under Abnormal Conditions," NACA Yearbook, 1921, p. 224.

14 Ibid., p. 225.

15 J. P. Jordan, "Discussion," NACA Yearbook, 1921, p. 231.

16 C. M. Finney, "Discussion," NACA Yearbook, 1921, pp. 235–236.

17 H. G. Crockett, "The Distribution of Overhead Under Abnormal Conditions," NACA Yearbook, 1921, p. 219.

18 P. F. Clapp, "The Distribution of Overhead Under Abnormal Conditions," NACA Yearbook, 1921, p. 226.

19 The term "MAAP" is used here to indicate clearly that, at least during the Golden Era, management's needs took precedence over traditional financial accounting concerns. The tension between MAAP and GAAP was so created.

20 Jordan, op. cit., p. 241.

21 Ibid., p. 242.

[22] Williams, op. cit., p. 203.

[23] W. H. Alden, Jr., "Handling the Expense of Idle Facilities," NACA Yearbook, 1924, pp. 118, 119.

[24] C. H. Scovell, "Question Box," from the 1926 Annual Meeting of the NACA, reprinted as Article 18 in Richard Vangermeersch's *Relevance Rediscovered*, Vol. I, Montvale, NJ: National Association of Accountants, 1990, p. 260.

[25] F. L. Sweetser, comments in "Question Box" from the 1926 Annual Meeting of the NACA, reprinted as Article 18 in Richard Vangermeersch's *Relevance Rediscovered*, Vol. I, Montvale, NJ: National Association of Acountants, 1990, p. 261.

[26] H. A. Bullis, ibid., p. 259.

[27] C. VanZandt, ibid., pp. 259–260.

[28] F. L. Sweetser, ibid., p. 263.

[29] C. H. Scovell, op. cit., p. 266.

[30] Ibid., p. 265.

[31] A. H. Church, "Overhead—The Cost of Preparedness," *Factory and Industrial Management*, January 1931, pp. 38, 40.

[32] Ibid., p. 39.

[33] J. M. Clark, "Some Central Problems of Overhead Costs: An Inquiry into Aspects of One of the Most Delicate Problems of Business Policy," *Bulletin of the Taylor Society*, February 1927, p. 288.

[34] R. J. Bernard, "New Haven Accountants Debate Disposition of Unabsorbed Overhead," *American Accountant*, April 1933, pp. 113–114.

[35] G. Preshaw, "Unabsorbed Overhead—Should It Be Charged to Inventory?" *American Accountant*, June 1933, pp. 179–180.

[36] A. H. Church, *Overhead Expenses in Relation to Costs, Sales, and Profits*, New York: McGraw-Hill, 1930, pp. 383–384.

9
THE ERA OF CRISIS: 1933–1952

...If you want to know where the consuming power of America went, you need only look around you and see it congealed in icebergs of unnecessary buildings and un-needed plants—and in the dead leaves of the worthless securities which financed them....How could we reverse our situation? Obviously, by a plan to obliterate its causes—an amendment to the rule of laissez-faire.[1]

In the New Haven debate of 1932 between Bernard and Preshaw, warning signs of a troubled future for the development of capacity reporting were evident. Preshaw, regardless of his efforts to tie capacity reporting practices to management's need for information, lost the debate to Bernard. Bernard and the accounting-centered view of cost reporting emerged victorious. Yet the 1932 debate was simply that, a debate. It was no more nor less important than earlier discussions between Gantt and Church or those that had been featured in prior NACA meetings and publications. In retrospect, though, this debate and its impact were different, for it served as a visible signal of the shift away from logic and economic rationale as the basis for cost management practices.

In any review of the historical development of capacity reporting, the nagging question that appears is, why? Why did the elaborate capacity reporting models developed during the first three decades of the 1900s disappear? What force was strong enough to push management reporting off the front page of the management accountant's list of priorities in preference to meeting external demands for information? Was only one person or argument responsible, or was there a progression of incidents that resulted in the death of capacity reporting? It is this latter explanation that appears most likely, and as suggested by the events of the 1933–1952 period, it is the most convincing and yet troubling basis for these changes.

In this chapter, the macroeconomic events that so vividly defined the Roosevelt era in American history serve to shape the discussion (see Table 9-1). The major influences on capacity reporting in this era of economic and political crisis didn't end with the federal government, though. The year 1940 saw the publication of the seminal monograph *An Introduction to Corporate Accounting Standards* by Paton and Littleton, a document that continues to shape GAAP today. On an international level, World War II began and ended, closely followed by the Korean conflict. Capacity reporting faded from view in this turbulent time of great events.

The Blue Eagle Soars

History probably will record the National Industrial Recovery Act as the most important and far-reaching legislation ever enacted by the American Congress. It represents a supreme effort to stabilize for all time the many factors which make for the prosperity of the nation and the preservation of American standards. Its goal is the assurance of reasonable profit to industry and living wages for labor, with the elimination of the piratical methods and practices which have not only harassed honest business but also contributed to the ills of labor.—Franklin Delano Roosevelt, 1933, upon signing the NIRA into law.

Table 9-1. Timetable of Macroeconomic Events, 1933–1952

1933   Adolf Hitler becomes chancellor of Germany.

The Bauhaus, the art and design school of Weimar and later Dessau in central Germany (1919–1933) is dissolved by the Nazis.

The Agricultural Adjustment Act allows farmers to remove acreage from cultivation in return for federal payment. This law is ruled unconstitutional in 1936.

It is stated later on in Hughes's *American Economic History* that the "War Industries Board would reappear in 1933 as the National Recovery Administration."

FDR scuttles the World Economic Conference by dropping the gold standard and increasing the U. S. domestic price level by the NRA and the Agricultural Adjustment Administration.

The National Industrial Recovery Act becomes law on June 16.

1934   Hugh S. Johnson, administrator of the NRA, appoints R. H. Montgomery chief of the Research and Planning Division.

Montgomery warns against the increase in prices due to the NRA.

Montgomery, in his fifth edition of *Principles of Auditing*, stresses an equitable basis for distributing factory overhead and keeps the same wording as used in 1927 for the treatment of under-absorbed or over-absorbed costs.

Small business objections to the NRA lead FDR to appoint Clarence Darrow—the celebrated criminal lawyer—as chairman of the National Recovery Review Board.

1935   Benito Mussolini publishes *Fascism: Doctrine and Institutions,* in which he comments on the NRA: "The American experiment should be followed very closely. In the U. S., government intervention in business is direct; and sometimes it takes a preemptory form. The [NRA] codes are nothing more nor less than collective contracts to which the President compels both parties to submit. We must wait before passing judgment on the experiment."

The NRA, then in a state of disarray, is ruled unconstitutional by a unanimous vote of the Supreme Court in the Schechter case.

The collective bargaining provisions of the NRA are put into the Wagner Act by Senator Robert Wagner from New York. The proper title for this act was the National Labor Relations Act.

1936   The Robinson-Patman Act disallows unjustified price cutting to large buyers.

1937   The Miller-Tydings Act legalizes retail price maintenance in interstate commerce.

1938   The Fair Labor Standards Act establishes a maximum work week before overtime must be granted, as well as setting the first minimum wage.

Japan has great successes in its invasion of China.

1939   World War II starts, leading the United States out of a serious economic slump.

1940   Two U. S. accounting theorists, William A. Paton and A. C. Littleton, promulgate their "costs attach" and "costs have the power of cohesion" theories in their *Introduction to Corporate Accounting Standards.*

1941   The Lend-Lease Act and the Ship Warrants Act involve the United States in economic warfare.

On December 7 Japan bombs Pearl Harbor, leading to the American declaration of war against Germany, Japan, and Italy.

1942   The NACA holds an all day-session at its annual meeting on "Accounting Problems Arising from War Contracts" and "Wartime Cost Problems."

1944   The Bretton Woods System for the world economy is adopted.

1945   World War II ends.

The NACA annual meeting is on "The Postwar Problems of the Industrial Accountant."

1946   The first civilian digital computer appears.

The Full Employment Act passes.

Winston Churchill gives his "Iron Curtain" speech.

1947   The sun sets on the British Empire as India and Pakistan are granted independence.

Transistors are invented.

The Marshall Plan involves the United States in the European economic reconstruction.

Accounting Research Bulletin No. 29, "Inventory Pricing," states that "as applied to inventories, cost means in principle the sum of the applicable expenditures and charges directly or indirectly incurred in bringing an article to its current condition and location" and "...under some circumstances, items such as idle facility expense...may be so abnormal as to require treatment as current period charges rather than as a portion of the inventory cost...."

1948   A computer predicts for TV that Truman will beat Dewey, but the newscasters are afraid to publicize the prediction.

Tito leads Yugoslavia out of the Soviet bloc.

1949   Montgomery, in his seventh edition, equivocates on the issue of direct costing, mentions the machine-hour method, and rules the charge-off method for unabsorbed overhead to be usual.

The North Atlantic Treaty Organization is formed.

The USSR acquires the atomic bomb.

Mao Tse-tung chases Chiang Kai-shek to Formosa and takes over China.

1950   The Korean conflict starts and leads to a renewed surge in the U. S. economy that lasts until 1960.

Hughes states, "From World War II until the end of the sixties, American economic progress was the envy of the world."

Within 40 years the world population will double from about 2 billion. The population is expected to reach and stabilize at 10 billion by 2030.*

---

*   Eric J. Hobsbawm, *The Age of Extremes: A History of the World, 1914–1991,* New York: Random House, Inc., 1994, p. 568.

One of the most significant years in the development of the American economy was 1933. That year saw the passage of every major element of Roosevelt's New Deal program, which was his plan for battling the Great Depression. The first of the Security Exchange Acts was passed in 1933, as well as the Agricultural Adjustment Act. But of all the bills and laws passed, the National Industrial Recovery Act (NIRA) was the most ambitious. Targeted at developing rules and regulations that would affect the very essence of the laissez-faire model of competition that had shaped the first 150 years of the American adventure, the NIRA represented the first real attempt by any government to regulate business activities on a micro level.

The NIRA's target was the so-called "predatory competition" of the pre-Depression era, seen by Roosevelt and his followers as the major cause of the market failures of 1929 and 1930. In the words of the time, the driving force behind the NIRA and its operations was the belief that free market capitalism had failed:

> Among the avowed purposes of the National Industrial Recovery Act none stands out more clearly than the declaration of intention to revise the nature of competition in American business…. [I]ts purpose was to "civilize industry," to "write a new merchant law" for American business….
> As a consequence of this purpose of the law, NRA codes have contained, either under the title of trade practices or otherwise, provisions designed to regulate trade activities. Indeed the codes are called codes of fair competition.[2]

Franklin Roosevelt was elected based on his promises to get the country back to work, and he did. But it is less well known that the basis for this recovery was a direct attack on the competitive market mechanism. Given that the capacity reporting models developed during the Golden Era were intricately tied to the logic of the market, it is clear that the NIRA, if successfully implemented, would affect these practices.

And affect them it did, in a very basic way: through the development of uniform costing practices. In fact, one of the main enforcing mechanisms of the NIRA, as defined by Hugh Johnson, its director, and the array of prominent individuals involved in its framing,[3] was the development of a broad number of industrial cost codes. In all, about 600 separate code items dealing with the concept of "cost" were developed during the two short years that the NIRA functioned.

The development of uniform costing practices was the backbone of the NIRA's attack on the free market structure. And it was not simply any form of costing that was to serve the NIRA's purpose—*full cost recovery* became the accepted means of measuring, and hence setting prices on the basis of incurred costs. The implications of this change in the role and method of costing in business enterprises were clearly understood by those shaping the economy.

> It is highly probable that in every instance in which the NRA guaranteed cost protection to industries it was expected that such protection would bring about a price higher than the competitive price. It is needless to say, therefore, that it is in effect price fixing. Unless the cost systems...included elements of cost that *were not being earned* [emphasis added], there would be no demand on the part of industries for such provisions. The precise extent to which no-sales-below-individual-cost provisions bring prices above competitive prices depends in part upon the elements included in costs.... An analysis of the first 16 accounting systems approved indicates that in each cost system elements of "cost" specified not only all direct labor and material costs, but a large proportion of indirect manufacturing expenses....[4]

The NIRA relied on full cost recovery practices to redefine the competitive marketplace, a fact that provides a potential explanation for the shift away from a rich, economics-based theory of costing, as detailed and promoted by Church, Gantt, and Clark, toward one that promoted full cost recovery as the basis for price setting.

The accountant took on a new role under the NIRA, described by Taggart: "The accountant's voice, formerly crying unheard in the wilderness, would be the voice of a dictator—it must be listened to to keep out of jail....For the first time in history cost accounting had become law."[5] In this telling discussion by Taggart of the NIRA and cost accounting, it is clear that business was behind the codes because they provided a quid pro quo for business's acceptance of wage and hour legislation. Business would abide by the cost codes because they provided companies with a way to recover the excess costs incurred meeting Roosevelt's "back to work" programs. For accountants, the benefits were immense, as significant referential and professional power was shifted to them. No longer locked in a debate with engineers as to who had the "right" to define cost practices, accountants found themselves on the "side of the eagle" in creating and defining business practice.

☐ The NIRA, the Blue Eagle, and Capacity Reporting

The essential elements of the NIRA with respect to capacity reporting were its reliance on full cost recovery costing methods and its promotion of "cost plus a fair profit" approaches to setting market prices. In sharp contrast, the capacity reporting model or MAAP developed during the Golden Era was a far cry from full costing. It assigned idle capacity costs (unearned burden) to period expenses rather than product. The goal of capacity information in the Golden Era was not to spread costs (which, in fact, was ridiculed as a naive objective) but rather to provide solid information on how well management had used the resources at its disposal to generate revenues and profits.

Just as important to the writers of the Golden Era as the concept of a "true product cost," devoid of charges for idle capacity and related forms of waste, was their reliance on free market mechanisms in defining price. Gantt was very clear in his view that waste could not be passed on to customers via inflated market prices: *price was a function of value delivered to customers, not cost incurred*. It was this tie between value and price that the NIRA attacked. In attacking the concept of a "true cost" and the role of the market in shaping management reporting practices, the NIRA effectively destroyed the foundations of capacity reporting as defined during the Golden Era.

The NIRA, though, appears as a transitory blip in economic history. Signed into law as a temporary action in June 1933, it was terminated in 1935 on the heels of a series of legal and legislative battles that brought its constitutionality directly into question: "The NRA was declared unconstitutional as an excessive delegation of law-making power to private groups and government agencies."[6]

The reach of the NIRA legislation, however, went beyond the physical legislation. While the formal legislative structure of the NIRA was dismantled, it was not the only way that the Act and its intentions were enforced. Specifically, the development of the NIRA by Hugh Johnson was framed around the use of a symbol: the Blue Eagle.

The 1930s can be seen as an era of symbols. From Hitler's swastika to Mussolini's fascis to the hammer and sickle that still represents the Russian state, symbols helped move nations to action. The Blue Eagle, the symbol of the NIRA, was a symbol with far-reaching effects, one that far outlived the act that spawned it:

> The clothes would have looked different, the women's skirts a little shorter, the men's coats sporting small black-velvet collars, perhaps. The automobiles would have been square and black. The shop windows would have carried the blue eagle of the National Recovery Act. There would have been small differences, but a city does not really change much over the years, because a city is only a collection of people and people are timeless. And the way the automobile came around the corner, it could have been 1937.[7]

It is the Blue Eagle and its ongoing use throughout the period leading up to World War II that provide the second and perhaps most interesting part of the story of the NIRA and its impact on capacity reporting practices.

□ The Birth of the Blue Eagle

> In war, as in the gloom of night attack, soldiers wear a bright
> badge to be sure that comrades do not fire on comrades. On
> that principle those who cooperate in this program must
> know each other at a glance.—Franklin Roosevelt on the
> Blue Eagle, fireside chat, July 13, 1933.

To understand the role played by the Blue Eagle in enforcing the
intent, if not the letter, of the law written in the NIRA codes, it
is best to turn to the autobiography of Hugh Johnson, the man
who was charged with the formation, operation, and success of
the NIRA by Roosevelt. His book, aptly named *The Blue Eagle
from Egg to Earth* provides unusual and at times troubling insights into the logic and motivations of the persons who shaped
the New Deal era.

In Chapter 21 of *The Blue Eagle*, Johnson focused on the
reasons for the Blue Eagle and the precedents for its use:

> Mobilization of public opinion becomes important. If it is
> commonly understood that those who are cooperating are
> soldiers against the enemy within and those who omit to
> act are on the other side, there will be little hanging back.
> The insignia of government approval on doorways, letter-
> heads, and invoices will become a necessity in business. This
> method was a success in 1918. It is a short cut to action and
> to public support without which no such plan can succeed.
> By this method a large part of the emergency job can be
> accomplished in short order.[8]

In this passage, Johnson seems to suggest that the fate of the
NIRA was inextricably tied to the Blue Eagle. As described, it
would appear that the Blue Eagle's role was to serve as an iden-
tifier of those loyal to the tenets of the NIRA, a necessary part
of bringing pressure to bear on them to conform with the new
market structure proposed by the New Deal. The importance of
this pressure is revealed in Johnson's own words:

> When a change like NRA comes along—raising wages, short-
> ening hours, and inevitably increasing costs—one company in

an industry cannot accept it unless practically all other companies in that industry accept it.... There was a political reason far deeper and more subtle.... The Blue Eagle put the enforcement of this law [the NIRA] in the hands of the whole people.[9]

Roosevelt reinforced this view of the role of the Blue Eagle, stating, "There are adequate penalties in the law, but I am asking the cooperation that comes from opinion and from conscience. These are the only instruments we shall use in the great summer offensive against unemployment. But we shall use them to the limit to protect the willing from the laggard and to make the plan succeed."[10]

The Blue Eagle, then, appears to have been a very vital part of the mobilization of public opinion to support the NIRA and its directives, as once again suggested by Johnson's own words:

Men might argue about how many business angels could stand on the point of an economic needle—and let the chance go by, but a woman in support of her home is about as safe for triflers as a Royal Bengal Tigress at the door of a den full of cubs. When every American housewife understands that the Blue Eagle on everything that she permits to come into her home is a symbol of its restoration to security, mercy on the man or group of men who attempt to trifle with this bird.[11]

In its intent and functioning, the role of the Blue Eagle within the development of the NIRA appears to have been to identify "recalcitrants," the enemy in the battle to restore prosperity. So while the NIRA was dismantled, its influence appears to have remained as a driving force in the shape of the Blue Eagle symbol. It is hard to argue that a simple symbol would in itself be enough to reinforce or create the major shift in the economic markets desired by the New Deal proponents. It is equally difficult to argue that these forces reshaped capacity reporting, until the voluntary adherence to NIRA principles is considered.

□ A Mutual Agreement

While no doubt many industrialists had a greater or lesser degree of hope, if not faith, that increases in wages might be conducive to recovery, and while there is no doubt that many individuals were moved to take what they regarded as the added risks of wage increases, it is equally without a doubt that for the most part codes of fair competition would not have been 'voluntarily' brought forward and would not have been voluntarily agreed to unless they contained what the industrial groups regarded as a quid pro quo. This quid pro quo was in many cases permission to do as a group what was at least of questionable legality before the passage of the Recovery Act....[12]

Pulling the threads of the argument together, it appears that the Blue Eagle may have provided a mechanism beyond 1935 for the continued influence of the NIRA, including its pursuit of uniform costing methods as embodied in full cost recovery. To gain acceptance from business, it seems that there was a need to pass the increased costs of doing business inherent in the NIRA through to the public in the form of price increases that effectively moved prices above the competitive market level.

By tacitly agreeing to compete on a cost-based definition of market value or price, business appears to have been creating a safety net for itself that would effectively remove it from the harsh realities of the free market system. In its early phases, then, the NIRA was supported by business because business itself stood to benefit. Proof of this ongoing adherence to the NIRA is evident in the excerpt from U. S. Steel's annual report dated 1935.

The business of the subsidiary manufacturing companies continued for the early part of 1935 to be conducted under the provisions of the Code of Fair Competition of the Iron and Steel Industry, to which references were made in previous annual reports. In accordance with the decision rendered by the Supreme Court on May 27, 1935, declaring the National Industrial Recovery Act unconstitutional, the

Iron and Steel and other codes were rescinded. The subsidiary companies concerned have, however, continued in their policy of retaining and promoting those working and industrial relations which tend to maintain such of the advantages as have resulted from code operation.

U. S. Steel is remarkable in its consistent history of capacity reporting, beginning with its earliest published financial statements in 1900. Yet even U. S. Steel abandoned its reporting of idle capacity costs when the New Deal legislation came into being. The only remaining issue was the extent of this agreement and the consequences of failing to comply with the NIRA.

From H. S. Johnson, *The Blue Eagle from Egg to Earth*, Garden City, NY: Doubleday, Doran and Company, 1935, p. 256.

Figure 9-1. Non Member, We Don't

From H. S. Johnson, *The Blue Eagle from Egg to Earth*, Garden City, NY: Doubleday, Doran and Company, 1935, p. 229.

Figure 9-2. Working on His Eagle, Again

☐ The "Recalcitrants"

Not all business could be argued to benefit from the NIRA. In fact, those businesses that were thriving under the free market were likely to lose, if not profitability, at least control over their destiny should the NIRA succeed. These successful business-men formed the core of the "recalcitrants" that the Blue Eagle and subsequent government sanctions sought to "reveal." Fig-ures 9-1 and 9-2, which originally appeared in Johnson's work, provide perhaps the most powerful vision of the Blue Eagle and its role in enforcing the tenets of the NIRA.

Of all of the recalcitrants who brought on the pressure and ire of the NIRA and its proponents, Henry Ford was perhaps the most noteworthy. Clearly Schechter Poultry's challenges led to the undoing of the formal body called the NRA, but it was Henry Ford who ultimately bore the brunt of the pressures—on whom the Blue Eagle truly landed. Ford would not adhere to the rules created under the NIRA for reasons stated so eloquently by his spokesman, William J. Cameron: "There can be no doubt...that proposals are being made in the name of recovery that have nothing to do with recovery, and that seriously affect the fundamental American idea. We doubt that it is necessary to scrap America in order to achieve recovery." [13]

Ford adhered to his conviction that the free market or "American ideal" was the best and only economic system viable in the United States. He refused, in spite of increasing pressures and the economic risks they represented to his own firm, to sign the codes that attempted to place cost and price controls on the automobile industry, an act that "prevented him from displaying the Blue Eagle on his products.... Without the Blue Eagle, the government initially refused to purchase Ford cars, and there was considerable uncertainty whether the public would buy them either. Hugh Johnson's appeals to individual consumers to boycott products that did not display the Blue Eagle had been relatively effective at the time Ford was refusing to place the emblem on his vehicles." [14]

Essentially, then, the Blue Eagle was purposely used as a mode of identifying and punishing "recalcitrants" through the withholding of vital government contracts for business as well as governmentally supported public boycotts of products, as suggested by the following: "Non-compliance! Dereliction of statutory duties—it is not just a misdemeanor—it is failure to *play the game in a great national crisis*." [15] There is no need to create or assume this nefarious intent into the Blue Eagle and its use; these objectives are freely and openly stated by Johnson in his autobiography and by Roosevelt in his speeches and actions.

☐ Summary: Capacity Reporting Under the Blue Eagle

One of the most troubling aspects of any study of capacity is the sharp shift in reporting practices after 1933. Most people tend to believe that progress in thinking and the development of management tools means a movement forward in time, but capacity reporting practices appeared to take a major leap backward in 1933. While many reinforcing and complementary events tied to changes in capacity reporting practices, only the NIRA so clearly focused on changing cost practices and hence, implicitly, capacity cost management techniques.

In enforcing a full cost recovery model, the NIRA went against the logic and wisdom of the Golden Era. How could the position of the NIRA be accepted in a world that spawned Gantt, Church, and Scovell? How could the same set of managers who had developed the MAAP on capacity reporting described in the previous chapter and who referred to full costing models with derision, agree to abandon the logic of the market? Clearly, Church and Gantt, had they been alive, would not have agreed to abide by the NIRA rulings, any more than Henry Ford did. But with the giants gone, industrial engineering on the decline as the dominant management technique, and the intense pressure of the Roosevelt administration brought to bear on business, it is not that hard to believe that idle capacity reporting would fall victim. It was a regrettable reversion, however, because it was to take more than 60 years for the topic to regain even a small part of the ground lost in 1933.[16]

The NIRA alone seems unlikely to have been a large enough force totally to overturn the search for "true" cost that defined the Golden Era of capacity reporting. In fact, a number of reinforcing events and changes in the economy at large, in the focus taken by the accounting profession, and in the development of textbook material to train new accountants combined effectively to divorce cost accounting from its historical roots. The NIRA may have provided the initial thrust toward the full cost recovery model in accounting, but it was not the only event of import in this turbulent time.

Capacity Reporting and
the Development of Accounting Theory

> Accounting historians should examine carefully the extent
> to which the writings and teachings by academic accoun-
> tants (as distinct from auditors and managers) have contrib-
> uted to cost accounting's lost relevance for cost management.[17]

Underlying the changing tides of capacity cost and reporting
practices during the 1933–1952 period was the development of
elaborate professional training programs in accounting. Focused
on the general ledger and the demands of financial reporting,
these programs emphasized product costing under a full cost
recovery approach. Prior to 1933, this financial orientation was
present, but there was little real-world reinforcement of it. Post-
1933, a number of government-driven regulations and programs
elevated the importance of financial reporting in the American
economy. The SEC Acts of 1933 and 1934 are most often cited
in this regard, but the Miller-Tydings Act, the Federal Wage and
Hour Act, and the Robinson-Patman Act were equally influential
in shifting the emphasis of industrial accountants away from serving management and toward a financial markets orientation.

In the "real world" of management accounting there appear
to have been marked shifts in the emphasis placed on supporting management versus adherence to professional accounting
standards. Reviewing the academic literature of the time, as captured in leading textbooks and publications of the then-infant
American Accounting Association (AAA), no real shift in emphasis can be found. If anything, it appears that financial accounting-based cost models were from their infancy simplistic
in nature. The textbooks continually focused on product costing
as a technique used to attach the costs of production to the
output of the period. While arguments were made repeatedly
about how this "accounting-centered" information had relevance
for management decision making, there is no evidence that managers felt this to be the case.

In reviewing the literature of the Era of Crisis, it is important to remember that Gantt had made a significant distinction between the cost accountant and the engineer in discussing the development of cost standards. Prior to 1933, cost accounting simply recorded historical transactions and balanced the books for inventory. The major thinkers and developers of cost theory were engineers, not accountants. While the thinking on cost and its meaning had been quite rich throughout the first 30 years of the 20th century, it is not clear that accounting was the source of innovation or even relevance in costing practices. Cost theory was developed not as part of accounting but as part of sophisticated management practice under the auspices of the Scientific Management movement. Actual accounting theory developed along different lines.

□ Developing Accounting Theory

Two major publications in the 1933–1952 era, both by Paton and Littleton, were to shape the future of capacity reporting: "A Tentative Statement of Accounting Principles Affecting Corporate Reports" (*Accounting Review*, June 1936, pp. 187–191) and *An Introduction to Corporate Accounting Standards* (American Accounting Association, Monograph #3, 1940). Reflecting the emphasis of the AAA and its members, these two pieces are notable in their lack of concern for management accounting issues. Focused on developing standards for accounting, their authors made short work of any "nonobjective" method for creating accounting reports. Accounting was not to focus on value—it was intricately tied to historical cost and the "proper" treatment of all period and product expenses. Since capacity costing during the Golden Era had been driven by a concern for customer-perceived value, it was clear that these methods would fail to meet the objectivity threshhold set by Paton and Littleton.

The 1936 Statement by Paton and Littleton was the first attempt to homogenize the financial reporting practices of companies. In making this attempt, the Statement placed its emphasis on comparability of data between companies and the objective measurement of income and equity:

> ...that the purpose of the statements is the expression, in financial terms, of the utilization of economic resources of the enterprise and the resultant changes in and position of the interests of creditors and investors. Accounting is thus not essentially a process of valuation, but the allocation of historical costs and revenues to the current and succeeding fiscal periods (p. 188).

Given the fact that the capacity reporting models of the Golden Era were based on *value*, not cost, the developing accounting theory was in direct conflict with earlier positions and interests. In an accounting world built on the tenets of historical costs, value- or management-driven cost reports became undesirable in their inaccuracy, incomparability, and nonobjectivity.

The publication of the Statement set the stage for a more elaborate development and codification of accounting standards. This refinement took the form of Paton and Littleton's seminal work on accounting standards, still used today by FASB and others as the source of acceptable solutions to accounting problems. Paton and Littleton's monograph provided the basic framework of accounting as practiced and taught today. To understand the impact of this monograph on capacity cost reporting, several comments are useful:

> Costs are not marshalled to show value or worth.... Some costs, like manufacturing overhead, in which an affinity with the product can be detected, are allocated directly to a product.... Therefore costs are assembled by products or time intervals as if they had a power of cohesion, not because, as regrouped, they express values, but because they express parts of the total effort made to bring about a subsequent advantageous sale (p. 14).
>
> Ideally, all costs incurred should be viewed as ultimately clinging to definite items of goods sold or service rendered.... In economics, the total "cost of production" is usually conceived of as the price-influencing cost effective at a point of

time in a given market area—a cost which includes all elements which the price paid by the purchaser must cover if
production is to continue. From this standpoint cost clearly
becomes identical with the selling price of the marginal producer.... This is in contrast to the position taken by the
accountant. Accounting exists primarily as a means of computing a residuum, a balance, the difference between costs
(as efforts) and revenues (as accomplishments) for individual
enterprises (p. 15).

True cost is measured by the amount of cash that will
have to be expended if final settlement is to be reached at
once (p. 26).

The overemphasizing of last increments or differentials
is another phase of the tendency to rank costs improperly.
Impressed by unutilized capacity and the accompanying
array of inelastic costs, the management sometimes becomes
convinced that the assignable cost of a possible increment
of revenue is restricted to the amount by which the total of
operating charges will be increased if it is decided to under-
take to produce the additional volume of business in question (p. 68).

Several key ideas are embedded in these comments. First,
"true cost" is redefined away from a concern with the economic
value of the resources required to make a product to a focus on
cash outlays, the objective baseline of all accounting. Gone is
Gantt's position that cost reflects resources used in production
under ideal conditions; production is not even an issue in Paton
and Littleton's world.

A second and perhaps more important concept embedded in
Paton and Littleton's treatise is the attachment of all costs of
production to units of output. Explicit in these production costs
is the globally defined notion of "overhead." Overhead attaches
to product, period. Why is this the case? Because overhead has
an affinity with the product made. Reinforcing the attachment
process is the comment that consumption of a resource does not
necessarily mean that it should be assigned to revenue; in some
way Paton and Littleton appear to suggest that resources that

have already been used still have future value. This position would undoubtedly have troubled Gantt and Church alike.

Finally, in rejecting incremental or differential costing, Paton and Littleton appeared to reinforce the primacy of full cost recovery approaches. In reality, though, a careful reading of Paton and Littleton actually leads to a far different conclusion. In addition to the notion of cost "affinity," several other comments in the monograph open the door to interpretation:

> The flow of cost factors, in other words, needs to be appropriately divided between the pool of charges to be held back, deferred, and those representing elements from which the utility has been fully exhausted (p. 16).
>
> Until revenue has been generated by the effort expended, costs merely accumulate. If no revenue appears, costs may still represent an investment. But at the extreme, the cost-forms may be such that they are currently useless to the suppliers of capital, as well as ineffective in producing future revenue; in such case the investment is lost (pp. 32–33).
>
> There are lean years and fat years in business operation and it is a function of accounting to disclose this condition sharply, not to cover it up. The standing and reputation of an enterprise must be maintained by performance, not by statistics (p. 77).
>
> Segregation of costs which have the nature of losses is especially desirable when inefficient management is responsible (p. 80).
>
> A loss may be defined as an expiration of cost incurred without compensation or return, in contrast to charges which are absorbed as costs of revenue (p. 93).
>
> ...all expired costs are chargeable to revenue so long as conditions are not too far out of line with ordinary standards of management (p. 94).

Are the costs arising from idle capacity part of normal business practices and therefore chargeable to product, or are they nearer to losses that bear no future benefit or ability to generate revenues? The "proper" accounting treatment of idle capacity costs rests in the answer to this question. Does reporting idle capacity costs violate or support GAAP as so forcefully defined by Paton and Littleton? The answer to this question lies in the definition of "normal" practice and the perceived ability of the cost accountant to separate losses due to normal conditions from those of an abnormal nature.

Embedded in this second set of quotations from Paton and Littleton, then, lies the key to disconnecting capacity cost reporting from the full cost model: If inefficient management is the source for the losses, then idle capacity costs, among others, should be immediately expensed. Are the costs associated with idleness a "normal" part of doing business? Then they should be assigned to inventory with all other forms of regular damage and obsolescence charges. Where one draws the line on the counterposing arguments of potential future value of idle capacity costs and the extent to which these costs are a reflection of "normal" practices or management inefficiency defines the type of capacity costing treatment followed.

In reality, it would appear that all that Paton and Littleton's monograph does for the capacity costing issue is to pinpoint the issues that would underlie a debate of best practice in capacity reporting. There are no answers in these phrases but rather an identification of the issues that underlie this complex topic. In closing this section, it seems appropriate to recognize Paton and Littleton's views on cost accounting:

> The computation of standard costs, as interpretative devices, is not objectionable provided the income statement reports costs actually incurred (p. 118).
>
> The typical enterprise is a closely knit institution composed of interdependent factors.... There is always danger that cost assignments, however carefully worked out, will not reflect essentially long-run relationships (p. 120).
>
> It seems clear that no matter how penetrating and complex may be the work of the cost accountant there is slight possibility of developing dependable causal connections between particular costs and segments of that revenue.... Revenue cannot be obtained without business activity, and business activity involves the occurrence of costs (p. 121).

Cost accounting cannot, according to Paton and Littleton, be based on causality. Why? Because dependable causal connections between segments of revenue and the resources used to generate them cannot be developed. In the eyes of these authors, there's no point at all to the costing exercise, so why do it? If for no other reason, the dismissal of cost accounting in this series of passages sealed the fate of capacity cost reporting. To believe that capacity cost reporting, including the careful identification and separation of idleness costs from productive resource uses, is possible one would have to believe that costing can be done with some sort of accuracy in the first place. Clearly, Paton and Littleton don't have a great deal of enthusiasm for the costing process and its value; accounting is, after all, concerned with objective "fact" based on historical records, not market forces.

☐   The Loss of Relevance in Costing—Fact or Fiction

The fine line between a period loss and an asset capable of generating future revenues is difficult to discern given Paton and Littleton's position. Clearly, only items that can generate future revenues should be assigned to work-in-process inventory. On the other hand, this demarcation cannot be based on the consumption of the resource, the logical point for making this assessment of future revenue-generating ability. It would seem that while Paton and Littleton did not disallow the direct expensing of idle capacity costs on the income statement, neither can it be said that they believed cost accounting could, with any sort of accuracy, sort out idleness costs from the other sundry costs stored in the overhead account. And if management intends to have idle capacity then these costs are not extraordinary but, rather, a normal cost of doing business. A careful analysis of Paton and Littleton leaves us with the option to expense unexpected or excess idle capacity and the burden it causes, but the treatment of other forms of idleness remains poorly defined.

Gone in these accounting-centered remarks is a concern for the customer-defined value of the goods and services provided by an organization, a concern that was the defining feature of the Golden Era. Gone, also, is the practical mind of the engineer that believes a "true cost" can be defined—that resources can be causally attached to the goods and services that consume them. Replacing this practical, management-centered view of costs and capacity is a financial accounting model that promotes actual costs as the basis for inventory valuation (the average of all resource costs per item produced) over standards and attaching all overhead costs to inventory, regardless of whether the customer would reimburse the company for these costs in the price paid for the goods. When combined with the dominant focus of textbooks of the period on full cost recovery methods, as well as the dramatic and pervasive influence of the NIRA and the Blue Eagle, the message delivered by Paton and Littleton was clear: Attach idleness costs to good production.

Turning now to the remaining capacity-based literature of the 1933–1952 period, the pervasiveness of these views becomes clear. Paton and Littleton, in rejecting the possibility that effective, accurate costing could be developed, laid the groundwork for the increasingly irrelevant nature of management accounting.

Capacity Reporting in Retreat

Completing the analysis of the capacity reporting literature during the period 1933–1952 (see Bibliography), it is clear that World War II interrupted the debate on capacity. Prior to the war, capacity issues were still presented in light of the burden attached to the use of machines and equipment. Post-World War II, the dominant focus turned to variance analysis and reconciling financial and cost accounting records.

To state that capacity reporting methods were in retreat after World War II is perhaps an understatement. In the articles reviewed, the shift in perspective and emphasis on key capacity issues is marked. By 1946, little of the logic and structure of the Golden Era's debates and agreements remained. Replaced by increasingly dominant financial reporting practices, a formalization of the accounting profession around the theory developed by Paton and Littleton, and the tacit acceptance of full cost plus pricing methods, the logic of the market and the dominant role played by value in setting prices were lost. In comparing cost to price, the NIRA and then Paton and Littleton shattered the basic assumptions of market-based economics, replacing them with a cost-based focus that placed little or no emphasis on customer rights.

☐ A Final Debate

In 1945, the NACA hosted its final debate on the issues of capacity and costs. Edwin Nourse, an economist, was pitted against Charles James, a cost accountant. In the four parts making up this debate, the emphasis was placed on the interplay between various definitions of capacity and the market demand and price for goods. Nourse began the discussion, noting that current capacity utilization in most companies was bordering on 70%, and that this translated to excess cost and hence reduced competitiveness for a company. Arguing from an average cost position, Nourse suggested that market cycles and long-term unemployment result from failing to utilize capacity completely and consistently.

James took a counterposition, noting that Nourse's view of cost was simplistic at best and wrong at worst. Noting that the high level of variable and stepped costs inherent in most companies' cost structures might actually make full capacity a higher cost basis for operation than some lower level of utilization, James also argued that the iron laws of supply and demand would determine price, regardless of cost. In this position, it appears that James was arguing for efficient markets as the key to understanding demand and prices, not cost.

Nourse's rejoinder pointed to the fact that while average costs might be a bit simplistic, James's view that there is only one set of market supply and demand curves was equally naive. In the end, the debate added little to the overall understanding of capacity and how management should frame its use, focusing instead on macroeconomic issues that bore little resemblance to the concerns and hence logic of the Golden Era.

This final debate ushered in a period when management accounting's concern with capacity linked through budgets and variance reporting, while economists turned their attention to macroeconomic trends. Lost was the concern with providing decision-relevant information for the needs of the individual business. Articles such as Stevenson's 1950 discussion of a cycle reserve harkened back to arguments soundly rejected by the Golden Era debates as incorrectly holding over costs that have no future value. In general, then, the issues surrounding management of capacity in a single firm seeking to compete effectively in the market faded as the prosperity of post-World War II washed across the American landscape. There was little demand for information on capacity, idleness, or waste.

It seems, in reviewing the events of the Era of Crisis, that the newly formed market structure of the New Deal was comfortable for business and government alike. With cost clearly defined and cost-plus pricing established as the preferred basis for setting market prices, as well as the high demand for American products across the war-ravaged global marketplace, the United States settled into a period of prosperity and growth. It was a trend that served to underscore the fact that, in upending laissez-faire capitalism, Roosevelt had created an economic structure that would ensure the long-run health and stability of the nation.

In leaving the Era of Crisis, the shift in the nature and intent of capacity reporting practices remained as one of the most visible signals that the economics of business had changed. These rules were to hold sway for the next 30 years, giving way only when the force of the global marketplace began to erode share and profits for American firms. Marked by an acceptance of the dominance of financial reporting in the accounting profession and a belief that standard costing, budgets, and responsibility accounting were the essence of management accounting, the dawning Full Cost era was to be as different from the Golden Era as two such periods could be.

> A final warning may not be amiss. The primary justification for cost accounting has been and must continue to be that it is an essential tool of management. Cost accountants can make a good case for themselves, in the long run, only in this field. Cost accounting is not primarily a price-making device. The present emphasis on this function is not healthy. Cost systems set up and installed with an eye to price-making are bound to lose caste when the emergency is over and the emphasis on prices as a basis of fair competition is past....Cost accountants must continue, as in the past, to prove their worth to management on the grounds that they furnish facts for the guidance of internal policies.[18]

☐ References and Notes

[1] H. S. Johnson, *The Blue Eagle from Egg to Earth*, Garden City, NY: Doubleday, Doran and Company, 1935, p. 160.

[2] L. Lyon, P. Homan, L. Lorwin, G. Terborgh, C. Dearing, and L. Marshall, *The National Recovery Administration: An Analysis and Appraisal*, Washington, D. C.: The Brookings Institution, 1935, p. 551.

[3] Bernard Baruch, William Lybrand, Robert Montgomery, Joseph Kennedy, John Lewis, Louis Kirstein, Arthur D. Whiteside, Malcolm Muir, and Major General C. C. Williams were just a few of those involved. Lybrand was to be central to the development of the costing practices of the period, while Montgomery has since been declared "a Pioneer Leader of American Accounting." Lybrand would have worked behind the scenes through his partner, Montgomery.

[4] Lyon et al., op. cit., p. 588.

[5] H. F. Taggart, "The Relation of a Cost Accountant to the NRA Codes," *Accounting Review*, June 1934, p. 152.

[6] T. Lowi, *The Politics of Disorder*, New York: Basic Books, 1971, p. 75.

[7] E. McBain, *Killer's Payoff*, 1974, p. 5.

[8] Johnson, op. cit., p. 251.

[9] Ibid., pp. 253, 261.

[10] Ibid., p. 262.

[11] Ibid., p. 263.

[12] Lyon et al., op. cit., p. 563.

[13] This passage appears in Sidney Fine's work, *The Automobile Under the Blue Eagle: Labor, Management, and the Automobile Manufacturing Code*, Ann Arbor, MI: University of Michigan Press, 1963, pp. 76–78.

[14] The source for many of these insights on Ford is Donald Brand's work, *Corporatism and the Rule of the Law: A Study of the National Recovery Administration*, Ithaca, NY: Cornell University Press, 1988. The noted quotes in this section appear on page 171. In addition, Hugh Johnson (1935) makes reinforcing references to his ongoing dispute with Henry Ford, such as that made on p. 237 of his work.

[15] Johnson, op. cit., p. 362.

[16] A number of authors and researchers have suggested that World War II, with the impact of the War Board, was the pivotal period in the changing tide of capacity reporting. But, in reviewing source documents from companies that openly adhered to the Golden Age approach to capacity reporting (for example, U. S. Steel), the NIRA and the Uniform Cost Codes underlying it emerge repeatedly as justification for changing capacity reporting methods. No similar management explanation appears in the annual reports for the 1941–46 period.

[17] H. T. Johnson and R. S. Kaplan, *Relevance Lost: The Rise and Fall of Management Accounting*, New York: McGraw-Hill, 1987, p. 145.

[18] Taggart, op. cit., p. 157.

10

THE DARK AGES OF CAPACITY
REPORTING: 1953–1978

There is an urgent need to reduce the gap between the task
of accounting to serve managerial decision-making and the
somewhat narrow and self-centered attitude of many accounting practitioners who are in danger of losing sight of
those really important tasks of the profession.[1]

Serving as an omen of events to come, Weinwurm's comments
are a fitting introduction to the fourth major period in capacity
reporting: its "Dark Ages." Standing in stark contrast to the en-
lightened discussions prior to 1933, the 25-year period between
1953 and 1978 is characterized by a rapid decay of capacity
reporting thought and practice. As distressing to watch as the
deterioration of a human brain is this downward spiral in the
memory of the accounting "collective mind." Gone is the rich
understanding of the relationship between capacity and the firm's
long-term success, replaced by an increasingly myopic focus on
variances and control.

The 25 years spanned by the Dark Ages contain two major
subperiods. The first of these periods (1953–1964) was shaped

by the full cost/direct cost controversy that dominated the accounting literature during this period. In this "all or nothing" battle, the middle ground of debate was all but ignored. As the dust settled on this debate, the dominance of the full cost model in shaping the next 13 years of accounting thought was assured. Having put to rest the troublesome issue of how best to "cost" the activities of a firm, the focus of the profession turned toward elaborating and fine-tuning the full cost approach.

The full cost paradigm that emerged during the 1965–1978 period was dominated by a concern with control. Variance reporting models, in ever-increasing levels of complexity, took center stage in the literature. Capacity, once the domain of sophisticated debate, was reduced to an intricate game best described as "how many variances can dance on the head of a pin?" The pages that follow show how the good, the bad, and the ugly of the Dark Ages of capacity reporting commingled to create a fertile ground for the renaissance in accounting practice that would be launched by Johnson and Kaplan's work, *Relevance Lost*.

A Losing Proposition

> The idle capacity loss is considered to be the unutilized portion of fixed manufacturing overhead costs.... The objective of this article is to set forth the general view that there is no such thing as a loss due to idle capacity for purposes of income measurement.... If one were to disagree with this conclusion, he would be admitting that absolutely necessary cost input could be considered as a loss or waste.[2]

The 10 years spanning 1953 to 1964 were a period of transition in capacity reporting. Reflecting macroeconomic shifts as the war economy wound down (see Table 10-1) and the consumer-driven market reemerged as the driving force of commerce, capacity

Table 10-1. Timetable of Macroeconomic Events, 1953–1978

1953   Soviet tanks crush East Germany.

Stalin dies.

Mussadiq is overthrown in Iran by an Anglo-American secret service coup.

1954   The CIA overthrows the government of Guatemala.

The French lose Indo-China.

1955   The Bandung conference is held.

1956   Nikita Khrushchev denounces Stalin.

The Hungarian revolution is crushed by Soviet armed forces.

The United States makes France, Britain, and Israel back off the Suez Canal.

1957   The eighth edition of the retitled *Montgomery's Auditing* (sans Montgomery) favors simplicity in overhead accounting and states that the direct costing method is unwarranted.

The USSR launch of Sputnik I startles the United States.

The Treaty of Rome marks the beginning of the European Economic Community.

1959   President Eisenhower gives his "military industrial complex" speech.

1960   China breaks with the USSR.

1961   The Bay of Pigs invasion fails.

The Berlin Wall is built.

1962   Algeria gains independence from France.

The Cuban missile crisis is settled.

President Kennedy makes U. S. Steel roll back its price increase and calls businessmen "sons-of-bitches."

1963   President Kennedy is assassinated.

1965   President Johnson escalates U. S. involvement in Vietnam.

1968   The Czechoslovakian revolution is crushed by the USSR.

Student uprisings occur throughout the world.

An inflationary period starts that lasts until 1970.

1969   Man walks on the moon.

1970   The Cost Accounting Standards Board (CASB) is founded under the impetus of Admiral Hyman G. Rickover and Senator William Proxmire (D-Wisc.) to achieve uniformity in costing for defense contracts.

Hughes writes, "In the 1970s, the massive invasion of American markets by foreign manufacturers indicated that somehow our industrial house was not in order" and "In the years since the mid-1970s the country has been alarmed by successive crises involving the manufacturing industry's supposed decline, and it is even advocated that government policies should now be formed that aim at the 'reindustrialization' of America."

1971   President Nixon has the United States abandon its obligation to sell gold internationally at a fixed rate.

Nixon declares price controls to be needed and enacts these measures.

1972   Nixon visits China.

1973   Allende is killed in Chile.

An IRS regulation covering both direct costing (explicitly forbidding it) and capacity costing (quite complex) is issued.

OPEC succeeds in raising the price of crude oil by more than a factor of 3.

APB #28 on Interim Statements continues AICPA ambivalence on accounting for capacity variances.

1974   Nixon resigns because of Watergate.

1975   Saigon falls.

A new surge of price inflation begins, which lasts about eight years.

In the ninth edition of *Montgomery's Auditing*, direct costing is ruled to be not encompassed within GAAP, although the AICPA never really specifies this as so. However, both the SEC and IRS say that this method is unacceptable. The book also notes: "The more common practice is to treat the (unabsorbed overhead) variance as a proportionate adjustment of the aggregate cost of goods sold and ending inventory."

1976   Milton Friedman wins the Nobel Prize for economics.

Deng Xiaoping starts his new course for China.

1978   The first Polish pope in history is Karol Wojtyla (John Paul II).

reporting moved into the realm of theory. In examining the writing during this period, the potpourri of concepts, opinions, and approaches is evident (see Bibliography). Key themes embedded in the literature of this period include:

- Recognition that a search for one "true" definition of capacity was destined for failure;
- Increasing focus on analysis, rather than practical management concerns;
- Preference for a full cost, income statement-centered approach in the treatment of capacity costs;
- Enhanced concern with the impact of capacity measurement on the external financial statements and the picture they paint of organizational performance;
- Increased emphasis on macroeconomic rather than firm-specific treatment and analysis of capacity.

In moving away from firm-specific to macroeconomic capacity models, the justification for idle capacity reporting was lost.

Idle capacity and the productive capability that it holds hostage affected the fortunes of individual firms, not nations. At the abstract level, idle capacity was troubling but not life-threatening. In relegating the firm and its managers to the back burner of academic and professional concern, management accounting abandoned its implicit covenant to provide decision-relevant information to managers charged with creating value for the firm's stakeholders. It was a shift that ultimately was to lead to the professional crisis embodied by the charge of "relevance lost."

□ An Economic Lens

Of the articles reviewed for this time period, roughly one-third assumed an economic lens in their approach to capacity reporting. Focused on the impact on market prices and firm profits of various levels of capacity utilization, these articles provided little or no practical guidance on how to define or measure capacity. In fact, writing as part of the Subcommittee on Economic Statistics, Norton noted:

> Enough complications have been introduced, however, to indicate that no single, all purpose definition of physical capacity seems possible. Explicit definitions have to be tailored to the conditions which pertain to particular products or established groups.... Capacity is not directly observable. Its measurement depends on an appropriate set of rules. The uncertainty and ambiguity which abound with respect to capacity may be traced to the lack of an accepted set of rules.[3]

Norton's observations on the difficulty of developing an all-inclusive definition of capacity, as well as his recognition that context and "rules" (e.g., criteria) are the key to attaining an unambiguous definition, provided a marked departure from the confidence of the Golden Era in the existence of a "true" capacity, and hence a "true" cost of production.

Throughout the 1962 Subcommittee on Economic Statistics hearings, the difficulty with developing one comprehensive measure of capacity was reiterated in statements made by the experts called to testify. Creamer attempted a definition, noting that "capacity...is an economic limit to the rate of output with the existing facilities of a sector." This logical comment was immediately followed by a more troubling one, once again by Creamer. "It [capacity] is the rate after which capital additions would tend to be made."[4] Capacity is not a definable concept in this approach. In fact, even as capacity became measurable (at the point of adding new capital), it was becoming unmeasurable (except when new capital was again required). It isn't difficult to see that this circular logic would make a poor basis for developing capacity measures.

Apparently the subcommittee members agreed, for Creamer was then asked just exactly what current statistical measures of capacity utilization, widely published as a leading indicator by the government, actually mean. Responding, Creamer stated, "In general the procedure is to establish a fixed capital-output ratio for each industry classification for a benchmark year which independent evidence indicates was a period when capacity was virtually fully utilized"(p. 538). Upon this shaky foundation of estimates, guesses, and procedures, the health of the general economy was judged.

Klein, who appeared after Creamer, made another attempt to scale the slippery slope of capacity measurement, noting:

> ...Capacity utilization, unlike the unemployment rate, is an output measure. It shows the extent to which an output potential is being realized through the use of all factors of production...yet...a difficulty would remain in that we are not sure what is meant by capacity.... In any given production unit or small sector of the economy there may be no realistic limit to potential production if we put our efforts exclusively toward increasing activity in that branch.[5]

To solve this seemingly impossible puzzle, Klein invoked the "cost concept" and cost-benefit analysis as a means to establish realistic limits on capacity growth.

The attempts during the Full Cost Era to use economic logic to define, measure, and analyze capacity and capacity utilization at a macroeconomic level ended up yielding little, if any, concrete results. Yet several core concepts emerged from the economics-based capacity literature of this period. During the 1953–1968 period, Baumol[6] completed his work on economic theory, which built from a belief that the short-term/long-term dichotomy in economics is an insufficient basis for economic theory building. Noting that there is, in reality, a third, or intermediate, time period, Baumol went on to illustrate how capacity decisions change over these three time frames. In the short term, per Baumol, a company is bound by prior decisions, while in the long term total freedom exists to create capacity and activity. In between these two extremes lies the intermediate term, where some constraints exist, but ample freedom to change policies and procedures is present. The three-pronged approach to the planning and decision horizon created by Baumol provided a much more realistic basis for developing capacity models.

Phillips, writing in 1963, suggested that current efforts to measure capacity were too vague, too global, and useless in focusing attention on individual, manageable items of excess and idle resources. He indicated that the capability of a set of resources to create value is the key criterion. Specifically, he noted, "It is clear that the appropriate output measure is value-added, not gross output."[7] This focus on the value-creating ability of a set of resources reflected the same concerns and approach taken by Church so many years before. While Phillips remained in a minority during this time period, his concern with value creation, not solely utilization of resources, provided the basis for redeveloping the strategic view of capacity analysis (see Chapter 5).

Schultz in 1963 provided the last of the major economic views of capacity reporting reviewed for this period. Schultz put an interesting spin on the topic, noting that from the viewpoint of resource utilization, excess capacity represents misallocation of the factors of production or economic waste. In addressing this waste, Schultz noted that a company and its management

cannot base their actions solely on internal issues but must recognize that these policies have to make sense in view of the likely
actions of competing firms. Schultz's arguments served as a precursor to the value-based approach to capacity measurement and
analysis developed earlier in this monograph.

In total, these articles provided a less than clear picture of
economic measures of capacity. While there appeared to be consensus that it is hard to measure capacity, little constructive advice was given to organizations seeking to understand the basic
economics of their market or industry. When in doubt, each
economist in turn pointed to a better understanding of the costs
of capacity as the only way out of the maze created by an economic approach to the topic. Relying on a "cost" as a firm, tightly
defined concept, these economists took solace in knowing that a
practical solution to the knotty theoretical problems was inherent in measuring and managing capacity. The accountants could
solve this problem, or so they believed.

☐ The Cost of Capacity

While it is doubtful that economists' wistful search for a cost-
based definition of capacity could generate activity in management accounting circles, in 1963 the National Association of
Accountants (NAA) did fund a research study on the topic. *Accounting for the Costs of Capacity*, NAA Research Report No. 39,
represents one of the most exhaustive treatments of the topic in
the accounting literature. In the study, capacity costs were defined as "the continuing costs of having capacity to manufacture and to sell." Reflective of Baumol's position, the study's
authors noted that the nature of capacity costs differs significantly with respect to the timing and types of actions that can
be taken to control future costs. The terms "managed costs" and
"committed costs" were used to denote the relative manageabil-
ity of a specific capacity cost in the short and long term.

The essential assumption underlying this research report was
the renewed belief in the logic of "different costs for different

purposes" first suggested by Clark in 1923. Clearly attempting to find a means of sidestepping the then hotly contested issue of whether direct or full cost approaches were superior, the authors of this research study tried to focus attention on the need for various types of capacity measures (e.g., practical, normal, or budgeted) to meet the diverse information needs of the organization. In a work that appears to be destined to sit on a shelf collecting dust, this research was lost in the melee following on the heels of victory by the "full costers."

The 1963 study is not the only bright spot in the literature of this period. Churchill, writing in 1968,[8] argued for a return to comprehensive reporting of idle capacity costs and causes. He promoted the separation of idleness costs from product costs based on the belief that this approach would best serve management's information needs. Concluding his article, Churchill noted, "Data in which too much has been merged will be meaningless for many of these purposes" (p. 87). To what purposes was he referring? The varied decisions and analysis that management is required to make every day formed, to Churchill, the only defensible basis for measuring and reporting capacity costs and the impact of idle capacity on profits.

While reminiscent of the arguments made during the Golden Era, the message delivered by these accounting authors was washed away in the floodwaters of full costing. Capacity costing, some argued, is not direct costing and should remain as a viable and important cost management tool. Jones, writing in 1957, suggested that capacity costing could serve as a midpoint between direct and full costing. Arguing for the need to place idle capacity costs on the income statement, Jones noted:

> Its [capacity costing's] advantages are, first, that it is similar to direct costing as to the stabilization of product costs. Further, only one cost is needed for each product. Then, too, inventory is valued at a conservative amount, as all abnormal or unused fixed costs are excluded. The valuation basis is an acceptable accounting practice.... Beyond this,

unused or idle capacity is highlighted for management as to areas and cost.[9]

Jones's position harked back to the MAAP established at the 1921 meeting of the NACA, with the added insights born of participation in the ongoing debates about "best" accounting practice that dominated the latter part of the 1950s.

In stark contrast to Jones's position was a series of articles written by Ferrara.[10] The first part was aptly titled "Idle Capacity as a Loss: Fact or Fiction?" In the last of the three parts in this series, Ferrara stated:

> ...but let us specify which purposes are served by an idle capacity concept and then let us not confuse the concept of idle capacity as it relates to decision-making, production planning, and even socioeconomic analyses with the process of income measurement. The concept of idle capacity as a loss is inconsistent with the process of income measurement.

Markedly not a "direct coster," Ferrara argued that the use of units-of-production depreciation as well as balance sheet deferral of some idleness costs was the best way to develop reliable income numbers that would deal realistically with all the invariable costs of production.

The task of rebutting Ferrara's position fell to Weinwurm. His primary position was that theory and reality are often very different. Noting that Ferrara's model might sound good in theory, Weinwurm argued that it did little to address the critical and very real issues embedded in the capacity reporting process, as the following comments suggest:

> ...management has a vital interest in the amount of idle capacity cost which will always be a determining factor in decision-making. The concept is not merely an engineering problem, as asserted by Professor Ferrara, but one of significance to accounting as well.... Experience has shown it is one of the important but often difficult tasks of the industrial accountant to make operating people aware of the un-

deniable fact that existing idle capacity involves a constant accumulation of costs.[11]

Cast within the larger picture of the complete history of capacity reporting, one could envision the implicit debate between Ferrara and Weinwurm taking place in the chambers of the NACA conference of 1921. These positions were fully argued during that period, with Weinwurm's view winning out. Yet in the environment of the 1960s, Ferrara dominated the debate. If income measurement rather than management is the driving force behind capacity reporting practices, then idle capacity costs are a fiction. In the macroeconomic sense, idle capacity costs "distort" the income measurement process.

In the final analysis, even Ferrara's position was lost in the drive toward full cost-based accounting. The final debates between Ferrara and Weinwurm were interesting tidbits in the academic literature but were to have little or no impact on evolving practice. Full costing became the rule of the day, displacing all other models and the needs of all other information users.

The Darkness Deepens

The theory and practice of overhead costing has progressed at a somewhat slower pace and perhaps with less understanding than many other phases of cost accounting.... The concept of idle capacity has not been subjected to careful examination and there has been little philosophical development in this area.[12]

What a difference 45 years make! In 1921 a consensus emerged on "best practice" for capacity reporting after several focused days and many years of analysis and debate on the pros and cons of the various options available in this area. Yet by 1966, leading accounting professionals appeared unaware of the rich history of capacity reporting and the depth of the analysis underlying the 1921 MAAP.

By 1965, full cost-based models had won ascendancy in the minds and hearts of accountants throughout the western world. Having reached a comfortable decision on the one best way to account for product costs, management accountants turned their attention to fine-tuning variance reporting approaches. The rich variety of capacity reporting models that existed prior to 1933 had now been collapsed into one model and one measure: the volume variance.

During this period, industry practices remained shaped by the NIRA, leading to industry-unique modes of recording and reporting costs. This fact provides an explanation for the results of a research study completed by Purdy in 1963. Focused on determining whether industry patterns existed in the choice of capacity baselines or measures, Purdy surveyed more than 300 industrial firms to gather data on this question. The findings are best summarized in Purdy's own words:

> ...it appears that, if a comprehensive view of overhead costing is taken, differences in capacity choice cannot be explained on the basis of the different objectives of efficiency, pricing, and income measurement.... There seems to be some correlation between capacity measures and the overhead costing problems faced by the industry, but the results obtained by a certain choice in a specific industry may not vary greatly from those obtained by a different choice in a different industry.[13]

Purdy found common practices by industry and, to some extent, commonality across the entire population. The ongoing pressures for standardization of accounting practice that began with the NIRA and continued with the full costing/direct costing debates, reinforced by increasing simplification and standardization of the textbook treatment of these topics (see Vollmer 1996), culminated in the illogical results reported here. Regardless of how different an industry was or how unique a specific company might be within that industry, only one accounting approach was prevalent: full absorption costing.

☐ How Many Variances?

The "capacity" literature of the 1965–1978 time frame, if it can be so called, is a frustrating search through volume variances stated in ever-growing complexity (see Bibliography). Of the articles reviewed, more than 70% were tied directly to discussions of overhead variances. In an elaborate ballet orchestrated by leading accounting academics and practitioners, an answer to the question "How many variances can dance on the head of a pin?" is found—too many.

Petri and Minch, writing in 1972, represented the pinnacle in this variance-intensive approach to capacity reporting. They suggested four separate variances as a replacement for the current "volume" variance developed under the traditional standard cost model:

> ...the traditional volume variance was separated into four components. These include the production efficiency variance, idle capacity (marketing) variance, off capacity variance and the out-of-pocket spending variance [which are] unit sunk costs...as a form of "opportunity cost" that measure the aggregate present value of sales lost through inefficient production.[14]

Petri and Minch clearly recognized the information and responsibility accounting issues encapsulated in the generic volume variance reporting process. Yet the solution they suggested did little to change the nature of this information—unfortunately, more variances, like more controls, do not translate into more *control*.[15] The timing, nature, and focus of the variance reporting model was on balancing the accounting system, not on providing decision-relevant information. To be relevant, information has to arrive before a decision is made; variance information is, by definition, available too late to be of any use to management.

Ronen, writing in the *Journal of Accounting Research* in 1970, suggested another four-way variance analysis as a replacement for the volume variance. Focused on developing a series of ex-post capacity variances that "improve decisions regarding the design of capacity and its subsequent utilization," Ronen placed his emphasis on the creation of responsibility accounting data:

> ...optimization of the production function involves equating, at the margin, the marginal cost of any factor of production with its marginal revenue product....using the dimension of time to distinguish between costs of capacity and costs of operation does not appear useful. A better distinction can be made along a responsibility dimension.... From an evaluation and control standpoint, only controllable costs are relevant.[16]

The economics-based, control-oriented approach taken by Ronen was reflected in the variances he developed:

- An ex-post opportunity cost capacity planning variance that focused on foregone profits due to improper estimates of actual demand on a facility;
- Capacity implementation variance, which focused on the difference between planned and actual available capacity and its related opportunity costs;
- The total reduction in profit, given the first two; and
- The cost of not adjusting capacity to the level dictated by the ex-post information.

These variances, in Ronen's view, highlighted the potential sources of suboptimal output resulting from the interaction of capacity and operating decisions. While it is hard to argue with the logic in Ronen's paper, it is just as hard to envision its implementation in industry. Divorced from the harsh realities of the business world, this article reflects the widening gap between theory (academic) and practice that began in the early 1960s and continues, many would argue, through today.

Embedded in this debate over which and how many variances were the best replacement for the idle capacity charge of the pre-1933 period was the implicit acceptance of "budgeted" capacity as the baseline capacity measure of choice. While some firms were bold enough to use "normal" capacity (average utilization over a three- to five-year period), most firms developed their standards and created the basis for variance reporting using the planned output for the year. This decision, unconscious though it appeared to be, ended up embedding a significant amount of waste in the standard cost model.

Rather than measuring productive capability, as suggested by Church and others, common practice during this era was to substitute planned output for potential output. This shift in assumptions about the "correct" baseline capacity measure resulted in a ratchet effect (see Figure 10-1): Ever-increasing levels of waste were generated as companies, believing they were operating "at capacity," continued to build new factories at a rapid rate. Given the earlier links established between excess capacity and the Great Depression, this potential for unbridled growth in capacity represented a major threat to the stability of the economy. If the old saying, "Those who fail to study history are destined to repeat it," is accepted, the ever-growing mass amnesia of the Dark Ages of capacity reporting was opening the doors for economic crisis.

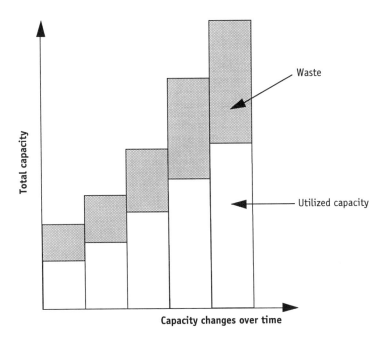

Figure 10-1. Wasted Capacity: A Ratchet Effect

☐ Practitioners Join the Fray

In the same period that Ronen was writing of marginal costs and multilevel capacity variances, practitioner-oriented articles were using full absorption costing as their departure point. One of the more notable of these "practice-based" articles was written by Bartenstein in 1978. Following on the theme of different costs for different purposes, he made a strong argument against the emerging practice of treating idle capacity as a long-run measurement problem:

> Even though it may be useful for control purposes to separate out the costs of idle capacity, it is not reasonable to consider them period costs or losses.... The establishment of capacity in any form is a long-range decision.... The problem resulting from uneven use of the facility and the related idle capacity costs are simply problems of measurement and have no place in a purely theoretical discussion. If all capacity costs are shared by products, we again reach the conclusion that all costs of capacity, including idle capacity costs, are product costs.[17]

The position described here as common by Bartenstein was the antithesis of best practice established before the upheaval set in motion by the NIRA. Gantt would have had little patience for this argument, nor would Church. To argue that all expenditures made in a period of production are *caused* by that production, all other factors being equal, is a leap few would venture to make today. Yet in the simplified world of full absorption costing the correct answer to any question regarding how to treat cost was always the same: Spread it over good units produced.

To Bartenstein, the negative impact of including idle capacity costs in product costs was significant:

> If inventory is burdened with idle capacity costs there is an unavoidable implication of value. An item is not necessarily worth more because it costs more to produce.... Because

idle capacity costs do not influence future costs or result in future cost avoidance, they cannot be assets or be added to the value or costs of assets such as inventory.[18]

Ferrara and many other experts of this period were convinced that idle capacity was, at worst, a measurement problem. But individuals such as Bartenstein, who were concerned with helping companies faced with the challenge of making a profit given existing capacity and process constraints, knew that capacity issues were much more complex than simply measuring activity and reporting variances from plan. If excess costs were incurred for any reason, profits would be negatively affected. As the logic of the global market and the demand for value-driven pricing began to reemerge as dominant forces in the late 1970s, a subtle shift in the capacity literature began to take place.

Warning Signs on the Horizon

> Today's management accounting information, driven by the procedures and cycle of the organization's financial reporting system, is too late, too aggregated, and too distorted to be relevant for managers' planning and control decisions.... And despite the considerable resources devoted to computing a monthly or quarterly income figure, the figure does not measure the actual increase or decrease in economic value that has occurred.[19]

The warning signs of the impending onslaught of global competition and its impact on the prosperity and viability of American business were increasing as the Dark Ages drew to a close. Major U. S. corporations such as U. S. Steel, Chrysler Motors, Xerox, Caterpillar, and Motorola, to name just a few, began to fall on hard times. The CEO of Xerox made the rude discovery that Panasonic was selling copiers in the market at a price lower than Xerox's "full cost" of production. This discovery brought about a revolution at Xerox, led by the quest for "six sigma" production. American steel companies were not as lucky as Xerox; the "rust belt" became a virtual ghost town as company after company folded under the intense pressure of foreign competition. Chrysler, under the able leadership of Lee Iaccoca, managed to obtain a government-funded bailout package that allowed it to recoup a sustainable position in the increasingly demanding automobile market.

With company after company facing major challenges to its market share and competitive position, it became increasingly clear that the financial measurement system had failed to provide a sound basis for managing a business. Looking for answers to its questions and solutions to its problems, management found itself with no usable information; accounting was giving the score for a game that was already over.

The hue and cry for accounting reforms began to echo in corporate boardrooms across the United States. Academics remaining close to business, while in a minority, were quick to realize that the mood in management circles had changed radically. Gone was the aura of precision and value that had surrounded the numbers generated by accounting, replaced by an increasingly vituperative demand for relevant information.

The first solution emerging from the profession scrambling to provide the type of information required was *activity-based costing* (ABC). As described in more depth in Chapter 11, this approach, promoted as a solution to all ills, was to place renewed emphasis on traceability and causality as the basis for attaching costs to the products and services of a firm. Reflecting the need to get costs assigned to the activities, products, and/or services that caused them, ABC was to be a first step on the path to regaining relevance in management accounting.

As was soon to be clear, however, the generation of more cost pools promoted by the ABC cadre would create another problem for the field: capacity measurement. A knowledge all but lost to the practicing accountant was now central to creating accurate cost estimates that would identify waste and opportunities for improvement. Returning to a problem that had been solved in the early 1900s for manufacturing processes, management accounting now found itself faced with not one capacity problem but as many capacities as there were cost pools in the newly created ABC systems.

The Dark Ages of accounting made it difficult for the profession to understand the source of its problems and to create effective solutions to them. Launching a period of discovery similar to the Renaissance of the 14th to 17th centuries in scientific knowledge, the book *Relevance Lost* generated an intense reexamination of accounting practice that would return capacity cost management to a central position in the literature. Rediscovering the roots of accounting was to prove a challenge worthy of able practitioners and academics alike, as the organizations they served began a frantic search for the key to competitive success in the global market.

> A foreign manufacturer, visiting our plants, said: "We have to fix our profits in advance, or we should not be able to pay our charges. Unless we can calculate on the basis of a certain output and certain profit, we should have to go out of business. How do you manage that?"
>
> The question was perfectly sincere, and the man meant well. But he was trying to drive with the cart before the horse. He had been setting out to gain…a certain profit instead of starting out to render a certain amount of service—and let the profit take care of itself.
>
> We regard a profit as the inevitable conclusion of work well done. Money is simply a commodity which we need just as we need coal and iron…. The stock market as such has nothing to do with business. It has nothing to do with the quality of the article which is manufactured, nothing to do with the output, nothing to do with the marketing, it does not even increase or decrease the amount of capital used in the business. It is just a little show on the side.—Henry Ford, *Today and Tomorrow*

□ References and Notes

[1] E. Weinwurm, "The Importance of Idle Capacity Cost," *Accounting Review*, July 1961, p. 421.

[2] W. Ferrara, "Idle Capacity as a Loss: Fact or Fiction?" *Accounting Review*, July 1960, p. 490. Ferrara now indicates that he has changed his views on this topic.

[3] J. D. Norton, "Capacity Statistics: Problems and Potential," in *Measures of Productive Capacity*, Hearings before the Subcommittee on Economic Statistics of the Joint Economic Committee, 87th Congress, second session, Washington, USGPO, 1962, p. 95.

[4] D. Creamer, "The Use of Capital-Output Ratios to Measure Manufacturing Capacity," in *Measures of Productive Capacity*, op. cit., p. 37.

[5] L. R. Klein, "Why Measure Capacity?", in *Measures of Productive Capacity*, op. cit., p. 54.

[6] W. Baumol, *Economic Theory and Operations Analysis*, 2nd edition, Englewood Cliffs, NJ: Prentice-Hall, 1965.

[7] A. Phillips, "Industrial Capacity: An Appraisal of Measures of Capacity," *American Economic Association: Papers and Proceedings*, 1963, p. 289.

[8] N. Churchill, "Another Look at Accounting for Idle Time," *NAA Bulletin*, January 1968, pp. 83–87.

[9] R. Kendall Jones, "Why Not Capacity Costing," *NAA Bulletin*, November 1957, p. 14.

[10] W. Ferrara, "Idle Capacity as a Loss: Fact or Fiction?" *Accounting Review*, July 1960, pp. 490–496. The argument made here is continued in a second article, "Overhead Costs and Income Measurement," published in January 1961 in *Accounting Review*, as well as a rejoinder to comments made on his position published in the July issue of this publication.

[11] Weinwurm, op. cit.

[12] D. T. DeCoster, "Measurement of the Idle Capacity Variance," *Accounting Review*, April 1966, pp. 297–302. This quote appears on page 302.

[13] C. Purdy, "Industry Patterns of Capacity or Volume Choices: Their Existence and Rationale," *Journal of Accounting Research*, 1965, pp. 237, 240.

[14] E. Petri and R. Minch, "Capacity Variance: Responsibility and Control," *Management Accounting*, April 1972, p. 41.

[15] This seemingly paradoxical view of control was first stated by Peter Drucker in his article, "Controls, Control and Management," in *Management Controls: New Directions for Basic Research*, Charles P. Bonini, Robert K. Jaedicke, and Harvey M. Wagner, eds., New York: McGraw-Hill, 1964, p. 294.

[16] J. Ronen, "Capacity and Operating Variances: An Ex Post Approach," *Journal of Accounting Research*, Autumn 1970, pp. 232–252.

[17] E. Bartenstein, "Different Costs for Different Purposes," *Management Accounting*, August 1978, p. 44.

[18] Ibid., p. 45.

[19] H. T. Johnson and R. S. Kaplan, *Relevance Lost: The Rise and Fall of Management Accounting*, New York: McGraw-Hill, 1986, p. 1.

11

THE ERA OF QUESTIONING:
1979–PRESENT

Asking what the practical capacity of a plant is may be like asking how much water a bathtub can hold without overflowing: It depends on who is in the tub at the time and what he or she is doing.[1]

The Era of Questioning, the period since 1979, has witnessed wide swings in the domestic focus of American politics and politicians, ranging from the last years of Carter through the conservative years of Reagan/Bush, to the modern liberalism of the Clinton White House. On the international front, the disintegration of the USSR has been only one of the major events shaping the last 20 years.

The business world has been equally turbulent, with the impact of globalization playing out in the decline of once major industries such as steel and consumer electronics and in the restructuring, reengineering, downsizing, and return to basics in business management. As corporate giants struggled to adopt lean manufacturing and management techniques, new industries emerged that built on the burgeoning information technologies of the late 20th century. A period of transitions, contradictions, and transformations, the post-1979 era has reinforced the basic tenets of business: (1) change is a way of life and (2) the more things change the more they stay the same (see Table 11-1). In capacity reporting, these seemingly contradictory statements are reflected in the movement away from traditional accounting to the rebirth of capacity reporting and relevant costing practices.

By 1979, books and articles were beginning to appear that decried a management out of touch with its people and processes and mired in out-of-date practices and beliefs. In a related development, the 1980s brought the rapid-fire development of new techniques to meet these challenges, with an abundance of three-letter acronyms to herald their arrival. MRP, CAD/CAM, JIT, CIM, TQM, TPM, and FMS[2] were just a few of the new management approaches that dominated the business literature during the 1980s. By the middle of the decade, accounting joined this alphabet soup with the development of ABC, SCM, EVA, and ABM.[3] Lagging the revolution on the plant floor by almost a decade, accounting has spent the last 10 years attempting to regain relevance. The rebirth of sophisticated capacity reporting practices bears witness to the progress the accounting reform efforts have made.

The Dark Ages of capacity reporting, from 1953 to 1978, represented an era when too much was assumed and too little known about the economics of the firm and the impact of global market pressures on company performance. Companies and the managers who ran them often did well in spite of themselves. Capacity was a problem only on one dimension: as a constraint to production. Management, often divorced from the factory floor, turned to numbers to run the business at the very time that those numbers were increasingly mismatched to the processes and products making up the firm.

Capacity reporting discussions mirrored this developmental path. Early in this era, operational concerns with measuring and managing capacity surfaced, followed closely by a financial market assessment of capacity as a use of scarce investment dollars

Table 11-1. Timetable of Macroeconomic Events, 1979–Present

1979	The Shah of Iran is overthrown by the revolution led by the Ayatollah Ruholla Khomeini.
	The Iranian hostage crisis shakes the United States.
1980	Iran-Iraq war starts, ending in 1988.
	Ronald Reagan wins presidency.
	The Cost Accounting Standards Board (CASB) dies when Congress does not appropriate funds for it in fiscal year 1980–81.
1981	Reagan fires air traffic controllers.
1983	Henry Schwarzbach and Richard Vangermeersch question if cost accounting is not 200 years behind the times and reintroduce Church's machine rate method.
	The United States attacks Grenada.
	Robert S. Kaplan publishes "Measuring Manufacturing Performance: A New Challenge for Managerial Accounting" and then in 1984, "The Evolution of Management Accounting."
	Eliyahu M. Goldratt and Jeff Cox publish *The Goal: Excellence in Manufacturing.*
1984	Reagan wins second term in office.
Mid-80s	The personal computer comes of age.
1985	Mikhail Gorbachev heads the USSR.
	In the 10th edition of *Montgomery's Auditing,* the authors present strong language for allocating underabsorbed overhead.
1986	Gorbachev and Reagan meet in Iceland to discuss nuclear disarmament.
	The United States bombs Libya.
	U. S. Steel becomes USX as U. S. Steel merges with Texas Oil and Gas.
	Relevance Lost by H. Thomas Johnson and Robert S. Kaplan is published, creating a groundswell of discontent with existing accounting practices that leads to a revolution in the field of management accounting.
	James A. Brimson and Callie Berliner edit and publish the first major CAM-I work, *Cost Management for Today's Advanced Manufacturing.*
	Bold Step projects are launched by the Institute of Management Accountants to discover emerging practice in the field of management accounting.
1987	On October 19, a drop of more than 500 points in the Dow-Jones occurs on the New York Stock Exchange.
	The IMA and AAA's Management Accounting Section begin two jointly sponsored meetings, one on developing trends/research in management accounting, the other a case workshop. Both continue today, attracting management accounting instructors from many different institutions.
1988	A new version of CASB is founded as a part of the Office of Federal Procurement Policy (OFPP). This version of CASB has had little impact as of the publication of this monograph.

The Government Accounting Office (GAO) undertakes a study of ABC costing for defense contracting, including training of current auditors, inclusion in doctoral and masters programs, and requirements for ABC-based bids and reports.

The IMA and APICS co-sponsor debates between Goldratt/Fox and Kaplan/Cooper on the pros and cons of ABC versus the theory of constraints.

Several major new management accounting journals are launched during this period, including *Journal of Cost Management, Advances in Management Accounting*, and *Journal of Management Accounting Research*. Warren, Gorham and Lamont begin two handbook series, *Emerging Practices in Cost Management* and *Handbook of Cost Management*, under the direction of Barry Brinker. These publications are part of an explosion, mirrored in *Management Accounting*, of interest, research, and theory development in management accounting.

1990   The 11th edition of *Montgomery's Auditing* seems to reopen the creative relationship between external auditing and public accounting in the area of cost accounting and inventory valuation.

Vangermeersch edits and publishes a three-volume compilation of the best articles in the archives of *Management Accounting* in conjunction with the IMA.

1991   The Gulf War results in a victory of Allied forces over Iraq.

1992   Bill Clinton is elected over George Bush in a hotly disputed election that includes the first major thrust by a third party in recent history.

Johnson publishes *Relevance Regained*, representing the first systemic, outside-in view of accounting.

1993   The North American Free Trade Agreement (NAFTA) passes.

Health industry reform comes, and goes.

A stand-off between David Koresh and his followers and the FBI in Waco, Texas, leads to disaster, as the facility is attacked and goes up in flames, killing all but a few of those inside (including women and children).

John K. Shank and Vijay Govindarajan publish *Strategic Cost Management*, creating a new, value chain-based view of accounting and its role in corporations.

1994   The United States appears to be number one again in industrial statistics.

Republicans gain control of the House and Senate for the first time in almost 50 years.

The *Journal of Cost Management* dedicates its entire summer issue to the discussion of capacity issues, including the reissuance of Gantt's 1916 work.

1995   Ongoing investigations into the Clinton White House, as well as ongoing struggles over the Contract with America, create uncertainty in the American economy.

Oklahoma City is the victim of a car bomb that destroys the government center, killing more than 100 people.

Budget battles in 1995/96 repeatedly shut down the government.

The Institute for International Research holds a series of workshops and conferences on capacity and capacity cost management.

C. J. McNair publishes *The Profit Potential*, which includes an in-depth discussion of waste in various parts of the organization, including capacity-based waste.

1996　The United States enters Bosnia as part of the U.N. peacekeeping mission.

Major eruptions between the Palestinians and Israelis lead to renewed tensions and concerns in this area.

The Dow Jones passes 6000 for the first time in history.

The Society of Management Accountants of Canada, in conjunction with CAM-I and the IMA, publishes *Management Accounting Guideline #42: Measuring the Cost of Capacity*, coauthored by McNair and Vangermeersch. It is published by the IMA as SMA 4Y. The guideline defines best practice in capacity cost management on the use of theoretical capacity baselines and the return of idle capacity charges that are reported outside of the cost of goods.

CAM-I publishes a *Capacity Primer*, edited by Tom Klammer, as part of its ongoing investigation into capacity cost issues.

by the firm. The theory of constraints (TOC) literature, such as *The Goal* by Goldratt and Cox, raised capacity management to a new level through an intense focus on bottleneck management and plant throughput. TOC's richness provided a natural bridge to accounting, leading to a rebirth of Church's 1931 view of capacity costing at the "point of the tool."

In this era, questions truly outnumbered answers, however, as "experts" battled to define the "right" measure of capacity and "best" method for managing it while practitioners struggled to reduce the waste and profitability erosion that excess or idle capacity represented. Supplementing the development of new management techniques was a veritable explosion in computer technology and capability. The enhanced computational abilities of the computer led to data-intensive capacity models that searched for *the* solution to capacity balancing and utilization. Like the search for the Holy Grail, management experts turned to the computer to resolve once and for all the age-old questions surrounding capacity.

The efforts to reengage capacity issues have emerged along three distinct fronts during this final era of the 20th century: operational, economic, and financial accounting-based. Affecting the developmental path of all three approaches is the "new science" of systems, complexity and chaos theories. The detail-oriented,

Scientific Management-based approach to understanding and shaping organizations has come into direct conflict with the holistic, systemic view of the world. These two themes—functional perspectives and overall world view—underlie the following discussion.

Redefining Capacity:
An Operational Perspective

It is usually difficult (and often misleading) to calculate... capacity. Bottlenecks tend to shift according to the product mix and so vary the capacity available.[4]

Four major movements have defined the operational perspective on capacity since 1979: material requirements planning (MRP-I and MRP-II), total quality management (TQM), the theory of constraints (TOC), and systems theory. MRP came on the scene first in the United States, reaching full-scale application and acceptance by the mid-1980s. MRP, which focuses on detailed scheduling, materials requisitioning, and shop floor control aspects of the manufacturing process, was the first major movement to rely extensively on the explosion in information technology for its development. Driven by complex algorithms that led to repeated computer system crashes among its early users, MRP represented, in many ways, a culmination of the Scientific Management view of the firm. Detailed in nature and very short term in focus, MRP implementations continue today, as company after company turns to the computer to integrate their material planning and production scheduling efforts.

The early MRP literature did not deal with the capacity issue, leading to the development of production plans that could not be effected in the real world of the factory floor. By the end of the 1980s, it was clear to MRP experts that this weakness needed to be redressed, optimally of course. Embedded in the MRP "solution" developed to meet this shortcoming was a precise definition of capacity. For the mathematics of MRP to work, key variables had to be clearly defined, leading to a need to define capacity in unambiguous terms. Comments by Veral and LaForge[5] illustrate the tenor and thrust of this literature: "It is well known that the basic logic of MRP is insensitive to capacity considerations.... Consideration of capacity in a closed-loop MRP environment can take place as the MPS (master production schedule) is being developed and as an extension of the MRP processing logic."

The detailed, short-run, operational view of capacity was well developed in the 1989 APICS publication *Capacity Management* by Blackstone. Dealing with issues such as capacity versus load, efficiency, and utilization, this document focused on MRP-driven capacity concepts. Throughout this literature, including Blackstone's seminal work, the MRP-based capacity discussions returned again and again to balancing the load across key areas with the demand placed on them. Reflecting the concerns underlying the TOC model, what set the MRP literature apart was the embedding of capacity in a complex web of algorithms and calculations and hence, the need to achieve precision in its measurement.

One example of the path MRP-based capacity analysis has taken is the work by Hill et al.[6] These authors stressed the need to establish a finite notion of capacity to improve the management of resources and scheduling problems in job-shop-based firms. Relying on a simulation model that embedded a series of rules and algorithms as well as precise definitions of capacity that were not bottleneck based, these authors utilized a simple case study to show the impact of their approach on the effectiveness of the firm. The key assumption these authors made was that "it is usually difficult (and often misleading) to calculate their [bottleneck operations] capacity. Bottlenecks tend to shift according to product mix and so vary the capacity available." To avoid the messiness of reality, this MRP-based approach simply defined away the complex interdependencies of product mix and production capabilities to ensure that a "solution" could be found to the scheduling problem.

In a similar vein, Veral and LaForge used the master production schedule to balance the trade-offs between inventory-related costs and work load variability. Specifically, this article stated:

> As the projected load exceeds normal capacity by a greater and greater amount, the feasibility of the manufacturing plan becomes more and more questionable....
>
> In general, the Dixon-Silver algorithm is designed to determine lot sizes for multiple items that are processed through a single facility such that inventory-related costs are minimized, no backorders occur, and capacity is not exceeded.[7]

Of course, achieving these ends once again depended on having a precise definition of capacity that could serve as a limit to the MRP scheduling algorithm.

Heavily focused on short-term problems and hourly production demands, then, the MRP school appeared limited in its application to other disciplines and other management concerns, as well as constrained by the very assumptions it made to achieve a solution to the capacity "problem."

☐ Capacity Issues Under TQM and JIT Production

The late 1970s and the 1980s witnessed a veritable explosion of Japanese management approaches, most commonly applied through two models: total quality management (TQM) and cellular or just-in-time production (JIT-P). Focused on identifying and eliminating waste wherever it occurs, these two models were among the first wave of "new science"-based approaches to managing the factory floor.

TQM and JIT-P were linked from the start. Where JIT-P focused on eliminating move and queue from operations, TQM concentrated effort on removing defects and errors from the work flow. Combined, these two management techniques built the philosophy of continuous improvement into the operational mindset.

The tie between these two techniques and capacity was embedded in the cellular design and the balanced flow and discipline required to maximize its potential. In its essence, JIT-P is capacity management in its purest form. Balancing the flow of product through a cell requires a careful analysis and assessment of the capacity of each workstation or individual in the manufacturing process. Pacing the flow through the cell to minimize variation and disruptions, JIT-P is the embodiment of systemic notions of capacity. By focusing on the events and product features that reduce available capacity, JIT-P moves toward improved capacity utilization, not by throwing more resources at the problem but rather by identifying the sources of variation and eliminating their impact.

JIT-P is Church's "little shop." The costing models that emerged as this technology was put into place took on a simple form: Total costs are divided by good units produced to create an actual cost estimate. The power of this approach is the way in which the historical standard was used. It was trended over time, with the goal of continuous reduction of the cost (and therefore, waste of resources and capacity) as the driving motivation for process improvements. Theoretical capacity for the cell was estimated by most companies employing the JIT-P model, providing a standard to assess the performance of the cell.

Merging the concepts of cost and capacity through the notion of velocity of materials through the cell, JIT-P converted repetitive manufacturing into an assembly line. In the process, overhead is attacked as the search for nonvalue-added activities and the costs they cause is undertaken.[8] As suggested by Adair-Heeley,[9] overhead and the capacity costs it entails are the untapped opportunity in many JIT-P operations. Defined on bottleneck operations and balancing work to offload these constraining areas or enhance their capabilities, JIT-P cells use capacity concepts to improve performance through the *balancing* of work, the elimination of idle capacity. It is the notion of balance that separates JIT-P from its cousin, the theory of constraints.

☐   TOC: Emphasizing the Role of Bottlenecks

Operational managers have always been aware that bottleneck operations pace the factory at large. What TOC, as created by Goldratt, did was turn attention away from detail-ridden, reductionist approaches to solving this old problem to a systemic view that simplified the production problem to one core concern: the flow of materials across the bottleneck resource.

Capacity and TOC were intricately linked from the start. Managing bottleneck resources ultimately came down to managing the available capacity of the plant, deploying this capability to those products and services that promised the greatest payoff per minute of bottleneck time consumed. Under the TOC approach, little attempt is made to balance the plant; excess capacity in nonbottleneck areas is, at worst, a necessary evil, and at best, a desirable use of resources. In fact, as suggested by Noreen, Smith, and Mackey, idle capacity is not an opportunity cost unless customer orders are not being filled.[10]

The essence of TOC is its emphasis on company profitability over keeping people or machines busy. To Goldratt, inventoried finished goods and work-in-process are liabilities, while "inventoried" productive capability is an asset. Idle capacity is not waste; only activated resources for which there is no real demand fall into this class.

Both TOC and JIT-P, then, rely on a "pull" approach to manufacturing that places an order or item into production only if demand exists for it. Capacity, defined at the point of the bottleneck operation, drives the operation of the plant. The key difference within these two models lies in the definition of excess systemic capacity (e.g., machines or operations that will never be used to their full potential). In Goldratt's model, these implicit opportunity costs receive little attention, while in the JIT-P model all forms of waste, including embedded systemic idle capacity, are constantly attacked through rebalancing of the line. Both models, however, limit their attention to a clearly defined constraint or bottleneck, leaving open the question of dealing with changing demand.

☐ Systemic Models of Capacity Management

The development of sophisticated simulation models and relational database structures represents the most current operational approach to capacity management. Two models currently compete for the honors in this emerging area: CUBES (capacity utilization bottleneck efficiency system) and the CAM-I capacity model. Both these models have been defined and implemented within the semiconductor industry, with limited applications outside this core application.

CUBES was developed by Sematech, the industry consortium for the semiconductor industry.[11] Integrating financial and nonfinancial data, this model uses activity-based costing, TOC logic, and dynamic simulations of shifting bottlenecks and capacity deployment profiles to identify the least-cost solution given current operating conditions. Capacity utilization is broken into 11 different categories in this model: nonscheduled time, scheduled downtime, engineering time, unscheduled downtime, standby/idle time, other time losses, tool speed loss, batching losses, quality losses, and actual CUBES efficiency defined against theoretical capacity. In retrospect, then, CUBES applies the logic developed by Gantt many years earlier to categorize and analyze capacity utilization.

The CAM-I model takes an approach similar to the CUBES approach but with an increased emphasis on strategic analysis of capacity deployment.[12] Built from activities at the operational level, the model is a collection of capacity data and includes the supply of capacity, the demand on that capacity by specific products, and the constraints within a process that limit the production of good units. The CAM-I model uses many of the same capacity categories in its reporting package, which emphasizes the communication aspects of capacity management.

These two models, combined with a number of other simulation-based decision support tools in the capacity area, merge detail with the logic of systems to create a complex analytical tool that helps management identify the impact of decisions and products on capacity utilization. While the underlying simulation models embedded in the systemic approach are somewhat complex, once defined, the models are easy to use and understand. Stepping away from the notion of one single, precise definition of capacity and the ability of the firm to maximize this potential, the systemic models provide the basis for implementing a flexible, decision-oriented operational capacity approach.

In moving away from the detail-oriented, finite, nonsystemic models of capacity, the emerging operational approach to capacity management promises to shift the debate away from a concern with finding the "right" measure of capacity to understanding how the dynamics of business affect the efficient and effective utilization of productive capability. The systemic models set the table for the movable feast.

Economics and Capacity: Macro Trends

Even for a single plant, a range of capacity concepts applies. At the high end of the range would be an engineering maximum based on the rated speed of machines in place and operated with minimum downtime. At the low end, economic concepts relate a firm's capacity to a quantity of output that minimizes the unit costs or beyond which its costs rise unacceptably.[13]

The inability to define and measure capacity precisely, while recognized in the macroeconomics literature, has been summarily ignored in the search for macro trends. The link between capacity utilization and inflationary pressure dominates this area, with authors such as Garner taking the firm position that inflation will start at about 82% plant utilization.[14] Orr, taking a more global view of the problem, argued that excess capacity abroad has reduced the inflationary pressures traditionally associated with high utilization rates in the United States.[15] In each case, the authors were comfortable in defining, at a macro level, a concept of capacity utilization that few operational managers would be comfortable accepting.

A second major thrust of the economics literature on capacity since 1979 has focused on the interplay between capacity expansion, the size of plants, and the value of the firm. An example of this stream of research is Pindyck, who noted in 1988 that:

> In effect, a unit of capacity gives the firm an infinite number of options to produce, one for every future time, each with exercise price equal to production cost, and can be valued accordingly.... These "operating options" are worth more the more volatile is demand, just as a call option on a stock is worth more, the more volatile is the price of the stock.
>
> ...and, in markets with volatile and unpredictable demand, firms should hold less capacity than they would if investment were reversible or future demands were known.[16]

It is hard to argue with any of these statements, but it is also difficult to see how these general comments can be applied in any specific setting to guide capacity investment decisions. Mills, writing in the *Rand Journal of Economics*, reinforced this conclusion, noting that the size and nature of capacity expansions in industry are "hard to predict a priori."[17]

In combination, then, the macroeconomic literature came out strongly in favor of suggesting that capacity utilization is linked to inflation and job growth at a conceptual level. The weakness in this literature, though, is obvious. Fraught with measurement problems, inconsistencies, and little or no definable pattern of investment at the macroeconomic level in plant and equipment, this literature bears a striking contrast to the MRP-based models. Where MRP defines the "one right" measure of capacity, the macroeconomic literature suggests that capacity is an ambiguous term that does not lend itself to measurement at all. In the world of econometrics, though, unmeasurability appears to be only a minor obstacle.

Capacity analysis took on a central role in both the operational and economic literatures after the Dark Ages. It was in the accounting arena, however, that the need to understand and apply capacity cost management emerged most strongly, for it was in accounting that the tie between capacity and profitability was born.

A Financial View of Capacity

> But the failure to increase profits is not due to costs being intrinsically "fixed." Rather, the failure is the consequence of managers being unwilling or unable to exploit the unused capacity they have created.[18]

A review of the capacity literature in the operational and economic arenas reflects an elaboration and expansion of capacity modeling as new information technologies became available. The development of these models was logical and evolutionary in nature, reflecting the ongoing recognition by operating managers and economists alike of the central role played by capacity and capacity utilization in defining microeconomic and macroeconomic trends.

The accounting literature varied markedly from this evolutionary path. As suggested in earlier chapters, the radical shift in accounting practices that followed on the heels of FDR's New Deal legislation separated accounting from its natural tie to capacity measurement and management. It was only the increasingly intense questioning of accounting relevance, exemplified by Johnson and Kaplan's seminal work, *Relevance Lost*, that served to reattach accounting and capacity cost management to their historical roots.

Reviewing the literature in accounting during the post-1979 period, the shift from standard cost, volume variance-driven views of capacity is evident (see Bibliography). Mackey, writing in 1987, provided a strong argument for the linkage of irrelevance in accounting and its failure to deal adequately with capacity issues. Typical of his comments is the following:

> Certain amounts of work-in-process represent stored capac-

ity, and are used to protect against perturbations in production activity and demand surges with semi-finished products.

...because of the high cost of automated and robotic machinery, accounting systems as a matter of practice should be generating variances that reflect the cost of carrying under-utilized capacity.[19]

Noting that traditional variances are not useful for operational managers, Mackey suggested that measuring and reporting capacity utilization is a key element of the financial manager's role.

Mackey's article was a precursor to a wave of accounting-based capacity articles emerging after 1990. While the reasons for this reemergence of capacity issues in accounting were many, it appears that the development of activity-based costing models provided the strongest explanation for this change. In creating activity-based cost estimates, companies were faced with defining not just one capacity measure for machines or physical processes but rather a multitude of capacities for the various activities of the firm. For every driver of costs, there had to be a preset capacity or capability to create value that would capture the underlying economic dynamics of the firm.

Early efforts in activity-based costing placed the dominant emphasis on traceability or ensuring that the resources consumed by activities were clustered in homogeneous pools. The capacity of these pools was simply assumed to be matched to the current demand on that area, with little attempt to measure whether the resources were fully utilized or not. By the mid-1990s, though, there was increasing concern that this treatment of driver capacity was inconsistent with the continuous improvement process and the recognition that high levels of waste were present throughout the organization.

Capacity and cost management became linked, then, for a very simple and basic reason: In defining the basic cost equation, capacity represented the denominator or "volume" of drivers that the costs (resources consumed) could support. The definition of capacity in the standard cost-based accounting literature—what was normally done or planned to be done for the coming year (budgeted capacity)—was no longer acceptable in an organization striving to drive out waste and improve performance. The focus in accounting, then, returned rapidly to the need to define capacity outside of existing practice—to embrace a conceptual view of capacity.

In 1994, *The Journal of Cost Management*, often a leading indicator of changes in management accounting focus, dedicated an entire issue to capacity cost management issues. The first article in this volume was a reprint of Gantt's 1915 treatise on the relationship between production and cost, followed by articles from various perspectives. A common theme among these articles was the need to abandon planned capacity as the baseline measure for practical or theoretical approaches that are more supportive of the continuous improvement model.

Dilton-Hill and Glad noted that there are different causes for capacity shortages and surpluses and that these causes determine whether or not surplus capacity costs should be included in standard costs. Taking a value chain view, these authors noted that some forms of surplus capacity are driven by macroeconomic or value chain pressures and are an unavoidable cost of being in an industry. Four causes of surplus capacity were explored: decline in demand/increase in productivity, policy decisions to retain flexibility or provide industry backup, nonbottleneck areas, and capacity purchased in advance of needs. The authors advocated charging surplus capacity costs from nonbottleneck areas or those due to industry backup to product costs, while the remaining idle capacity costs (defined on practical capacity) were not charged to product. Some comments of interest from these authors include:

> Establishing capacity amounts to a commitment to pay for the resources that are used to set up an infrastructure. To manage this commitment, it is essential to understand the capacity (and the utilization) of those resources.

…when surplus capacity is reported as a separate line item, the objective is to focus attention on the surplus resources to ensure that appropriate action is taken…. Surplus capacity costs should be included in the section of the income statement where the other general overhead costs that are not readily traceable to products or customers are reported. Any revenue that is earned from specific projects designed to utilize surplus capacity should be offset against the costs of surplus capacity and not included in normal revenue.[20]

Two key elements of the arguments made by Dilton-Hill and Glad were that capacity is a commitment to pay for or obtain resources and represents a capability to create value, and that most forms of surplus capacity costs should not be included in product costs. In taking these positions, the authors took both a giant step forward and back—to the future defined by Gantt and Church.

DeBruine and Sopariwala focused their attention on the relationship between capacity definitions and the average fixed costs attached to products. Taking the position that products should not be charged with idle capacity costs, these authors also promoted a return to the more elaborate capacity costing methods of an earlier time.[21] Both these articles deal with capacity as a measurable concept in the costing equation, an assumption that is, interestingly, under debate at the same time in the operational and economics literatures.

McNair, building off of work with Vangermeersch, took a systemic view of the capacity issue, focusing attention on eliminating capacity waste as the key to improving performance. The essence of the position taken in this article was that

Effective capacity management means maximizing utilization of the total capability of all resources. Managing capability is a far more challenging task than simply pushing more output through the production process. It requires an active, ongoing examination of the process of doing work and creating value…. Capacity management in the global marketplace is based on minimizing the costs of responding to demands for economies of scope....[22]

Taking a distinctly long-term view of capacity as the purchased capability to create value for customers now and in the future, McNair argued that measuring wasted capacity provides the most sustainable and continuous improvement-linked approach to capacity cost management.

In reviewing the accounting literature on capacity, then, the feeling is one of observing a process come full circle. This view is reflected in the Institute of Management Accountants' joint research project with the Society of Management Accountants of Canada, Statement on Management Accounting (SMA) 4Y, which juxtaposes both the old (Gantt and Church) and the new (CUBES and CAM-I) models of capacity within one overarching framework. The conclusion of this Statement—that best practice in management accounting requires the use of theoretical capacity and the separation of idle capacity costs from product costs—is a restatement of the MAAP developed more than 80 years ago by the NACA.

This 1996 SMA provides a summary statement of the best that has been written and developed on capacity and capacity costing since 1900.

A key comment is the following:

Management accountants need to reopen the debate of "best practice" in capacity cost managment—debates which led to elaborate idle capacity reporting practices early in this century. Management accountants need to recognize and address current misconceptions about GAAP and its implication for capacity reporting practices, and openly search for ways to better reflect economic reality in their reporting practices.

Where they will be effective, major changes in common reporting practices required to support capacity cost measurement include:

- use of theoretical rather than annual budgeted capacity as the capacity baseline measure;
- elimination of idle capacity costs from product costs...;

- analysis and reporting of the cost of capacity in different states of preparedness;
- reporting of all idle, nonproductive, and productive uses of capacity and their costs.[23]

Taking a broad view of capacity and capacity cost management, this SMA spans the operational, economic, and financial perspectives in the short, intermediate, and long term. A culmination of a collaborative and at times hotly contested process, this publication represents a statement of best practice as defined by the associations, companies, and academics that participated in its development.

One remaining article, published in December 1995, deserves mention before leaving this section. Kee, writing in *Accounting Horizons*, provided a capacity cost model that integrates activity-based costing and TOC concepts to arrive at an optimal capacity utilization figure. Using marginal revenue and a mixed-integer programming approach, Kee developed a hybrid model that incorporated the strengths of both TOC and ABC. The resulting approach was closely linked to the logic of the CUBES and CAM-I models, utilizing more accessible technology and existing ABC data as its baseline. The use of marginal revenue, though, sets this model apart from the CUBES and CAM-I approaches, suggesting that, in the end, it is the marriage of all three streams of capacity research—operational, economic, and financial—that ultimately will provide the richness required to make capacity cost management truly a movable feast.

The reincarnation of capacity cost management practices, the return to the well-reasoned logic of the early 20th century, and the adaptation of these best practice concepts into the technology-rich, systemic world of modern corporations is reflective of the rebirth of management accounting in many different arenas. Triggered by *Relevance Lost*, supported by *Relevance Rediscovered* and *Relevance Regained*, the development of capacity cost literature suggests that management accountants are reattaching to their roots, once again employing management theory and logic to drive accounting practices. It is a journey that we hope will avoid the circular logic, the politics, and the inconsistencies of the 20th century, replacing them with a continuous journey toward improvement.

> There is nothing more difficult to take in hand, more perilous to conduct, or more uncertain in its success, than to take the lead in the introduction of a new order of things.— Niccolo Machiavelli, *The Prince*, 1532, Chapter 6.

> Just because everything has changed doesn't mean anything has changed.—Irene Peter, *Peter's Quotations*, 1977, p. 75.

□ References and Notes

[1] R. D. Raddock and C. E. Gilbert, "Recent Developments in Industrial Capacity and Utilization," *Federal Reserve Bulletin,* June 1990, p. 425.

[2] JIT: just-in-time manufacturing/inventory; TQM: total quality management; FMS: flexible manufacturing systems; CIM: computer-integrated manufacturing; MRP: material requirements planning; CAD/CAM: computer-aided design/computer-aided manufacturing; TPM: total preventive maintenance.

[3] ABC: activity-based costing; SCM: strategic cost management; EVA: economic value-added; ABM: activity-based management.

[4] Hill et al., "Strategic Capacity Planning and Production Scheduling in Jobbing Systems," *Integrated Manufacturing Systems,* Vol. 3, No. 3, 1992, p. 22.

[5] E. A. Veral and R. L. LaForge, "The Integration of Cost and Capacity Considerations in Material Requirements Planning Systems," *Decision Sciences,* Vol. 2, 1990, pp. 507, 519.

[6] Hill et al., op. cit., pp. 22–26.

[7] Veral and LaForge, op. cit., pp. 507, 513.

[8] See J. Myers, "Fundamentals of Production That Influence Industrial Facility Designs," *Appraisal Journal,* April 1994, pp. 296–302.

[9] C. Adair-Heeley, "Overhead: The Untapped Opportunity for JIT," *Production & Inventory Management Review,* May 1989, pp. 26–27.

[10] E. Noreen, D. Smith, and J. T. Mackey, *The Theory of Constraints and Its Implications for Management Accounting,* Montvale, NJ: Institute of Management Accountants, 1995.

[11] See J. M. Konopka, "Capacity Utilization Bottleneck Efficiency System— CUBES," *JEEE Transactions on Components, Packaging and Manufacturing Technology,* Part A, September 1995.

[12] See T. Klammer, *Capacity: A Manager's Primer,* Arlington, TX: CAM-I, 1996.

[13] Raddock and Gilbert, op. cit., p. 425.

[14] C. A. Garner, "Capacity Utilization and U. S. Inflation," *Federal Reserve Bank of Kansas City,* Fourth Quarter, 1994, pp. 5–21.

[15] J. Orr, "Has Excess Capacity Abroad Reduced U. S. Inflationary Pressures?", *FRBNY Quarterly Review,* Summer-Fall, 1994, pp. 101–106.

[16] R. S. Pindyck, "Irreversible Investment, Capacity Choice, and the Value of the Firm," *American Economic Review,* December 1988, pp. 970, 983.

[17] D. E. Mills, "Capacity Expansion and the Size of Plants," *RAND Journal of Economics,* Winter 1990, p. 556.

[18] R. Cooper and R. S. Kaplan, "Activity-Based Systems: Measuring the Cost of Resource Usage," *Accounting Horizons,* September 1992, p. 12.

[19] J. T. Mackey, "11 Key Issues in Manufacturing Accounting," *Management Accounting,* January 1987, pp. 33, 35.

[20] K. G. Dilton-Hill and E. Glad, "Managing Capacity," *Journal of Cost Management,* Spring 1994, pp. 33, 39.

[21] M. DeBruine and P. R. Sopariwala, "The Use of Practical Capacity for Better Management Decisions," *Journal of Cost Management,* Spring, 1994, pp. 25–31.

[22] C. J. McNair, "The Hidden Costs of Capacity," *Journal of Cost Management,* Spring 1994, p. 21.

[23] SMA 4Y, "Measuring the Cost of Capacity," Montvale, NJ: Institute of Management Accountants, 1996, pp. 47–48.

PART III

ANNOTATED BIBLIOGRAPHY
OVERVIEW OF
CAPACITY LITERATURE

ANNOTATED BIBLIOGRAPHY

OVERVIEW OF CAPACITY LITERATURE

1900–1919

Church, A. H. 1901. *The Proper Distribution of Expense Burden,* six articles originally published in *Engineering Magazine.*

Proposes a system for overhead treatment that includes the following points: (1) treat each man/machine couplet as a "little shop"; (2) establish a machine rate that includes machine costs, labor, and traceable indirect costs; (3) charge stable rates to products that use machine capacity (assuming normal capacity); (4) put idle costs with other untraceable indirects into a supplemental rate charge on direct labor hours or dollars to entire plant's production.

_____. 1910. *Production Factors in Cost Accounting and Works Management.* New York: *Engineering Magazine,* pp. 113–125.

This writing is a good early example of how financial accounting considerations have clouded cost/management accounting. Notable quotes include: "If profit is to be made anywhere in manufacturing it must be made at the point of the tool" (p. 115). "Its [supplemental rate for idle time] distribution is in fact a concession to those who like to see every item of expense "distributed" over work, without regard to whether such distribution teaches anything or not" (p. 123).

_____. 1911. "Distribution of the Expense Burden." *American Machinist*, May 25, pp. 991–992, 999.

Here, Church backs off from his supplementary charge approach and clearly states it is best to face the music of idle time (wasted capacity). Notable quotes include: "Expense burden represents, not the cost of production, but the cost of capacity to produce" (p. 992). "This idle time represents wasted capacity to produce.... In my idea waste is waste and when you have separated it out, face it squarely and admit that it is none the less waste if you arbitrarily spread it over jobs" (p. 999).

_____. 1912. "Direct and Indirect Costs." *American Machinist*, May 9, p. 763.

This brief piece states that the focus of the cost system should be on each machine. Church represents a tight argument for "scientific" machine rates, noting: "Each machine is a 'production center' making use of the subsidiary activities in a proportion different from its neighbors."

_____. 1915. "Mr. Gantt's Theory of Expense Burden." *American Machinist*, July 29, pp. 209–210.

First of Church's parleys in his debate with Henry Gantt. He feels Gantt has oversimplified the complex problem of idle capacity and unabsorbed burden. Key comments include: "It [undistributed burden] is of course mere waste. It represents unused productive capacity.... The amount of burden charged to the supplementary rate, or to profit and loss, can be determined when, and only when, some mechanism exists to attach to each order the proportion of burden that properly belongs to it" (p. 210).

_____. 1915. "Relation Between Production and Cost." *American Machinist*, Sept. 2, p. 431.

In this article, Church takes issue once again with the ratio-based approach to charging idle expense that Gantt proposes. Notable comments: "In many kinds of business there is always a more or less floating loss of burden, due to idleness, which is inseparable from the running of the business and must therefore be paid for out of profit.... it must be recovered through the cost of what was actually made."

_____. 1917. "Costing on Method C" from his book *Manufacturing Costs and Accounts*. New York: McGraw-Hill.

While Church remains embroiled in the controversy about how best to handle the charge for idle time, he also begins to emphasize the need for immediacy to solve this problem (e.g., charging to P&L). Notable comments: "[Idle machines imply] wasted opportunities.... In other words, the cost of idle machines should be separated from the process-cost of work" (p. 71). "And the particular variety of waste it represents is wasted manufacturing capacity. The price of this wasted capacity is the balance remaining in the burden account after the machine earnings charged to orders have been credited" (p. 349).

Cole, William Morse. 1915. "Principles Illustrated in Factory Accounting," in his book *Accounts: Their Construction and Interpretation*. Boston: Houghton Mifflin Company, pp. 283–313.

Cole puts intense focus on each resource used in manufacturing and how best to tie it to the productive process. While the writing itself is tortured, Cole is one of the few authors of the time to tie his arguments directly to the logic of the market, arguing for different treatment of costs in conditions of competition versus noncompetitive markets. Notable comments include: "The chances of unknown waste in factory administration are alarming and the purpose of cost accounting is quite as much to forestall them as to determine actual costs" (p. 283). "The most effective stimulus for reducing waste is to show that it costs something.... if idle costs are not so treated, accounting fails" (p. 285).

Edtterson, J. 1912. "Direct and Indirect Costs." *American Machinist*, March 7, pp. 387–88.

Focusing on the costing practices in navy yards, his primary concern is identifying who actually controls a cost. Notable quotes include: "It is at once apparent that the cost of material is not controlled by the plant superintendent, but rather by the designer, customer or maker of the specifications that the plant superintendent is required to meet" (p. 387). "...the plant superintendent does not have it in his power to greatly influence the indirect charges.... it leaves him only direct charges with which to obtain his efficiency" (p. 388).

Federal Reserve Board. 1919. "Percentage of Plant Capacity in Operation." Various items in the *Federal Reserve Bulletin*. In the March 1 issue, pp. 189–201; in the April 1 issue, pp. 331–336, 1137–1139.

Outside of this author's interest in the citation of Babson's composite plot of general business conditions, this document is notable for its use of capacity utilization as one of the key leading indicators of manufacturing health. The first time capacity is so noted is in the 1919 Bulletin. It continues to be so used today. Only during wartime did the Federal Reserve Board withhold capacity utilization figures from its reports, noting security reasons.

Gantt, Henry L. 1915. "The Relation Between Production and Costs." American Society of Mechanical Engineers, *Proceedings*, June. Buffalo, NY: pp. 109–28.

In this, Gantt's first published work of his views on costing, he suggests that it is illogical to attach the costs of idle capacity or "those costs not needed in its production" to a unit of good output. Laying the groundwork for the notion of a "true cost," this article also provides a detailed look at Gantt's position on capacity reporting and the placement of idle capacity costs on the P&L. Notable comments include: "Idle capacity should be charged to profit and loss directly" (p. 112). "The only expense logically chargeable to a product is that needed for its production when a plant is running at its full or normal capacity" (p. 117). "To do efficiently something that should not have been done at all, benefits nobody" (p. 128).

_____. 1915. "Relation Between Production and Cost." *American Machinist*, June 17, pp. 1055–56, 1061–62.

Following on the same logic as the piece noted above (both articles are based on the same speech), Gantt argues for the charging of idle capacity costs directly to the P&L using a ratio of idle time to total time available, a percentage, to charge idle costs. Notable quotes include: "The view of costs so largely held, namely, that the product of a factory, however small, must bear the total expense, however large, is responsible for much of the confusion about costs and hence leads to unsound business policies.... If we accept the view that the article produced shall bear only that portion of the indirect expense needed to produce it, our costs will not only become lower, but relatively far more constant, for the most variable factor in the cost of an article under the usual system of accounting has been the overhead, which has varied almost inversely as the amount of product" (p. 1056). This amount becomes "substantially constant if the overhead is figured on the normal capacity of the plant.... Of course, a method of accounting does not diminish the expense, but it may show us where the expense properly belongs and give us a more correct understanding of our business" (p. 1061).

_____. 1915. "Relation Between Production and Cost." *American Machinist*, August 25, pp. 385–386.

As part of the second major piece of the Church-Gantt debate on the treatment of idle capacity and the unabsorbed burden it creates, Gantt attacks the accounting position, noting that it is too heavily focused on the past. Notable comments include: "A disinclination to do a thing that is in itself right should not be used as an argument for not doing it. As a matter of fact, a man who does the thing which is economically right, whether it is disagreeable or not, will soon outdistance his competitors who do only those things that are both economically right and agreeable.... If this excess burden is mere waste, it certainly is an expense not of the parts of the works being operated but of the part not being operated, and which is not turning out any product.... The industrial organization that is guided by what has been done (accounting) will soon be left far behind by the competitor whose policy is based on what can be done (engineering)" (p. 386).

_____. 1915. "Relation Between Production and Cost." *American Machinist*, October 21, p. 737.

In this last commentary, Gantt suggests that while he believes he and Church are actually quite close in terms of overall views on idle capacity and its undesirable nature, he uses this last piece to hone in on the argument that accounting (e.g., Church) serves the financier, not the business. Also, he restates the belief that actual production cannot be made to bear the cost of idle facilities if a company is to remain competitive in the market. Notable comment: "Mr. Church is really defending his method of putting the unabsorbed expense in a reserve fund to be distributed later, which he practically admits was a concession to the financier. I absolutely fail to see why this reserve fund, which is really an 'idleness charge,' should be spread over product with which it had nothing to do" (p. 737).

_____. 1919. "Influence of Executives." *Annals of the American Academy of Political and Social Sciences*, September, pp. 257–263.

In this final article, Gantt turns his attention to convincing executives to take responsibility for idle capacity costs, removing them from the concerns of the plant. Gantt is finally addressing, then, Church's comment that business would not easily accept the P&L treatment of idle capacity costs. Notable comments include: "We have comparatively accurate methods of measuring the performance of workmen; but until recently we have had almost no methods of measuring the effectiveness of executives except the profits made by the business. If the business does not make profits, we naturally blame causes we can see, and ignore those we can't see; this is the reason the shop gets the blame, and the office goes free" (p. 258). "...a cost system which puts upon the product of one machine the expense of maintaining in idleness another machine which did not in any way influence the product, is fundamentally false" (p. 259). "...a study of idleness is much more effective in increasing the output of the plant than the study of efficiency as it has been studied" (p. 260). "...a recognition of the cost of idleness and the allocation of this expense to those who are responsible for it, is the most important economic fact that has been brought to the attention of the business world for many years" (p. 262). "The adoption of such a policy is in the hands of the executives, and the executives are of large enough caliber they will see that it is the strongest force they can use to oppose socialism, communism or bolshevism" (p. 263).

Kent, William. 1918. *Bookkeeping and Cost Accounting for Factories.* New York: John Wiley and Sons, pp. 99–107.

In this early text on cost accounting and its tie to the bookkeeping process, Kent assumes the increasingly popular opinion of Gantt, suggesting that idle costs be charged to the P&L. Notable comments include: "When costs are figured on the second basis [idle costs to the P&L], great activity immediately ensues to determine why machinery is idle, and to see what can be done to put it in operation" (p. 105). "If the idleness time in the ensuing year is greater than the amount estimated, the excess should not be apportioned to the cost of goods in any month, or in a year, but should be charged to profit and loss, either directly or through a subordinate account, such as 'Loss due to Idleness of Plant'" (p. 106).

McHenry, William E.M. 1915. "Relation Between Production and Cost." *American Machinist*, September 23, p. 564.

As the only outsider to venture into the Gantt/Church debate, McHenry suggests a compromise position, one that allows that while Church is taking care with the use of a theory, that Gantt is more correct in his single-minded focus on charging idle costs to the P&L directly. Notable comment: "But after reflection, my mind has settled to the strong conviction that it is wrong in principle and absurd in practice to add to the true cost of doing a thing the wholly misleading cost of not doing that thing or any other thing" (p. 564).

Scovell, H. Clinton. 1916. *Cost Accounting and Burden Application.* New York: D. Appleton and Company. "Fixed Charges," pp. 76–95; "Interest Charged to Cost," pp. 96–133; and "Unearned Burden," pp. 175–196.

Scovell takes a look at the determination of total manufacturing cost. He includes a computation of interest for amounts invested in buildings and machinery. He also calls for close approximation of depreciation, especially to the useful lives of fixed assets. Finally, Scovell joins the growing list of experts suggesting that idle costs be expensed, as suggested by the following: "The unearned burden, or the balance still remaining in the departmental accounts, should be closed to Loss and Gain for the period, since these charges represent the cost due to idle capacity for manufacturing" (p. 194).

Whitmore, John. 1906. "Factory Accounting Applied to Machine Shops." *Journal of Accountancy,* Part I, August, pp. 248–258; Part II, September, pp. 345–357; Part III, October, pp. 430–441; Part IV, November, pp. 20–31; Part V, December, pp. 106–114; Part VI, January 1907, pp. 211–217.

This is a highly underrated series of articles. Focused on developing a complete treatment of factory accounting, Whitmore reflects Church's concern with the machine hour rate and his overarching focus on identifying and eliminating waste in manufacturing. While many comments could be used, a select few capture the essence of Whitmore's views: "...and the object of the accounts is always the same, to eliminate waste from the operations. This then may be said to be the purpose of all factory accounting: to produce records in which waste shall be plainly shown as waste" (Part I, p. 249). "...it is useful to bear in mind that it is through the study of factory capacity, and through the accounting that may be set up in relation to it, that the most perfect test of efficiency is arrived at" (Part I, p. 250). "If this is the feeling, it fails to take into account influences which have their effect upon human effort: the sense of opportunity, the sense of necessity, and the exact knowledge of what ought to be done. It is for one thing to set at work these influences, to show exactly what factory capacity is underutilized and what the resulting loss is, that the accounting for factory capacity is set up" (Part III, p. 433). "For this purpose a record of the non-running time is kept in the shops..." (Part IV, p. 27). "...and the cost figures are freed from the fluctuating and confusing element of the expense of capacity idle that ought to be operated" (Part IV, p. 31).

_____. 1907. "Some Details of Machine Shop Cost Accounts." *Journal of Accountancy,* February, pp. 294–96.

This articles relates the idle time charge to the machine rate system of A. H. Church yet uses the percentage approach embraced by Gantt to deal with idle charges. Representative comment is: "One should charge to idle shop capacity as machines are idle, by the simple use of the machine rate" (p. 295).

_____. 1908. "Shoe Factory Accounts." *Journal of Accountancy*, May, pp. 12–25.

This article stresses the importance of the machine rate method once again, this time within a specific setting. Comments include: "The development of cost accounting must begin from simple methods and simple ideas and definitions" (p. 12). "Accidents and blunders occur and the cost, as in some instances the cost of unused factory capacity, may be so great that it would be absurd to state it as a part of the cost of the product" (p. 14).

1920 –1932

Alden, William H. 1924. "Handling the Expense of Idle Time." NACA Yearbook, 5th International Cost Conference, pp. 115–120.

The author argues that separating idle capacity charges is the key to developing sound information for management's use, evaluating shop floor performance, and assuring correct assignment of costs to inventory. Shows deep concern with knowing the relationship between standards and action. In favor of using "true costs" in reporting. Key notation is author's reference to the impact of idle capacity on income taxes, as the boom period surrounding World War I winds down.

Atkins, Paul M. 1923. "The Taylor Method of Expense and Burden Distribution." *Industrial Management*, October, pp. 217–223.

Atkins' primary concern is with documenting the fact that Taylor had created a cost system to accompany his Scientific Management approach and that this approach included the machine labor-hour method claimed by Church. He notes that Taylor's major failing in this regard was his failure to include changes in capacity utilization in his analysis.

Bennett, George E. 1926. "Some Observations on the Application of Manufacturing Expense of Production." *Accounting Review*, March, pp. 1–8.

The article makes several interesting comments of a practical nature but focuses on an academic view of "normal" operating conditions, reaching no sound conclusions. The author supports the use of 100% theoretical in costing, passing all idle costs so defined to the P&L but in doing so recognizes that practicality may call for the use of 80% of theoretical as the baseline. His desire to see multiyear reporting as the basis for cost reporting, separate from the financial system, is the major contribution. Finally, he is concerned that it is necessary to formalize the Science of Accounting, one that allows a debate on the meaning of terms and the best treatment of events, one that recognizes the impact of context on results.

Bernard, R. J. 1933. "New Haven Accountants Debate Disposition of Unabsorbed Overhead." *American Accountant*, April. pp. 113–114.

Bernard, who represents the winning side in this debate that takes place in the waning moments of 1932, argues the "negative side," namely, that idle capacity costs or unabsorbed burden should be charged to product. He goes on to reject the use of standard costs, arguing for the merits of actual costs instead. He is a direct proponent, then, of the move to eliminate even a standard-cost proxy of the idle capacity charge from the income statement and, as such, represents the first clear statement of a position that is to be dominant until the early 1990s.

Church, Alexander H. 1931. "Overhead—The Cost of Production Preparedness." *Factory and Industrial Management*, January, pp. 38–41.

In this article, Church recants his prior position in favor of the supplemental rate method for handling idle capacity costs. It is interesting that he moves away from his prior position at this time when, as noted above, just one year later he effectively "wins" the debate with Gantt by default. Yet, as this article suggests, Church seems to recognize that his supplemental rate is increasingly used to create a "full cost" product model in companies, rather than being used to track the waste of idle capacity. As such, then, Church's worst nightmares appear to be coming true, a fact that this article cannot prevent. This article is an essential "must read" for anyone interested in the capacity reporting area.

Clark, John Maurice. 1923. "Some Social Aspects of Overhead Costs: An Application of Overhead Costs to Social Accounting with Special Reference to the Business Cycle." *The American Economic Review,* March, pp. 50–59.

In this paper, Clark translates the concept of idle capacity and its consequences out of the realm of one business into the economy at large, and its impact on society. Noting that the cost of an idle man is greater than the cost of an idle machine because a man must be fed no matter what and hence has a higher cost of preparedness, Clark makes several major points: (1) Idleness is always waste for society, therefore it is always better to produce no matter what the cost on the financial statements. (2) Residual cost is total cost less the sum of the differential costs of the production. (3) Efficiency always requires putting idle overhead to work, whenever the product is worth the differential or variable cost (p. 51). (4) Most of the costs of industry are constant. (5) Labor, relatedly, is a constant cost to society that is transferred as a variable cost to a company via the system of wages (p. 54). (6) The treatment of labor and material as variable costs and capital costs as constant are a matter of accident, a function of how contracts are drawn rather than the true cost to society.

_____. 1923. *The Economics of Overhead Costs*. Chicago, IL: The University of Chicago Press.

This seminal work on overhead costs has one major theme, namely that there needs to be a new logic in accounting, one that supports the theme of "different costs for different purposes." Clark goes into tremendous detail on all aspects of overhead costs in this treatise, moving far beyond the abilities of this monograph to capture his thoughts. However, several notable comments pertaining to this discussion are: "There have been too many absolutes in accounting as in other arts and sciences, and an absolute generally means a conception which may be adapted to one purpose, but is arbitrarily used for other purposes for which it does not fit" (p. 194). "Change itself costs something" (p. 186). "We have to deal with cost in different aspects and no one formula for cost will fit in all cases" (p. 201).

_____. 1927. "Some Central Problems of Overhead Costs: An Inquiry into Aspects of One of the Most Delicate Problems of Business Policy." *Bulletin of the Taylor Society,* February, pp. 288–292.

The theme of this article is that to manage idle capacity fully, a company needs to gauge its differential costs, not standard or actual costs. Key comments made include: "The whole business, or the whole production process, must pay all of the costs incurred or it does not meet the basic test of economic self-support" (p. 287). "It is key to have a measure of cost that builds in idleness" (p. 288). "Whenever the overhead is not being fully utilized, which is most of the time, differential cost is less than average cost; often a great deal less" (p. 289). "The economic waste of idle time is vastly greater than the accounts show" (p. 292).

Clark, Wallace. 1927. Discussion of J. M. Clark's article noted above, *Bulletin of the Taylor Society,* February, pp. 292–293.

The author notes that the cost of idleness leads to a change in practices in a company. He suggests a series of idleness accounts, including lack of help, lack of materials, lack of power, lack of tools, repairs, and lack of orders. Honing in on J. M. Clark's concern with idleness as an unrecoverable cost, Wallace Clark provides a practitioner's response on various ways that these troublesome issues are handled in industry.

Cornell, C. H. 1924. "How is Over- or Under-Absorbed Burden to be Applied with Regard to Inventory at the End of the Fiscal Year?" NACA Yearbook, pp. 194–198.

Stressing the use of burden-based numbers in analysis and management reporting, Cornell argues that unabsorbed burden does not belong in inventory. Key comments in the article include: "Considering first that part of the under-absorbed burden which is due to idle plant or unused capacity, there seems to be no good reason for including any part of it in inventory" (p. 196).

Eggleston, D. 1920. "Machine Hour Rates," in *Cost Accounting,* Vol. III. New York: Ronald Press, pp. 267–298.

Eggleston's major concern is with the use of normal operation conditions as the baseline in capacity measurement, rather than theoretical. In this setting (using normal), idleness due to shutdown is argued to be best charged to profit and loss directly, while temporary idleness should be considered part of the normal, or average, cost of doing business. Specific quotes in this chapter include: "When computing the charges at the number of hours of operation, the figures in both cases should be based on normal operating conditions" (p. 289). "Loss due to idle capacity on account of shutdowns is charged to Profit and Loss" (p. 294). "This method throws into relief the wasted manufacturing capacity of the factory.... the loss due to the temporary idleness of machines is part of the cost of manufacture which must be recovered in the selling price of product" (p. 295).

Fiske, Wyman P. 1931. "Accounting for Unused Facilities." *NACA Bulletin*, November 15, pp. 355–369.

Fiske's key concern is with the causes of idle time, whether due to production, administration, or economic events. He notes that for accounting to support administrative control processes, it has to record the key elements of idle capacity both on the income statement and in operating reports. Fiske is also one of the earliest writers to focus on the bottleneck in a process as the key defining feature of capacity costs.

Jordan, J. P., and Gould L. Harris. 1920. *Cost Accounting: Principles and Practice*. New York: Ronald Press.

This is a hands-on textbook that argues for immediate recordings and reactions to the idle time on each machine. In a very detailed manner, the authors represent one of the most aggressive attempts at promoting and supporting the prevention of idle time. While it doesn't go so far as to reward this prevention, it does suggest it is the key to prosperity. Notable comments include: "It has also been stated that 80% of the causes of idleness of equipment are the fault of the management" (p. 418). "The principal objective to be secured in connection with delays in the use of equipment is to stop the delays" (p. 419).

Knapp, C. Howard. 1924. "Variations from Predetermined Standards of Burden and Manufacturing Costs." NACA Yearbook, pp. 206–219.

Part of the 1924 debate, this article takes a look at idle capacity and how to account for it, as well as how to price an off-schedule job, given the presence of idle capacity. The writer favors using the title "Idle Capacity" each month on the profit and loss statement. Specific comments include: "Some cost accountants advise the creation of a reserve account to which is charged or credited the item of over- or under-absorbed burden. It is the writer's opinion that idle capacity is a better name for this account, and that it should be cleared each month to profit and loss" (pp. 216–217).

Martin, R. F. 1932. "Industrial Overcapacity." *Bulletin of the Taylor Society,* June, pp. 94–99.

This articles provides a detailed description of the varied ways capacity is defined across the key industrial sectors of the 1930s. Noted are very low capacity utilization rates in all cases, even assuming a one-shift, 40-hour baseline for plants/industries surveyed. Key also is the author's view that, while most notable during the Depression, excess capacity had existed at very high levels during the preceding period of prosperity. The graphs included in the article show steel working at 12–40% of capacity (20% average), textile machinery at 30–40%, paper at about 60%, and all others at between 18–60% of available capacity (under "normal" operations).

May, George O. 1932. "Influence of the Depression on the Practice of Accounting." *Journal of Accountancy,* November, pp. 336–350.

Dealing predominantly with the need to write down physical assets and inventory in the face of the prolonged Depression, May's article suggests that such writedowns should provide a psychological boost to the use of machines because now they would be cheaper to run, thereby making products cheaper to make. No proof is offered for this philosophical position.

Nicholson, J. Lee, and J. F. D. Rohrbach. 1920. "Lost and Idle Time of Production." *Cost Accounting.* New York: Ronald Press, p. 131, pp. 188–190.

While this article is perhaps overly detailed with its focus on the accounting treatment of various expenses and events, it is notable in its concern that idle time be correctly recorded rather than being directly charged to product cost. Clearly, the authors believe that placing idleness costs into general product costs will reduce the informativeness of the system. Notable quote: "It is far more important to know the amount of this idle time than to have all productive time treated as a direct element of cost. The wastage of time can only be avoided if the time so lost is properly recorded" (p. 131).

Preshaw, G. 1933. "Unabsorbed Overhead—Should It Be Charged to Inventory?" *American Accountant*, June, pp. 179–180.

As part of the New Haven debate, Preshaw's paper is one of the last clear arguments against charging idle capacity costs to inventory in the form of unabsorbed overhead. Concerned with the tie between value creation and price, as well as the definition of a "true cost" for a product, Preshaw notes that idle capacity is waste, not cost.

Sanders, T. H. 1926. "Overhead in Economics and Accounting." *NACA Bulletin*, April 15, pp. 241–249.

The focus of this article is on the need for information from accounting that identifies capacity and planning problems and that pinpoints the departments where improvements can be made. He argues for total costs as the basis for price, even though he notes that most people feel this is an abandonment of "true cost." He also notes that in the case of Henry Ford, all the information needed is the speed of autos off the line. In many ways, then, he recognizes the role of throughput in the costing process.

_____. 1930. *Problems in Industrial Accounting*, 2nd edition. New York: McGraw-Hill.

Of greatest interest in this book is the author's development of six specific cases of idle capacity and its treatment. These cases allow for different treatments under different conditions within the firm and the industry in which it operates. The cases are presented in debate format, allowing the students to suggest the best treatment for the idle capacity in each unique setting. Outside of these cases, little additional insight is added into capacity issues.

Scovell, H. Clinton. 1926. "Question Box." *NACA Bulletin*, pp. 251–268.

Scovell chairs a session at the 1926 NACA annual meeting that focuses specifically on the treatment of idle costs or unabsorbed burden. The debate captured in this article provides an early snapshot of the reasons for choosing various levels of "capacity" as the baseline for costing. Theoretical capacity is argued to be the best basis for management purposes, while practical or "balanced production" appears to be most preferred for all other reporting formats.

Stock, A. P., and J. M. Coffey. 1925. "Overhead During Low-Volume Production." *NACA Bulletin*, Feb. 16, pp. 3–11.

Using a CVP-based approach, this author suggests the use of "normal" capacity under expected operating conditions as the basis for capacity reporting. Notable quotes include: "Cost accounting must consider and stress the selling viewpoint. ...customer buying must be stimulated effectively. When the selling price meets the consumer's viewpoint of value at a given moment, it cannot help but stimulate sales. Future business will never be forthcoming to make use of idle equipment unless sales prices anticipate future costs" (p. 3). "...the correct general basis on which to obtain sufficient future business...is to bring it somewhere near its capacity point" (p. 4).

Thompson, R. R. 1925. "Various Wage Systems in Relation to Factory Indirect Charges." *NACA Bulletin*, December 15, pp. 283–296.

A worthwhile read, this article gives a solution for handling capacity increases over a given time period. It gives a good description of wage systems at the time, a long since forgotten accounting topic. Primary focus is on the tradeoff between labor and capacity, stated in terms of the impact on indirect cost.

VanZandt, Charles. 1922. "Normal Burden Rates: Some Problems in Their Application." *NACA Bulletin*, July 1, pp. 3–12.

This article makes an interesting plea for help in setting the normal amount, or burden rate. There is more than one reference to the use of balance sheet accounts to smooth the impact of volume shifts between years. VanZandt, who participated in the NACA debates, continued to hold to the view that unabsorbed burden due to the vagaries of volume in a year should be booked to a balance sheet account, "storing" this value until future volume could absorb it. He was alone in this stance, facing significant pressure during the 1926 debate to recognize the need to place idle capacity costs directly on the income statement.

Williams, C. B. 1921. "The Distribution of Overhead Under Abnormal Conditions." NACA Yearbook, pp. 199–206.

As with most articles of this period, the author argues for a separation of utilized versus idle capacity, with a direct charge of idle costs to the profit and loss statement. In addition, he notes the faulty assumptions inherent in full costing. He does assume some level of waste into his cost standards, as is typical of this period. Notable comments include: "I contend that it costs no more to manufacture an article when only one of ten machines is working than it does when all are working. If the sales price is based on the cost of manufacturing, idle expense excluded, instead of on total expenditures, possibly it can be made low enough to attract buyers and at the same time not show a loss" (p. 200).

1933–1952

AICPA. 1947. ARB No. 29, "Inventory Pricing," reprinted in *The Journal of Accountancy*, September 1947, pp. 196–201.

This AICPA publication focuses on defining inventory costs and the proper matching of these costs to revenue in a period. Inventory is defined as "goods awaiting sale" and "goods to be consumed in the course of production." "...the inventory at any given date is in effect a residual amount remaining after the matching of absorbed costs with concurrent revenues.... The primary basis of accounting for inventories is cost, which has been defined generally as the price paid or consideration given to acquire an asset.... under some circumstances, items such as idle facility expense, excessive spoilage, double freight, and rehandling costs may be so abnormal as to require treatment as current period charges rather than as a portion of the inventory cost."

Avery, Harold G. 1940. "The Problem of Idle Equipment." *Accounting Review*, December, pp. 469–473.

A classic article that shows the weakness and sterility of the financial accounting approach to the puzzle of idle capacity. Avery's concern is not with management's need to bring business in to fill capacity but rather how to treat the *depreciation* charges tied to idle equipment by traditional depreciation methods. No mention is made of the unabsorbed burden associated with idle machines. Instead, units-of-production depreciation is seen as the only solution needed.

Baridon, F. E. 1948. "A Capacity Budget Procedure to Set Task for Plant and Sales Force." *NACA Bulletin*, August 1, pp. 1483–1492.

Reflecting the increasing focus on budgets as the key to improving company performance, Baridon's article deals with the unique problems of new companies or small companies with very little backlog. Budgets, which are capacity driven, are seen as the most effective way to encourage and monitor performance. Noting that plant capacity is defined neither by bottlenecks nor machine hours, Baridon emphasizes the total productive capability of the plant, defined in practical terms, as the "capacity" to be managed.

Blodgett, Ralph H. 1943. "The Value of Economics for the Accountant." *Accounting Review*, pp. 324–330.

Blodgett argues in this article that accountants need to be exposed to economic theory, where assumptions and their implications for current and future outcomes are explored. These assumptions serve to simplify the issues at hand, providing the basis for identifying trends and key factors. Key comment with implications for capacity is: "...the costs of an enterprise consist of the competitive valuations of the services of all the production factors used in the enterprise, so that their use involves money expenses, or are owned inside the business, so that the remuneration for their services is retained by the enterprise itself" (p. 327). In addition, Blodgett points out that spreading fixed costs over individual units, even if it is done at capacity, places accounting at odds with the logic of economics and the development of long-run average cost curves.

Coan, Norman A. 1950. "Variances Must Be Forged into Familiar Tools." *NACA Bulletin*, June, pp. 1223–1236.

The article is based on the premise that volume-based variance analysis techniques have not worked for organizations. Coan suggests eight separate variances that focus on operating differences between standard and performance, stated in terms that support the search for underlying causes. Coan notes that variance analysis is a management tool and should be defined based on management needs, not accounting logic. The variances noted are expenditure of units variance, performance (output) variance, methods variance, length-of-run variance (deals with setup impacts), price variance, volume variance, calendar variance, and ratio or mixed variance.

Columbia University. 1934. *Economic Reconstruction: Report of the Columbia University Commission*. New York: Columbia University Press.

Responding to the impact of various New Deal efforts, including the NIRA, this study attempted to deal with the overcapacity of the nation as a key determinant in economic reconstruction. Comments of interest include: "[There are] two major sources of economic waste, one directly associated with the productive process itself, the other inherent in the economic conditions which control the general volume of productive output" (p. 7). "The writing into codes under the National Industrial Recovery Act of prohibitions upon sales below cost has opened the path to a modified control; but this power lies at the moment mainly with the code authorities that are permitted to prescribe methods of calculating costs" (p. 16). "There should be no illusion with regard to the fact that a general rise in prices through such measures is not a sign of increasing prosperity.... they involve a tax on the rest of the community" (p. 17).

Downie, L. W. 1944. "Normal Capacity and Its Uses." *NACA Bulletin*, September, Section I, pp. 3–11.

The writer skillfully brings in effective demand and warns against cutthroat pricing in his discussion of normal capacity. He raises the question of accounting for fully depreciated machinery and its effect on capacity. Comments include: "In approaching this subject of normal capacity, we should bear in mind that...it must be defined in terms of ability to produce, sell, and collect" (p. 3). "Normal burden rates should not include any expense of inefficient operation of any nature, including equipment not required for the business" (p. 8).

Glover, J. G., and C. L. Maze. 1937. "Control of Idle Costs" in *Managerial Control, Instruments and Methods in Industry*. New York: Ronald Press, pp. 394–408.

Taking a high-level approach for a textbook, these authors promote the use of theoretical capacity in their definition of idle capacity. Interesting comments include: "Idleness may be defined as the failure to use properly the available facilities and energy in whatever form to secure the necessary maximum results at the minimum cost and effort" (p. 395). "The premise should be that no idleness is necessary" (p. 398). "Management may find it profitable to compare the cost of output at maximum capacity with the cost at standard and operating capacity" (p. 406). "The responsibility for reducing idleness to the minimum is very definitely up to the management of a plant" (p. 407).

Hanley, E. J. 1938. "Control of Factory Overhead at Varying Volumes of Production." NACA Yearbook, 19th International Cost Conference, pp. 154–158.

This article presents a great many hands-on solutions to the problems of managing capacity. The solutions are right down to the individual machine and foreman levels, providing a microanalysis of events. It provides good advice on the rigor of the definition of the problem and also stresses a wider range of level of capacity usage. Notable comments include: "...since mechanization tends to convert variable labor cost into fixed cost, we are increasing fixed charges and simultaneously making it less possible to control factory overhead under conditions of decreased volume which always come" (p. 166). "Dispose of the equipment and get rid of the facilities when you are sure they are definitely idle, because a shrinkage in capacity will occasion a shrinkage in organization and hence a shrinkage in the expense of standby labor...." (p. 168).

James, Charles C. 1941. "Application of Overhead in Periods of Abnormal Activity." NACA Yearbook, pp. 339–359.

Contrary to the 1932–34 period when companies were forced to write down assets due to subnormal activities, the beginning of the war effort had these companies on overtime. But what to charge? In this summary article on the 1941 NACA overhead debate, focus turns toward standard costs in periods of excess demand. "The fundamental rule under which so-called indirect or so-called nonproductive expenditures may be made is that a dollar spent for that type of service or facility should save more than a dollar of direct cost" (p. 340).

_____. 1945. "Capacity, Costs, and Prices." NACA Yearbook. Reprinted in *Relevance Rediscovered*, Vol. III. Montvale, NJ: Institute of Management Accountants, 1992, pp. 146–153. Rejoinder to Nourse, pp. 158–159.

In this second part of a 1945 debate on capacity and costing practices, James focuses on Nourse's position that incorporating idleness costs in product costs results in refusing business that would be profitable under full capacity conditions, leading to a long-term loss in business profits and an increase in unnecessary idleness. James's response to this position is summarized in three basic points: "(1) The effect on unit costs of variations in volume of output after a normal range of operating activity is reached is much less than many people think. (2) Price reductions made possible merely by increased production would not release enough purchasing power to buy the increased output. (3) Nobody has yet been smart enough to run a business successfully in defiance of the law of supply and demand" (p. 153).

Lewis, W. A. 1948. *Overhead Costs: Some Essays in Economic Analysis.* New York: Augustus N. Kelley Publishers.

In this article, Lewis notes that the increased use of capacity, if this use does not generate an excess over long-run costs, is not a good thing. Specifically, he notes: "The economist's costs are those which can be escaped; fixed costs are those which cannot; escapability is the essence of the distinction" (p. 9).

NACA. 1938. Research and Technical Service Department. "Practice in Applying Overhead and Calculating Normal Capacity." *NACA Bulletin*, April 1, pp. 917–934.

This article was based on a survey study of definitions and measurements of capacity in use at that time. Interesting results are summarized, including the fact that 10/224 respondents used bottleneck practical capacity as the basis for their plant capacity definition, although they did not charge permanently idled capacity in other areas as part of this area's caused cost. Of the 224 responding, 48 used one plantwide rate based on direct labor dollars or hours, and 69 of 224 eliminated the fixed charges on equipment from overhead and treated them separately as idle equipment costs. Of these, 55 charged the P&L directly for idleness, while 10 posted the expense through to COS (Church supplementary method).

Nourse, E. G., et al. 1934. *America's Capacity to Produce*, special edition. New York: Review of Reviews Corporation.

This publication represents the best thinking about capacity by economists. The definitions of capacity and capacity utilization are vaguely defined in economic terms, using practical capacity as the baseline. Serious doubt is raised about the national figures on capacity utilization.

Nourse, E. G. 1945. "Cost Finding and Price Determination." NACA Yearbook. Rejoinder to James's comments, reprinted in *Relevance Rediscovered*, Vol. III. Montvale, NJ: Institute of Management Accountants, 1992, pp. 135–145; 153–158.

This paper is an economist's offering of hope to accountants from an action viewpoint. He believes accountants can make a positive contribution to increasing throughput. Specific comments include: "The mere financial accountant is a sort of hod-carrying historian of business, not an imaginative and creative architect of more enduring, more efficient, and more satisfying business and economic structures. It is in cost accounting, or, better, cost analysis, that we find the upper crust of the accounting group, and there is no ceiling that stops, or will even check, the cost analyst's rise into the ranks of professional economics and the farthest reaches of social science" (p. 135). "Just as soon as you write plant idleness (beyond that due to technical causes) into your cost sheets, you are headed for trouble.... This requires that the product as a whole be priced at actual and necessary costs under the conditions of full activity" (p. 145).

Paton, W. A., and A. C. Littleton. 1936. "Accounting Principles Affecting Corporate Reports." *Accounting Review*, June, pp. 187–191.

Summarizing the conclusions reached by the AAA Executive Committee, this article is a precursor to the seminal monograph on corporate reporting published in 1941. While vague in defining specific costs and treatments for abnormal expenses, the statement does promote the direct writeoff of assets that have lost usefulness; waste was not to be included in product cost. Key comments in this article include: "Accounting is thus not essentially a process of valuation, but the allocation of historical costs and revenues to the current and succeeding fiscal periods.... [A] company...should eliminate from its accounts those costs which are applicable to assets no longer useful or salable" (pp. 188, 189).

Paton, W. A., and A. C. Littleton. 1940. *An Introduction to Corporate Accounting Standards*. Sarasota, FL: American Accounting Association.

This monograph is the defining work in financial accounting theory, serving as the basis for ongoing development and regulation of the field. Embedded in the work is an ongoing concern with "normal" operating conditions as defined by management policies. Paton and Littleton provide ample room for booking idle capacity costs directly to the P&L, as unstorable costs that will not generate future revenues. The entire monograph is a must read.

Peloubet, Maurice E. 1942. "Trends in Accepted Accounting and Their Relation to Cost Accounting." *NACA Bulletin*, February, pp. 835–847.

This article is a statement by the public accounting profession of their expectations for cost accountants. In its language and thrust, it is indicative of the rise of financial accounting needs as the dominant force defining cost practices. Illustrative comments include: "All that the public accountant expects of the cost accountant is complete co-operation and full, prompt and accurate statements of costs and inventories adequately supported" (p. 835).

Schumpeter, J. A. 1939. *Business Cycles: A Theoretical, Historical and Statistical Analysis of Capitalist Process*. New York: McGraw-Hill.

Schumpeter, the leading pro-capitalist economist of the 20th century, stresses excess capacity as a function of technology changes. He also notes, "the National Recovery Act which stressed the importance of set prices above full cost and decried cutthroat competition...the NRA of 1933 was far more significant in accounting than the...Securities Acts of 1933 and 1934. Hugh Johnson of...NRA was much bigger than Joe Kennedy of the SEC.... [T]alks about overproduction and lack of purchasing power to support given to certain types of corporative action and planning, were eventually to find expression in the NRA legislation, the idea of which characteristically enough originated in business circles" (p. 802).

Stevenson, H. F. 1950. "A Cycle Reserve to Replace Annual Burden Charges." *NACA Bulletin*, September, pp. 79–83.

This article gives an excellent explanation of the long-term cycle theory of burden allocation. Comments include: "[I]f above average years are made to absorb more than the full amount of the fixed and semifixed burden charges of the year and the below-average years less than the full amount of those charges, the burden could be spread equitably over the product cycle of the manufacturer.... It is immaterial that accountants are accustomed to thinking in terms of a single fiscal year" (p. 81).

Taggart, Herbert F. 1934. "The Relation of the Cost Accountant to the NRA Codes." *Accounting Review*, pp. 149–157.

This article does an excellent job of capturing the mood of the times and the attitude with which cost accountants greeted the NRA. Taggart notes that the overall view of the NRA and its impact was, "The NRA was going to do for cost accounting what the income tax law had done years before for general accounting.... Prior to the NRA, however, cost accounting in the historical sense has, with few exceptions, been thought of as strictly a private matter. Its primary use has been as a guide to management in the internal control of business operations. Cost accounting has been used very little as an instrument of public control..." (p. 149). "[T]he accountant's voice, formerly crying unheard in the wilderness, would be the voice of a dictator—it must be listened to in order to keep out of jail.... These optimists lost sight of just one thing: for the first time in history cost accounting had become a law" (p. 152). Taggart notes that the representatives of industry viewed the cost codes and NRA as follows, "We have given you wages and hours, now give us cost protection. Our members are not interested in the code without something in it for them" (p. 155).

1953–1964

Baumol, William J. 1965. *Economic Theory and Operations Analysis*, 2nd edition. Englewood Cliffs, NJ: Prentice-Hall.

This book's contribution is the development of three distinct time periods: short-, intermediate- and long-term, according to their relative degree of freedom in decision making. Baumol uses capacity decisions as a way to illustrate the differences in these time periods, noting that in the short term a company is bound by prior decisions and can only shift the utilization of resources, while in the long term total freedom exists to create capacity and activity. The intermediate term is where some constraints exist, but where ample freedom to change policies and processes is present (see pp. 263–266).

Blodgett, Ralph H. 1955. *Our Expanding Economy.* New York: Rinehart and Company.

Blodgett places great emphasis on developing the economics of business in the intermediate period, noting that "in the intermediate period supply is based upon the rate of production which firms producing a good can achieve with the fixed productive facilities already at their disposal" (p. 278). In this period, then, Blodgett believes that the rate of production can be varied considerably, but that fixed elements of capacity are fixed. The goal is to attain the lowest average total cost, in the intermediate term, or the point of production at which both fixed and variable agents of production are used most effectively, as long as this goal is in line with long-term profitability goals.

Brummet, R. Lee. 1957. *Overhead Costing: The Costing of Manufactured Products*. Ann Arbor, MI: University of Michigan Press.

In this comprehensive book on overhead, Brummet deals with the concepts of idle capacity costs and their treatment, starting with late 19th century ideas through practices prevalent in the 1950s. The primary point made in this piece is that standard costing methods appear to have muddled the concepts of capacity and idle capacity costs, a confusion in concepts and terms that did not exist prior to 1930.

Churchill, Neil. 1958. "Another Look at Accounting for Idle Time." *NAA Bulletin*, January, pp. 83–87.

Churchill begins this article by defining idle capacity as "the length of time a given quantity of the company's resources have not been furthering the enterprise's objective during any period." He notes that Fiske (1931) identified three types of idle capacity: production, administrative, and economic. The costs of idle capacity arise from idle employees and idle facilities, including the use of highly skilled labor in low-skill jobs, which Churchill calls idle capacity cost by policy. Arguing for the use of a capacity baseline that allows for segmentation of idleness costs to productive and nonproductive periods (e.g., theoretical), he suggests absorption should be restricted to the overhead associated with productive periods. He promotes separation of idleness costs from product costs, noting such treatment best supports management needs for information. "...Data in which too much has been merged will be meaningless for many of these purposes. It is for this reason that the proper determination of the costs attributable to idle capacity is important" (p. 87).

Davidson, Sidney. 1963. "Old Wine into New Bottles." *Accounting Review*, April, pp. 278–284.

Focused on reviewing and commenting on Clark's (1923) treatise on overhead costs, Davidson places emphasis on Clark's chapter on "Different Costs for Different Purposes," specifically on Clark's statement, "if cost accounting sets out determined to discover what the cost of everything is and convinced in advance that there is one figure which can be found and which will furnish exactly the information which is desired for every possible purpose, it will necessarily fail, because there is no such figure. ...a figure which is right for some purposes...must necessarily be wrong for others." The essence of Davidson's position is, as suggested by Clark, that attention should be shifted from a search for the "correct" cost figure to one that focuses on identifying the correct cost concept. The tie to capacity in this article lies in Clark's own belief that "unused capacity is his central theme." In assessing the impact of various opportunities on total cost, the role of utilizing idle capacity plays a pivotal role in both Davidson's and Clark's views. Good review of Clark's key contributions to management accounting.

Day, C. F. 1959. "'Shadow Prices' for Evaluating Alternatives Uses of Available Capacity." *NAA Bulletin*, May, pp. 67–76.

Day's concern is that pure financial analysis of investments may fail to generate improved profitability if these assets/expenditures do not enhance existing capacity. "It is fatal to go blindly ahead. Although proper plant and equipment are certainly most important to profitable operations, the fact remains that the purchase of a particular piece of equipment, even if economically justifiable, may not represent the best possible use of money" (p. 67). Using a simplified example of a process with four bottleneck processes, Day suggests the solution Goldratt ultimately uses to make his fame—that the best investment is one that improves the capacity of the bottleneck to create throughput. As with Goldratt's model, Day bases his analysis on contribution margin baselines, which form the heart of his shadow price solution. The solution is no surprise; this early accounting application of the concept in the pre-Goldratt era is.

Devine, Carl T. 1961. "Boundaries and Potentials of Reporting on Profit-Volume Relationships." *NAA Bulletin*, January, pp. 5–14.

Typical of the direct/variable costing approach to capacity issues of the 1950–1960 time period, Devine's concern is with developing accounting reports that support reaching organizational objectives and with the value of direct costs in reaching this goal. During this period, capacity discussions are reduced to the issues tied to CVP analysis—the proverbial "fixed costs over more units" view of the capacity problem. Devine's primary concern in this article is the need for complete disclosure in accounting, specifically, "Accountants have been especially careless about explaining output limits, time horizons, and initial conditions upon which and over which their predictions may have validity" (p. 13). Focused on the need to detail the capacity assumptions that lead to specific CVP solutions, Devine is one of a meager number of writers during the "direct cost" years to recognize the impact these estimates had on the decisions they support.

Eldridge, Charles D. 1951. "The Complex Problem of Idle Machine Time." *NACA Bulletin*, December, pp. 427–433.

In the opening comments of this paper, the editor notes, "Machines which are not running are not producing. In these days which feature unprecedented demand for production, process delays are the concern of all groups in management." This article, concrete in its illustration of the frequent difficulties of locating causes for downtime, outlines a procedure under which a staff engineering activity supplements analysis available from the accounting data on operations. This accounting-centered view of capacity reporting is interesting, if nothing else. Eldridge notes that accounting reports should include idle machine time by cause, such as setup time, lack of material, lack of manpower, lack of work scheduled, lack of proper tools, and machine breakdown. These are the self-same accounts and titles that appear in Gantt's idleness charts but with no reference to their source or creator. In the end, the article simply suggests that the accounting records should include this engineering-based information on utilization and provide it as part of the monthly reporting package to management. Little is added to the thoughts about or understanding of capacity cost management.

Ferrara, William. 1960. "Idle Capacity as a Loss: Fact or Fiction?" *Accounting Review*, July, pp. 490–496.

Ferrara argues that idle capacity losses are a fiction by artfully dividing these expenses into costs best charged through "units of production" methods of depreciation (due to their long-term value) and those chargeable to period production (e.g., semivariable expenses) that have no future benefit. Of interest is the author's dominant income statement focus and belief that idle capacity (due to differences between current and planned production) should be booked as a deferred item on the balance sheet. Key arguments made include: with reference to prior positions taken on idle capacity, "The idle capacity loss is considered to be the unutilized portion of fixed manufacturing overhead costs.... The objective of this article is to set forth the general view that there is no such thing as a loss due to idle capacity for purposes of income measurement" (p. 490). "If one were to disagree with this conclusion, he would be admitting that absolutely necessary cost input could be considered as a loss or waste" (p. 491). In the end, Ferrara's position revolves around the issue of the underlying volume-defined behavior of costs rather than specific concerns with actual utilization; idle capacity is reduced to the fixed asset cost, which disappears with units of production depreciation approaches. This position is at complete odds with the findings, analysis, and theory of the pre-1950 eras but is rigorously defined and debated within the confines of the literature and writers of the full cost era.

_____. 1961. "Overhead Costs and Income Measurement." *Accounting Review*, January, pp. 63–70.

In this second article in a series on capacity cost issues, Ferrara turns his attention to the interplay of definitions of capacity and idleness costs. Specifically: "Practical capacity: Idle capacity is in a strict physical sense considered a loss; Normal capacity: Idle capacity due to less than average use of fixed assets, considered a loss; Cycle capacity: Unused costs due to less than average use of fixed assets, considered deferred fixed costs to be utilized in the future when greater than average use of fixed costs occurs" (p. 64). Returning to the earlier themes and concern with income measurement impacts, Ferrara decries the need to call "essential spending" of a lumpy, or stepped/semivariable form, waste. Markedly not a direct coster, Ferrara bases his position for deferral of some costs to the balance sheet and use of units-based depreciation on the need to develop reliable income numbers that realistically deal with all nonvariable costs of production (e.g., overhead).

_____. 1961. "The Importance of Idle Capacity Costs—A Rejoinder." *Accounting Review*, July, pp. 422–424.

Returning to his position that idle capacity charges are inconsistent within an income-centered view of accounting, Ferrara notes that idle capacity, to be useful, needs to be referred to in one of the following ways: (1) How much more output can be produced with existing equipment? (2) If present output of facilities could be increased to the physical output potential of facilities, how much would unit costs of production decrease? (3) If present output of facilities could be increased to the physical output potential of facilities, how much of our total cost could be transferred from present output to the incremental output? He ends with the following comment: "...but let us specify which purposes are served by an idle capcity concept and then let us not confuse the concept of idle capacity as it relates to decision-making, production planning, and even socio-economic analyses with the process of income measurement. The concept of idle capacity as a loss is inconsistent with the process of income measurement" (p. 424).

Garner, S. Paul. 1954. *Evolution of Cost Accounting to 1925*. University of Alabama Press, pp. 184–185, 201–243.

In this review of the development of cost accounting in the early 1900s, Garner provides a recasting of the key arguments behind the treatments of idle capacity that emerged in the

Golden Era. Garner's work provides a good starting point in understanding the early years of cost accounting and where key arguments developed. Interesting insights include: "Thus, it is recognized that the determination of burden rates in advance is indissolubly bound up with the theories underlying the techniques for handling idle time and capacity" (p. 202). "Cowan advocated also the setting up of certain compensating accounts and recoveries accounts which would assist in carrying the under or over absorbed burden from one year to another" (p. 214). "Whitmore...recommended that a separate account be set up on the ledger entitled 'factory idle capacity.' This is in contrast to Kent's position" (p. 219). "...all of these defects could be remedied he [Kent] stated by clearing the idle time charges through profit and loss instead of through the cost of goods produced" (p. 225).

Hearings before the Subcommittee on Economic Statistics. 1962. *Meaures of Productive Capacity.* Joint Economic Committee, 87th Congress, 2nd Session. Excerpts include Daniel Creamer (pp. 36–41), Lawrence B. Klein (pp. 52–59), John DeWitt Norton (pp. 90–120), Frank De Leeuw (pp. 121–131), and Robert S. Schultz (pp. 148–165).

This is must reading in the capacity literature; it shows both the possibilities and impossibilities of capacity reporting. Selected comments follow.

Creamer: "At least one economist gives as a reason for his interest in capacity measurements the possibility of using capacity as a basis for an estimate of the stock of capital—the problem of measuring the latter is regarded as insuperable. Others (and I count myself among them) despair of measuring capacity directly and estimate capital stocks as a basis for a measure of capacity" (p. 36). "Capacity for this purpose is an economic limit to the rate of output with the existing facilities of a sector. It is the rate after which capital additions would tend to be made" (p. 37). "Rather economic capacity must be determined in the context of practical operating considerations such as the normal number of shifts and 'downtime' for maintenance and repairs.... In general the procedure is to establish a fixed capital-output ratio for each industry classification for a benchmark year which independent evidence indicates was a period when capacity was virtually fully utilized" (p. 38).

Klein: "Capacity utilization, unlike the unemployment rate, is an output measure. It shows the extent to which an output potential is being realized through the use of all factors of production.... In terms of the economist's concept of a production function full capacity output is the highest output achievable with combinations of existing input factors" (p. 53). "...yet even if we had the series that we think we would need, a difficulty would remain in that we are not sure just what is meant by capacity.... In any given production unit or small sector of the economy there may be no realistic limit to potential production if we put our efforts exclusively toward increasing activity in that branch, yet there are realistic economic limitations to such enlarged production and that is where the cost concept plays an important role in our definition of capacity" (p. 54). "It is encouraging to see a wide diversity of thought and activity devoted to the premium of capacity measurement" (p. 57).

Norton: "...there remains, however, a conspicuous gap: statistics on the capacity and utilization of industrial plant and equipment" (p. 90). "Capacity is strictly a relationship between throughput and facility during a specified time period.... The capacity of any multiple process facility, whether at the shop, department, or establishment level, is limited to the capacity of the bottleneck component. One useful rule for determining capacity is to look for bottlenecks" (pp. 92–93). "Enough complications have been introduced, however, to indicate that no single, all purpose definition of physical capacity seems possible. Explicit definitions have to be tailored to the conditions which pertain to particular products or establishment groups.... Capacity is not directly observable. Its measurement depends on an appropriate set of rules. The uncertainty and ambiguity which abounds with respect to capacity may be traced to the lack of an accepted set of rules" (p. 95). "Unfortunately the process analysis approach to capacity at the equipment level proliferates too much detail to make it a practical means of capacity estimation at the present. But a qualitative classification of departments and an approximate measure of their importance by the number of workers employed seems feasible" (p. 97). "Controllers, production managers, and engineers may find different answers to the same questionnaire" (p. 98). "Intuition need not be lightly dismissed. If the respondent has the opportunity to observe the facility at varied rates of operation over an extended range, he may be able to provide an estimate as good as any produced by more elaborate calculations" (p. 99). "On the contrary, it is only by undertaking actual measurements of capacity that sufficient experience can be gained to interpret and evaluate the accuracy of the results" (p. 100). "The economics of computer operations upset preconceptions of what is feasible. Arithmetic has become very cheap" (p. 113).

De Leeuw: "The demand for capacity figures has been brisk in recent years, but the supply continues to be small and of uncertain quality. There is no doubt that we know much less about capacity than we know about output, prices, or employment. The primary problems of capacity measurement, therefore, are how to make judicious use of the limited supply of capacity figures available, and how to increase the supply" (p. 121). The so-called engineering definition of capacity interprets 'can produce' as 'can produce regardless of cost,' which really means can produce at less than what the engineer considers as prohibitive marginal cost" (p. 122). "Price and cost pressures are one important set of variables which appear to respond to changes in the degree of capacity utilization.... Another direction in which capacity utilization appears to exert a major influence is the demand for new plant and equipment" (p. 123). "Physical capacity data are simply not available for most industries" (p. 124).

Schultz: "Capacity is a very difficult thing to measure in any industry. The concept is not precise, to begin with. Does it refer to a maximum output under certain specified conditions, or to an optimum, most profitable output? Do you measure capacity with one 8-hour shift? Or two? Or three? What is the rate of seasonal factors? Of design changes; of shifts in the mix? How do you define your industry? Who is in it? What is the role of technological change?" (p. 148). "Capacity data on the 'maximum' basis would offer a more useful guide to effective capacity, and particularly to changes in capacity over time, than do the figures on the historic basis" (p. 158). "The capacity estimates so obtained should not be regarded as precise measures of capacity; as indicated, capacity cannot be measured with the precision the statistician would like" (p. 160). "In spite of problems of technological change, in spite of difficulties of concept and coverage, it is possible, on the basis of available data, to develop a consistent set of capacity figures for the paper industry.... These figures have been developed from trade association data, based on surveys of individual machines, and have been adjusted to reflect changing operating policies and practices. In total, these comments, plus the remainder of the testimony, point out the ever-growing concern with capacity that falls on the heels of any postwar economy" (p. 164).

Hickman, Bert G. 1964. "On a New Method of Capacity Estimation." *American Statistical Association Journal*, June, pp. 529–549.

Using a logarithmic approach, this article suggests a new method for capacity estimation, which in turn suggests that during the 1960 period under study most industries in the United States were operating well over capacity. Interesting insights include: "The first assumption is that real net fixed investment (change in real net capital stock) in any given year is proportional to the difference between actual and desired capital stock" (p. 530). "Owing to technical progress, new assets are generally more productive than older assets of equal real cost. One way to allow for quality improvements in capital goods is to weight the surviving capital goods of each vintage by a 'productivity improvement factor' that increases over time.... An alternative followed here is to measure the capital stock at its net depreciated value" (p. 531). "At any given time, then, capacity—an output variable—depends on the size of the capital stock, the level of production technique, and the prices of productive resources" (pp. 535-536).

Jones, R. Kendall. 1957. "Why Not Capacity Costing?" *NAA Bulletin*. November, pp. 13–21.

This article argues for "capacity costing" as a midpoint between full cost and direct cost. Capacity costing, or the assignment of direct cost plus utilized plant expenses, provides accurate, stable cost estimates and serves as a useful tool/proxy for utilization and efficiency (per the author). He argues for an idle charge on the income statement. Comments include: "He [the author] is looking for ways to eliminate excess standby or unusual costs from inventory value and, by doing so, to have more realistic product costs" (p. 13). "Its [capacity costing] advantages are, first, that it is similar to direct costing as to stabilization of product costs. Further, only one cost is needed for each product. Then, too, inventory is valued at a conservative amount, as all abnormal or unused fixed costs are excluded. The valuation basis is an acceptable accounting practice.... Beyond this, unused or idle capacity is highlighted for management as to areas and cost" (p. 14). "Unused capacity cost is calculated by the author as: [(practical capacity volume – actual volume) divided by practical capacity volume] times fixed expense = cost of unused capacity" (p. 16). (Practical capacity is defined on a 40-hour week with reductions for "unavoidable" downtime.) "In order to present a picture which will more closely depict the 'unused capacity cost,' a means must be devised of determining a monthly 'unused capacity credit' for each of the production departments. Not only will this relieve the department head of an unused expense for which he is not responsible but it will also readily determine a figure which can be used for the presentation of information to management" (pp. 18–19).

Keller, I. Wayne. 1958. "Capacity Utilization Studies for Cost Control and Reduction." *NAA Bulletin*, July, pp. 38–45.

This is an excellent piece on capacity for this period, containing many practical suggestions for managing the costs and transactions inherent in this complex area. Specific comments include: "In the factory nonoperating machine time not only increases the unit cost of production but also reduces the quantity of product which can be offered for sale" (p. 38). "Cost accounting literature is deficient in case material on the study of utilization of the productive capacity of individual machines" (p. 39). "The key to increased utilization of machine capacity is detailed analysis of what each machine is actually doing, or not doing, every hour and fraction of an hour of the day.... It would seem desirable to have every request for capital appropriations for additional machines supported by capacity utilization studies of the existing machines" (p. 40).

"Periodic analysis on a rotating basis throughout a plant will provide adequate data. In fact, very good results have been obtained by using work-sampling techniques in these studies" (pp. 40–41). "Our management reports are based on practical capacity utilization and the spread between this and absolute capacity is generally not discussed. Management has no idea how great it is" (p. 41). "With the advent of direct costing, the attention given to normal volume has tended to decline. This is unfortunate for normal volume is a vital figure under both direct and absorption costing.... Having determined practical capacity and normal volume, the significant consideration is the ratio of normal volume to practical capacity.... A very general range may be set at from 65 per cent to 85 per cent. Ratios above or below this range are signals that studies should be made" (p. 44). "Through capacity utilization studies we can control them—keep them from increasing and, in many instances, we can generate action to reduce or eliminate them" (p. 45).

Klein, L. R. 1960. "Some Theoretical Issues in the Measurement of Capacity." *Econometrica*, April, pp. 272–286.

Alternative approaches to the measurement of capacity are possible. Economic aspects of capacity measurement, as contrasted with pure engineering considerations, involve the introduction of cost considerations and limitations imposed by interdependence of different sectors of the economy. Some approaches to capacity measurement in terms of cost functions are explored, particularly as properties of a total cost function. A method of aggregating individual capacity, taking into account the interdependence of an input-output model, is outlined. Capacity measures so obtained are useful as descriptive statistics of economic efficiency and as explanatory variables in modern theories of investment behavior.

Other comments include: "Economic analysis is replete with use of the term *capacity,* yet comparatively little attention is devoted to a precise theoretical statement of the concept.... Capacity is a prominent variable in several modern business cycle theories, especially those based on a version of the acceleration principle. Capacity plays a less important role in the theory of the firm, but its statistical treatment has been more satisfactorily developed there" (p. 272). "Chamberlin gives an implication that imperfect competition causes inefficiency in economic organization and thus gives rise to excess capacity. Full capacity would be defined as the output level associated with full competitive equilibrium. For the individual firm this point would occur at the minimum of the average cost curve" (p. 273). "Technically, capacity for a firm or other small sector may mean very little in the absence of cost considerations" (p. 274). "Capacity output is thus the production flow associated with the input of fully utilized manpower, capital, and other relevant factors of production. ...[this] definition of capacity output in terms of a zero-profit competitive economy depends on the price system prevailing" (p. 275). "Suppose it is decided to measure capacity as the minimal point on a firm's cost curve" (p. 277). "A model developed...in terms of production functions will show how the capacity point changes when prices and unit costs change" (p. 280).

National Association of Accountants. 1963. "Digest of NAA Research Report No. 39: Accounting for Costs of Capacity." *NAA Bulletin*, May, pp. 8–10.

As a useful starting point for understanding the implications of RR #39, the entire article should be read. The key points it explores from the research report are controlling capacity costs through planning, improving profits by better use of capacity, assigning capacity costs to periods for measuring performance, and assigning capacity costs to product. In the study, capacity costs are defined as "the continuing costs of having capacity to manufacture and to sell." Noting that the nature of capacity costs differs significantly with respect to the timing and types of actions which can be taken to control future costs, the study breaks capacity costs into *committed* and *managed* cost components. This categorization provides the authors with the tools needed to meet the multiple demands placed on capacity cost numbers. Completely summarizing this document, and Research Report No. 39 underlying it, would take a book in itself. It is required reading.

Phillips, A. 1963. "Industrial Capacity: An Appraisal of Measures of Capacity." *American Economic Association: Papers and Proceedings*, pp. 275–292.

"In pure concept, the labor force and capital are much the same. Each is a stock of an economic resource available for the production of goods. Similarly, both the number of unemployed and the volume of excess capacity indicate the extent to which society is failing to use these resources" (p. 275). This opening comment summarizes the position taken in this paper. Phillips believes that the movement to measure industrial capacity in the mid-1960s was comparable to movements to measure labor efficiency in earlier times—too vague, too global, and useless in focusing attention on individual, manageable items of excess and idle resources.

He then goes on to overview five recent capacity studies, from the McGraw-Hill Department of Economics, the National Industrial Conference Board, *Fortune* magazine, the Wharton School Economics Research Unit, and the Division of Research and Statistics, Federal Reserve System. "In this context, capacity does not mean simply the 'maximum output under normal work schedules.' Given factor and product prices, capacity is an output rate which, if sustained with balanced facilities over a period of time, would induce neither net investment or disinvestment in real capacity in privately managed enterprises" (p. 287). "With this view, undepreciated values—as a measure of total equipment in place regardless of age—appear more relevant to physical output capability than do the net values. If the output concept is value-added and the capital is to be valued in terms of the current least cost alternative for producing that output, whether or not that alternative is in fact in use, the depreciated values seem the better. Current incremental capital-to-value-added ratios for balanced expansions multiplied by total current value-added might be a better way to obtain such an economic valuation of capital than any methods based on treating historical costs, but the relevance of this to current capability to produce goods is not at all clear.... It is clear that the appropriate output measure is value-added, not gross output, even if the ratio does not change" (p. 289).

Randelman, Carlton. 1956. "Achieving Benefits of Practical and Average Capacity in Burden Accounting." *NACA Bulletin*, November, pp. 376–383.

This article shows that direct costing did not capture all the companies in the 1950s. The difference between the needs of good management of capacity and of pricing is well stated. Is this a current problem? Specific comments: "Burden accounting on a 'full costing' basis remains a prevalent practice" (p. 376). "A normal burden rate is found by dividing normal rate of activity into the estimated burden for that rate of activity.... Balances in burden accounts charged off annually under this theory simply represent inaccuracy in rate determination.... To others, normal rate of activity means the volume at which the plant is equipped to operate or the maximum capacity attainable. Its corollary is that, if the plant operates at this rate of activity, all fixed costs will be charged to production but that, at a lesser capacity, the debit balances left in the burden accounts will be a fairly accurate measure of unused capacity and should be charged to profit and loss as such.... It [idleness cost] results from lack of sales orders required to maintain the maximum commercial demands which the plant could meet, possibly a capacity to produce more than the company can hope to sell. In this light it is nothing more than current cost of past mistakes and it is not wise to assume that this condition will correct itself within the economical life of the excess equipment" (p. 377).

"It is probable that a preponderance of companies using normal capacity based on ability to produce only define normal as the practical capacity of the plant as a whole (the practical capacity of each department considered individually), rather than to scale it down to the department of least capacity. Primary concern is with total productive capacity" (p. 378). "Lack of balance in activity between machines and processes will also be apparent from the same figures. Moreover, in setting up a procedure to accumulate the costs of idle time, the production man may fulfill his ultimate aim to eliminate idle capacity.... For price-setting purposes, then, and for purposes of establishing long-range price policies, normal capacity considered as capacity to make and sell, and based upon anticipated sales of a term of future years to approximate the period required for the realization of fixed investment, is the prerequisite for a sound price policy" (p. 379). "The degree to which he [the accountant] has informed management of the meaning of accounting information has a real bearing, for the efficiency and accuracy with which the theory of normal burden rates is to function and the adequacy of a particular interpretation of the theory of normal burden rates in serving the variety of purposes for which costs are used depends entirely upon management understanding of statistical and cost data" (p. 383).

Schultz, Robert S. 1963. "Profits, Prices, and Excess Capacity." *Harvard Business Review*, July-August, pp. 68–81.

In management circles, there are various shibboleths regarding the problem of excess capacity—for instance, "compete nicely" and "sell by service, not price." None of these shibboleths, states Schultz, is really useful for management. Focus is on using market logic and pricing to incorporate the very real impact increased capacity has on market prices and demand. "Sometimes one feels as if he is the only sane person in a lunatic asylum.... Capacity is difficult to define, and once defined, is still difficult to measure.... Economic theory treats the topic only implicitly, while the 'practicing economists' consider it only in a vacuum. Note, for example, the way many business economists in recent years have discussed under one heading the unfortunate fact of existing excess capacity, and then under another heading have called for higher levels of investment activity to 'get the economy moving again,' as though the cure for excess capacity were more capacity" (p. 68).

"From the viewpoint of resource use, excess capacity represents a misallocation of the factors of production, and thus economic waste.... But the aspect...with which this paper is concerned is the impact of excess capacity on prices, on profit margins, and on profits..." (p. 69). "Some commentators stress the favorable aspect for the nation as a whole: excess capacity is a curb on inflation.... The profit squeeze is not an independent, isolated phenomenon. The profit squeeze is the signal of the marketplace that there is too much capacity.... The short-range problem of living with existing excess capacity obviously differs from the long-range problem of attempting to prevent economic waste..." (p. 70) "These exhortations to behave like good little boys (e.g., to not compete on price when excess capacity is present, but rather to compete nicely) have about as much relevance to the real world of rough, tough, competitive business as the prayer that opens a political convention has to the subsequent proceedings."

Schultz then notes the ways companies try to deal with excess capacity problems in the short term: "(1) Compete nicely (won't work...), (2) Watch your costs. Certainly....an industry-wide cost reduction simply means a lower price. (3) Watch your costing. Know what it costs you to make what you sell. Again, certainly. This idea shows a touching faith in the ability of an industry or a company to charge whatever price it finds appropriate for its profit target—a faith which is widespread in prosperous times, but which in times of low operating rates seems to be shared only by Gardiner Means, Roger Blough, and President Kennedy. As any first year economics student knows, except in very special circumstances...overhead costs are given and, to use the terminology of economic theory, profits are maximized in relation to variable costs.... It is only after a company has decided on capacity that its overhead costs become fixed. (4) Sell by service, not by price.... Lower prices, longer terms, quicker delivery, greater variety—these are all part of the general marketing mix. There are many forms of competition, and the alert organization uses each and every competitive device to the fullest extent it finds appropriate. To emphasize quality and service when the customers want lower prices, and when the competition is offering lower prices, is a most distinguished road to bankruptcy. (5) Trust to industrial statesmanship.... Industrial statesmanship really means protection of the price structure by giving accounts to competitors....The company which sticks to list too long will lose valuable customers it should be able to keep, and may see competitive pressures ultimately force prices down anyway" (pp. 71–72).

"...these preachments suggest solutions which would work only by abolishing the laws of supply and demand...after a while, demand will rise to capacity levels. Capacity may not be excessive but only premature. If basic demand is strong and growing, growth should ameliorate, or terminate, the conditions of excess capacity." He then describes chiseling versus meat-axe competitive threats. "The chiseling approach (a tad more capacity) leads to reasonable price adjustments in the market. The meat axe (10% or more off the market price) leads to convulsions and demoralization as price structures are smashed. This threat cannot be met through industrial statesmanship" (p. 73). "...under the wild demoralization which characterizes the price structure of an industry when the cleaver is in use, prices probably get pushed, temporarily at least, below the equilibrium level" (p. 74).

"In preventing excess capacity, as in adjusting to it, management faces two types of problems: (1) the adoption of reasonable policies from its own immediate point of view; and (2) the adoption of policies that make sense in view of the actions or likely actions of competing firms" (p. 76). "The profitability of any expansion program must not be judged in terms of current prices, for it is a reasonable assumption that the price will be lower when the new capacity goes into operation.... New capacity while building is thus a kind of time bomb.... This general problem of price weakening as new capacity enters the market tends to be accentuated by business-cycle factors..." (p. 77). "The equilibrium level of capacity for an industry is the level where the going profit rate equals the interest rate (the cost of capital) plus whatever premium is needed to encourage risk taking in the particular industry..." (p. 78). "Sometimes expansion of capacity goes beyond the equilibrium level determined by capital costs and risk premiums; it is not justified by any sudden, sharp technological breakthrough. *Here there is social waste.... The answer is: Competition*" (p. 79). "The basic point of all action aimed at preventing excess capacity is to short-circuit the gestation period for capital goods, so that companies contemplating expansion will not be deceived by the strength of the current price level" (p. 80).

Subcommittee on Economic Statistics. 1962. *Measures of Productive Capacity*. Joint Economic Committee, GPO, Washington, pp. 1–8.

This book is a useful document for understanding macroeconomic issues and trends in capacity expansion and utilization. "Productive capacity is among the oldest, most used, and most important concepts in economic analysis" (p. 2). "Capacity is not directly observable…. Users of capacity measures find the available data inadequate for their needs because of lack of consistent definitions and rules of measurement, insufficient coverage, lack of detail in existing data, failure to report regularly, and at frequent intervals, and lack of integration with other economic measures—output, employment, etc.—at both the aggregate and detailed industry and product levels" (p. 3). "The Office of Statistical Standards of the Bureau of the Budget should take the lead in organizing a cooperative effort…directed toward early development of generally accepted standards covering the definition of capacity" (p. 4). "Reliable benchmarks for this work of measuring capital stock by the perpetual inventory method requires an inventory of the Nation's capital, whenever the technical problems can be solved" (p. 5).

Ulin, Robert P. 1955. "Are We Building Too Much Capacity?" *Harvard Business Review*, November-December, pp. 41–47.

Focused on providing analysis of, and solutions for, capacity expansion problems at the planning stage of the business cycle, this article provides a general commentary on capacity management. "Most important is an aggressive policy of research in plant and equipment design, aimed to reduce the future cost of a unit of capacity. Another important goal of this research should be to reduce the 'chunky' characteristics of new capacity so additions can be made in relatively small blocks as needed, and/or to increase the flexibility of capacity where relatively large units must be involved" (p. 46). "The way to keep excess capacity from becoming a general problem is to plan new capacity carefully. The men who do it are the production

and financial managers who screen new plant proposals....
But a wild rush to get on the bandwagon with more capacity—any kind of capacity, just to keep up with the next fel-
low—could lead us into serious trouble.... Only careful planning will ensure that this new capacity becomes a real asset
rather than a threat to economic stability" (p. 47).

Weinwurm, Ernest H. 1961. "The Importance of Idle Capacity Cost."
Accounting Review, July, pp. 418–421.

Focused on refuting many of the arguments made by Ferrara
in his July 1960 article, this rebuttal is concerned with the
fact that theory and reality are often different—and that while
Ferrara's model may sound good in theory, it does little to
address the critical and real issues that idle capacity represents. "...management has a vital interest in the amount of
idle capacity cost which will always be a determining factor in
decision-making. The concept is not merely an engineering problem, as asserted by Professor Ferrara, but one of significance to
accounting as well. It follows that the accountant is duty bound
to keep management constantly informed of current idle capacity costs..." (p. 419). "It would be a bad thing to avoid
showing these idle capacity costs for the particular period to
which they apply. To do so would be tantamount to depriving
management of one of its more important measures of operating and managerial efficiency.... Experience has shown it is one
of the important but often very difficult tasks of the industrial
accountant to make operating people aware of the undeniable
fact that existing idle capacity involves a constant accumulation of costs.... There is an urgent need to reduce the gap between the task of accounting to serve managerial decision-making and the somewhat narrow and self-centered attitude of many
accounting practitioners who are in danger of losing sight of
those really important tasks of the profession" (p. 421).

1965–1978

Bartenstein, Edwin. 1976. "An Annotated Bibliography for Historical Research in Accounting (with an Emphasis on Product

Costing under Conditions of Idle Plant Capacity)." Working paper No. 25, Academy of Accounting Historians.

This work provides a solid summary list of books and key articles for the 1930–1970 period. In general, we see an early preference for charging idle costs to profit and loss, giving way to full costing in the early 1960s. Ferrara and NAA concept statement #1 seem pivotal in the full costing push. NAA statement #6 states that "over the long run the full costs of all facilities have to be recovered in selling prices."

_____. 1978. "Different Costs for Different Purposes." *Management Accounting*, August, pp. 42–47.

The title of this article says it all. The author presents convincingly the arguments for full product costing as well as a very high-level discussion of why idle capacity charges should not be considered part of inventoriable costs. The key arguments suggest that, as purposes for information change, so should the numbers. The author ends with a forward-looking suggestion that cost data become part of a raw data bank that can be aggregated as needed only.

Of interest is Bartenstein's division of capacity into three key elements, physical, organizational, and financial, which he argues must be balanced if optimum capacity utilization is to be reached. "...[A] reiteration of the often stated position that, in the long run, all costs are variable...requires care and precision in use. As the costs of capacity increase, the potential for increased production is created. But production itself is not increased. Increased production may or may not result from increased costs of capacity. Thus it is questionable whether the costs of capacity can ever be considered to be variable costs, even in the long run..." (p. 43). "Even though it may be useful for control purposes to separate out the costs of idle capacity, it is not reasonable to consider them period costs or losses.... The establishment of capacity in any form is a long-range decision.... The problem resulting from uneven use of the facility and the related idle capacity costs, are simply problems of measurement and have no place in a purely theoretical discussion. If all capacity costs are shared by products, we again reach the conclusion that all costs of capacity, including idle capacity costs, are product costs.... idle capacity is that capacity which is not used productively at a specific time..." (p. 44).

"...idle capacity costs are not among those that are controlled at the manufacturing plant level. Much more valuable information for control purposes is made available to management if idle capacity costs are kept separate and are not included in product costs.... 'planned' idle capacity has nothing to do with the costs of manufacturing products. There is no good reason to inventory such costs which were knowingly incurred for an entirely different purpose.... If inventory is burdened with idle capacity costs there is an unavoidable implication of value. An item is not necessarily worth more because it costs more to produce.... The time relationship is accidental in that the product in question came through one production line when some other line was not operating at full capacity.... Because idle capacity costs do not influence future costs or result in future costs avoidance, they cannot be assets or be added to the value or costs of assets such as inventory" (p. 45).

Belt, Bill. 1976. "Integrating Capacity Planning and Capacity Control." *Production and Inventory Management*, first quarter, pp. 9–25.

This practical article suggests an input-output approach to capacity planning and control that is driven by an assumed level of optimal backlog. While interesting in development, the author clearly reflects a machine or work center focus that ignores actual plant throughput in its analysis. "Input-output planning, based on planned and released orders from MRP, with forward visibility of queue size, recognizes the stabilizing function of backlog in the shop and reduces capacity planning to the essentials—planned input, planned output, and planned queue" (p. 25). This assumes away JIT, cellular, or other modern manufacturing techniques and their impact. In summary, then, the article is very reductionist, pre-throughput-model oriented. It defines capacity as rate expressed in units per hour, while load is measured in hours. These two views of machine activity and control he finds incompatible.

Chiu, James, and John Talbott. 1978. "Factory Overhead Variance Analysis." *Managerial Planning*, July/August, pp. 36–39.

Reflecting the ongoing focus on standard costing typical of this period, this article suggests that the volume variance is superior to idle capacity charges. This judgment is based on a survey, which suggests that if three-way analysis of overhead variances is done, they use the volume variance. "The volume variance is the difference between the factory overhead budgeted for the capacity attained measured in standard productive hours and the factory overhead which has been applied.... As long as the labor hour is chosen as the independent variable in the measurement of factory overhead, the spending variance should be the difference between the actual factory overhead and the budgeted overhead at actual hours worked" (p. 36).

DeCoster, Don T. 1966. "Measurement of the Idle Capacity Variance." *Accounting Review*, April, pp. 297–302.

This article represents a very weak discussion with little awareness of the richness of the idle-time literature. "At the present time a disparity exists within accounting literature in quantifying the idle-capacity variance. The divergent methods used to calculate the variance indicate that, as yet, accountants have failed to agree on its meaning.... the heart of the problem lies with the volume measurement" (p. 297). "It assumes that the limiting factor of production is plant and equipment.... One group, and undoubtedly the first to focus attention on the subject, visualizes the idle capacity variances as measuring the cost of physical idleness.... The second group ascribes no physical connotation to the variance" (p. 298). "This assumption is not correct. Idle hours will result from maintaining productive facilities or capabilities that are not used to their maximum output potential. However, the cost of these idle hours is not apparent" (p. 299). "The volume base selected should be based upon the logically determined effort needed to achieve the planned output in an efficient manner over a pre-selected time period.... With the predetermined standard rate the idle capacity variance is best described as the amount of fixed overhead the company could have absorbed if the actual activity had been the same as the standard hours" (p. 300). "The efficiency variance is the difference between the standard hours in equivalent production and the hours multiplied by the variable segment of the overhead rate" (p. 301). "The theory and practice of overhead costing have progressed at a somewhat slower pace and perhaps with somewhat less understanding than many other phases of cost accounting.... The concept of idle capacity has not been subjected to careful examination and there has been little philosophical development in this area" (p. 302).

DeLeeuw, Frank, Frank E. Hopkins, and Michael D. Sherman. 1966. "A Revised Index of Manufacturing Capacity." *Federal Reserve Bulletin*, November, pp. 1605–15.

This article reiterates the vagueness of capacity measurement at the national level during 1960–1970. "This article describes a set of estimates of capacity and capacity utilization in U. S. manufacturing industries. The estimates represent a revision of a series maintained at the FRB for the past six years. They are crude and subject to much larger measurement errors than many other time series in common use.... The meaning of capacity as measured in these estimates is of necessity imprecise" (p. 1605). "There is no information available as to exactly what respondents to capacity surveys have in mind" (p. 1606). "The data for the construction of the gross capital stock series were obtained principally from an official census of manufacturers and from the surveys of manufacturers published in noncensus years since 1947" (p. 1608).

Grant, Philip C. 1974. "Minimizing Idle Time Costs." *Journal of Systems Management*, May, pp. 38–40.

Heavily quantitative in nature, this article focuses on idle time in the administrative area using queueing and reliability theory. The goal is to minimize the joint costs of delay, idle time, and failure costs in the management process. While interesting in focus, the paper leaves much to be desired in the area of depth and usability.

Grinnell, D. Jacque. 1975. "Activity Levels and the Disposition of Volume Variances." *Management Accounting*, August, pp. 29–32, 36.

This article establishes a framework for viewing the relationship between the choice of activity level and the year-end disposition of resulting variances, with an emphasis on product costing impacts. Three options for disposing of the volume variance are noted: charge the variance to income, apportion the volume variance between income and inventory, or defer it to future years on the balance sheet. "A proper choice among the three available options...is dependent on the activity level selected for establishing the fixed overhead absorption rate. ...the volume variance should be disposed in three parts, based on the nature of the expense based on expected annual capacity (budget), normal capacity, and practical capacity. Unexpected annual volume variances should be written off against income, while those due to longer term variances embedded in practical capacity decisions should be written off over time" (p. 29).

Huss, Jerry. 1969. "Planning and Controlling Overhead." *Journal of Accountancy*, July, pp. 83–85.

This piece misses the key issues in idle capacity totally. "While effective standards have generally been developed for evaluating material and labor costs, overhead is too often treated as a cost over which little control can be exercised" (p. 83). "More and more frequently companies are effectively using committees of operating managers to determine the course of and the cure for significant variances.... Management, of course, would be equipped with a much better control tool if it were told (as a result of variance analysis) exactly what causes variances rather than just which costs are out of line" (p. 85).

Johnson, Paulette. 1976. "Decision-Making Aspects of Overhead Variance Analysis." *Cost and Management* (Canada), November-December, pp. 49–53.

While predominantly concerned with variance analysis, this author suggests several useful ties between variance approaches, contribution margin, and idle/opportunity cost views of capacity management. She provides descriptions and examples of a "four-way" overhead variance model and its benefits, including spending, efficiency, effectiveness, and volume components. "Fixed overhead not applied because the plant did not operate at denominator activity is the volume

variance. The effectiveness variance represents fixed overhead not applied because actual hours differed from standard
hours.... [S]pending and efficiency...are incurred on a direct
cause-effect basis.... Rather than resulting from cause-effect
relationships, the volume variances have more of an opportunity cost concept. Fixed costs cannot be eliminated through
greater efficiency in the short run. They can only be spread
over more units" (p. 50).

"When choosing a denominator activity the decision maker
must remember that it influences two important factors: the
application of fixed overhead costs to products and the volume variance.... The volume variance, often used for performance evaluation and control purposes, influences activity in
the immediate future. When costing and pricing products,
any firm which hopes to be successful must recover its costs
in the long run" (p. 51). "Practical capacity adds relevance to
the volume variance, now the product of the fixed overhead
rate and the difference between practical capacity and actual
hours. It now represents the historical fixed costs of idleness"
(p. 52).

Klein, Lawrence, and Robert Summers. 1966. *The Wharton Index of
Capacity Utilization.* Philadelphia: Economic Research Unit,
University of Pennsylvania, pp. 1–4, 8, 49–51, 90–94.

A good bibliography of work in this area, this index and its
description play a prominent role in capacity analysis at the
macroeconomic level during this period. "In our present
econometric forecasting model, we find that our measure of
capacity utilization is an important variable in the investment
function, price equation, hours worked equation, and production functions. In addition, the industry measures of capacity
utilization have been found to be significant variables in industry investment and profit functions" (p. 1). "Our empirical efforts are directed at measuring the following concept:
the capacity of an industry at a particular time is the maximum sustainable level of output the industry can attain within
a very short time if the demand for its product were not a
constraining factor, when the industry is operating its existing stock of capital at its customer level of intensity.... Be-

cause the denominator, value (potential output) is observable only occasionally, it must be estimated somehow, and here is where the trend-through peaks method is used.… In this work, it was assumed, unless auxiliary information pointed strongly in a contrary direction, that a relative peak in an industry's time series of actual output, in fact, represents the potential output that the industry could produce at the time of the peak" (p. 2). "We feel that our figures are of the right order of magnitude, but we are primarily concerned with making sure that they show a good series of quarter-to-quarter movement in utilization rates" (p. 91).

Kravitz, Bernard J. 1968. "The Standard Cost Review—A Seldom Used Management Tool." *Management Accounting*, August, pp. 33–36.

This article is one more example of the poverty of thinking in volume variances, as compared to the idle time analysis that it replaced. "Varying opinions exist regarding the frequency with which standard costs should be revised. The conditions necessitating such revision may be classified as internal or external. Technological advances, design revisions, method changes, labor rate adjustments, and changes in physical facilities are among the internal conditions" (p. 33). "Ideally procedures enabling continuous review should be included when designing the standard cost system" (p. 34). "However, in the case of the overhead volume variance, the standard cost review can be facilitated by segregating the planned volume variance (resulting from the difference between practical capacity and the standard capacity level) and the operating volume variance attributed to scheduling errors and other manufacturing inefficiencies" (p. 36).

Lev, Baruch. 1969. "An Information Theory Analysis of Budget Variances." *Accounting Review*, October, pp. 704–710.

In this article, Lev suggests that control charting may be a useful way to graph and analyze variances. "… past data are usually not sufficient in volume and stability to define the statistical universe and to estimate the parameters needed in determining the significance of the variances" (p. 704). "[D]eviation of the decomposed variances from proportionality indicates their significance for further investigation" (p. 705). "The significance of variances of decomposition budgets for further investigation depends on the degree of interdependence within the decomposition. The weaker the interdependence, the more rewarding a detailed investigation..." (pp. 709–710).

Nielsen, Oswald. 1969. "The Role of Variances in Management Control." *Management Accounting*, October, pp. 26–28.

Another in the long stream of articles that illustrate the weakness of volume variances as a replacement for idle time information. "Controllability exists in the sense that management can either eliminate or minimize variances through positive, persistent action" (p. 26). "Putting it another way, the larger the variance is relative to the gross margin, the more important it is that the causes for variance be analyzed and eliminated. ...as long as cost of investigation and correction is less than the variance there is inducement to eliminate the variance. This applies particularly for low rate of gross profit margin activity" (p. 28).

Petri, Enrico, and Roland Minch. 1972. "Capacity Variance: Responsibility and Control." *Management Accounting*, April, pp. 38–41.

This article focuses on using normal capacity as the baseline measure and its impact on the capacity variance reporting process. It notes that there is an input approach to capacity reporting (actual labor and fixed costs at normal capacity) and an output approach (matching actuals against standard costs). The key point made in this article, though, is that true idle capacity, or available but unutilized, is marketing's responsibility and should be reported in such a way as to make this responsibility clear. The result is a series of complex variances aimed at providing data similar to those generated by Gantt in a much more usable format.

Interesting comments include: "Normal capacity is an expression of expected long run sales on an annual basis. Normal capacity considers productive facilities available, the normal efficiency with which they are used and the desired inventory levels. In essence, it is demand oriented. Practical capacity, on the other hand, considers the maximum operating capacity of the plant modified for unavoidable delays. Practical capacity is, therefore, supply oriented.... [C]osts not expected to generate revenues should be recorded as losses" (p. 39). "Fixed costs, costs that are not a direct function of volume, may be dichotomized as sunk costs and out-of-pocket costs. Sunk costs are those costs which have been incurred in the past and are now being allocated or written-off in the current time period. Since sunk costs have been incurred in the past, they will remain relatively stable and can be forecasted with a reasonable degree of certainty. ...out-of-pocket costs can and do change...[and] are incurred at discrete points in production, ...threshold points" (p. 40). "...the traditional volume variance was separated into four components. These include the production efficiency variance, idle capacity (marketing) variance, off capacity variance and the out-of-pocket spending variance. ... Our discount approach to unit sunk cost determination is a form of 'opportunity cost' that measures the aggregate present value of sales lost through inefficient production" (p. 41).

Prochaska, Fred J. 1978. "Theoretical and Empirical Considerations for Estimating Capacity and Capacity Utilization in Commercial Fisheries." *American Journal of Agricultural Economics*, December, pp. 1020–1025.

While this article may seem outside the realm of "business" issues, in reality it brings to life the key microeconomic issues surrounding capacity in a way that only a trained economist can do. Comments include: "Economic efficiency is often discussed in terms of optimum capacity.... The state of economic science with respect to capacity considerations has been summarized by Stigler as follows, 'The notion of capacity is widely used, but seldom defined precisely. Yet it is an ambiguous concept at best.' ... In the long run, optimum economic capacity generally refers to the scale of plant at which long-run average cost is a minimum" (p. 1020). "Dockside...prices directly affect through profit the rate of capacity utilization in the short run and the level of capacity in the long run.... Retail prices affect optimum capacity and rate of capacity utilization in the processing and marketing sectors.... In summary, the theoretical components which determine capacity and the extent of capacity utilization are the factors affecting individual firm cost structures such as input prices and catch per unit of effort, prices throughout the market system, prices and quantities of substitute products, and input constraints. This total or systems approach to considering capacity and its utilization is not inconsistent with empirical measures of capacity employed by economists interested in questions of capacity of total segments within the economy or the total economy" (p. 1021).

"Empirical estimates of capacity and its utilization are extremely difficult to make for any industry because of insufficient basic research, insufficient required data and inconsistent reporting procedures.... Storage, processing, and onshore holding capacity may limit or prevent the harvesting sector from fully utilizing its capacity during peak production seasons" (p. 1022). "Capacity is based on long-run considerations of expected prices and costs. There is little flexibility in plant and equipment size within production periods, especially in the processing sector. Rate at which capacity is utilized, however, is more flexible and can be changed in response to short-run changes in price, costs and other considerations" (p. 1025).

Purdy, Charles R. 1965. "Industry Patterns of Capacity or Volume Choice: Their Existence and Rationale." *Journal of Accounting Research*, pp. 228–241.

This article used empirical research to determine whether or not there were, as of 1963, industry patterns in the chosen capacity baseline. The database for the study was generated from 373 surveys mailed to industrial firms across various industries. The reasons put forward for expecting differences were: (1) the objectives of overhead costing, i.e., (a) efficient plant utilization, (b) pricing, (c) income measurement, and (d) compliance with law; or (2) the problems of overhead costing, i.e., (a) relative measurability of capacity concepts (as affected by type of product, manufacturing process, and relative stability of production), (b) cost structure-cost behavior, and (c) relative adaptability of capacity to changing demand.

Finally, since firms producing similar products were felt to face similar problems, the author suggested that industry patterns would emerge. "When practical capacity (a physical maximum based upon 100% time, three shifts, seven days a week) is used, the choice presumes relatively high fixed costs and considerable linearity in cost behavior. This results in a condition wherein minimum average cost and minimum average fixed cost occur at or very near the same output. On the other hand, the use of what I shall call a time-segmented capacity (e.g., one shift, five days per week) presumes curvilinear cost behavior with minimum average cost attainment when those segments are operated. The proof of this lies in the fact that such firms increase their capacity rather than consistently operating existing facilities at levels above these time segments" (p. 230).

The results: "It appears that, if a comprehensive view of overhead costing is taken, differences in capacity choice cannot be explained on the basis of the different objectives of efficiency, pricing, and income measurement..." (p. 237). "There seems to be some correlation between capacity measures and the overhead costing problems faced by the industry, but the results obtained by a certain choice in a specific industry may not vary greatly from those obtained by a different choice in a different industry. ...it may be that firms tend to make volume choices which, in view of their accounting problems, approximate minimum average cost" (p. 240).

Ronen, Joshua. 1970. "Capacity and Operating Variances: An Ex Post Approach." *Journal of Accounting Research*, Autumn, pp. 232–252.

Ronen's approach focuses on developing a series of ex post capacity variances that "improve decisions regarding the design of capacity and its subsequent utilization." Four capacity variances are suggested: (1) ex post opportunity cost capacity planning variances, which focus on profits forgone due to improper estimates of actual demand on the facility; (2) capacity implementation variance that focuses on the difference between planned and actual available capacity and its related opportunity costs; (3) the total reduction in profit given 1 and 2;

(4) the cost of not adjusting capacity to the level dictated by the ex post information. "What is common [to capacity variance discussions] is the underlying assumption of a fixed capacity; thus the main concern is how to control and motivate 'full utilization'" (p. 233).

"The optimal capacity for a given output is not achieved by building the plant for which the given output is provided at minimum short-run average cost. Rather it is the plant which has the minimum average cost of any possible plant for the given output" (p. 234). "...optimization of the production function involves equating, at the margin, the marginal cost of any factor of production with its marginal revenue product.... [U]sing the dimension of time to distinguish between costs of capacity and cost of current operations does not appear useful. A better distinction can be made along a responsibility dimension.... From an evaluation and motivation standpoint, only controllable costs are relevant.... This distinction suggests that the surrogates needed for planning and control of operation decisions differ from those required for the planning and control of capital decisions" (p. 237).

"If the output-price decision is delegated to the plant manager who does not control the capacity decision, he will maximize his apparent short-run profits...at the output at which marginal revenue equals the short-run marginal cost..." (p. 244). "When adjustment costs are introduced, the plant should not be expanded unless the additional profits exceed the adjustment costs" (p. 245). "We assume adjustment costs to be a function of the additional investment needed to reach the optimal level" (p. 248). "...it highlights the potential sources of suboptimal output as a result of interaction between the capacity decisions and operating decisions" (p. 252).

Shwayder, Keith. 1968. "A Note of a Contribution Margin Approach to the Analysis of Capacity Utilization." *Accounting Review*, January, pp. 101–104.

This note suggests a dichotomization of unused capacity into a volume variance (for control) and an expected idle capacity variance (for planning) to replace Horngren's fixed overhead efficiency variance.

Sisco, Anthony F., Jr. 1973. "Overhead Variance Analysis and Corrective Action." *Management Accounting*, October, pp. 45–47, 51.

One of many articles during this period to explore capacity issues from the perspective of variance analysis, this article focuses on the use of variances for correction of current behavior. "In other words, analysis is necessary to bring out the significance of the variance in terms of sources, responsibility, and causes. ... Variance analysis is not complete until a decision is made on corrective action to be taken. ... It [overhead performance report] originates from the company's budget plan based on the direct labor volume forecasted for the budget year" (p. 45).

1979–Present

Adair-Heeley, Charlene. 1989. "Overhead: The Untapped Opportunity for JIT." *Production & Inventory Management Review*, JIT Methods and Practices section, May, pp. 26–27.

This article is basically a "fight speech" for extending JIT techniques into overhead areas, in the same manner as they have been applied to direct labor management and reporting. While capacity is not directly addressed, a rigorous search for nonvalue-added steps in very broadly defined "overhead" will lead to a reduction of waste and, hence, lower cost of capacity. Also, the writer illustrates the oft-told tale of the dangers of the direct-labor method for allocating overhead.

Barlev, Benzion, and Jeffrey Callen. 1986. "Total Factor Productivity and Cost Variances: Survey and Analysis." *Journal of Accounting Literature*, Vol. 5, pp. 35–56.

While this article only tangentially refers to capacity, the writers do bring advanced econometric techniques to the readers. The writers raise the issue of using standards based on the newest technology rather than on current technology of the firm for the computation of variances. To the extent that a significant difference exists in capacity potential with the newest technology versus the current technology, that firm should consider entering the newest technology model into its information system. Clearly, if econometrics is used in the organization, this article has much merit. Key note is, "Little if any work has been done on measuring productivity of off-line departments such as marketing and accounting" (p. 53).

Baumol, William J., Sue Anne Batey Blackman, and Edward N. Wolff. 1989. "Productivity Growth as Measured by Productive Capacity." *Productivity and American Leadership: The Long View.* Cambridge, MA: The MIT Press, pp. 235–237.

This excerpt is similar to the preceding article which details the difficulty of measuring capacity at the level of newest technology versus the current technology of the firm. Key note is: "Then there simply exists no one number that can adequately measure the enhanced productive capacity" (p. 236).

Becker, Edward A. 1989. "Fixed Costs/Variable Costs: The First One Hundred Years," Working Paper No. 61. Academy of Accounting Historians.

This working paper gives an excellent summary of a topic, fixed and variable costs, that plays an important role in cost of capacity issues. It is interesting to note the ignoring of these classifications by such financial accounting writers as Henry Rand Hatfield and Roy B. Kester. Becker stated that much change in these concepts has occurred, and this change should continue in the future. This bibliography is quite detailed and useful.

Blackstone, John H., Jr. 1989. *Capacity Management.* Cincinnati, OH: APICS/South-Western Publishing Co.

This book-length document focuses on the key issues shaping operational capacity management in the short term. Dealing with issues such as capacity versus load, efficiency, and utilization, the focus is on MRP-driven capacity concepts. Topics covered include: capacity requirement planning, input/output control, operations scheduling, dispatching, synchronized production, and long-term capacity planning activities. Inclusive of several solid case studies, this monograph provides a comprehensive view of capacity management from an operational perspective. Recommended reading.

Blaxill, Mark F., and Thomas M. Hout. 1991. "The Fallacy of the Overhead Quick Fix." *Harvard Business Review*, July-August, pp. 93–101.

This article gives a strong rationalization for managing changes in overhead costs and, hence, the cost of capacity. The authors stress the importance of "process." They utilize the concept of the "robust company" as one that combines the best of big with the best of small. The authors relate three basic action steps: segmenting, mapping, and measuring each process. They also relate these step to some actual case studies.

Chakravarty, Amiya, and Hemant K. Jain. 1990. "Distributed Computer System Capacity Planning and Capacity Loading." *Decision Sciences*, Vol. 21, pp. 253–262.

This article relates the topic of capacity to a computer system. It is possible that one can gain some insight into a production system for capacity from an analogous look at a computer system.

Cheatham, Carole. 1987. "Profit and Productivity Analyses Revisited." *Journal of Accountancy*, July, pp. 123–124, 126, 128, 130.

This article is an example of the lateness of the computation of standard cost variances, including the volume variance. The variances are based on the data from the past year and not on a detailed engineering study.

_____. 1989. "Reporting the Effects of Excess Inventories." *Journal of Accountancy*, November, pp. 131–132, 134, 136, 138, 140.

This article attempts to penalize managers for building up inventories by associating the increased costs of inventory as an unfavorable variance for internal purposes only.

_____. 1990. "Updating Standard Cost Systems: Making Them Better Tools for Today's Manufacturing Environment." *Journal of Accountancy*, December, pp. 57–60.

While this article omits reference to variances for fixed costs, it does generate an unfavorable volume variance for variable costs when inventory is increased. As no financial statements are presented, the effects of the proposed system on the statements were not given. Be that as it may, this article at least raises the thought to the readers that a positive traditional volume variance caused by an inventory buildup should be a matter of concern.

Cooper, Robin, and Robert S. Kaplan. 1992. "Activity-Based Systems: Measuring the Cost of Resource Usage." *Accounting Horizons*, September, pp. 1–13.

This article proposes two presentations of income statement data, one for financial accounting and one for internal purposes, in which there would be an unused variance for each classification of committed resources. Usage is based on practical capacity. The authors caution against the use of a budgeted capacity approach and stress that the goal is to increase profits, not to obtain more accurate costs. They intend the activity-based model to be a central tool for management planning and budgeting. The authors note, "But the failure to increase profits is not due to costs being intrinsically 'fixed.' Rather, the failure is the consequence of managers being unable or unwilling to exploit the unused capacity they have created" (p. 12).

Coughlan, Pamela, and John Darlington. 1993. "As Fast as the Slowest Operation: The Theory of Constraints." *Management Accounting* (U.K.), June, pp. 14–16.

This article is an excellent summation of the theory of constraints and an excellent case study of its implementation. The authors' goal is to lay to rest the notion that the theory of constraints is valuable only for short-term decisions. The authors bring attention to the fact that more efficient setup time will lead to higher profits than will dropping products. They present a formula for capacity available:

Time available x efficiency x availability x activation

The authors end with 10 principles of synchronized production. A key comment is "The master schedule decides whether enough capacity exists at a few critical work centers to fulfill the demand placed upon them" (p. 15).

DeBruine, Marinus, and Parvez R. Sopariwala. 1994. "The Use of Practical Capacity for Better Management Decisions." *Journal of Cost Management*, Spring, pp. 25–31.

This article advances the argument that fixed overhead rates should be determined based on practical capacity measures, which should represent the maximum levels at which each plant (or shift, cell, or work island) can operate efficiently. This approach is illustrated by an example that compares the traditional approach to the approach based on practical capacity. The example points out how the practical capacity approach provides better cost information and thus leads the way to better management decision making.

Dilton-Hill, Kevin G., and Ernest Glad. 1994. "Managing Capacity." *Journal of Cost Management*, Spring, pp. 32–39.

This article points out that there are different causes for capacity surpluses or shortages. The appropriate response to surplus or shortage in capacity depends on the underlying cause. Similarly, the manner in which the cost of surplus capacity is reported and the decision whether to include the costs in product costs depend on the underlying cause. This article views capacity in the context of the value chain and activity-based costing. Key topics explored include the definitions of capacity, potential management responses to the different causes of surplus capacity, the impact of different ways of charging surplus capacity to products and services, the management of shortages in capacity, and how to report the costs of surplus capacity.

Dolinsky, Larry, and Thomas E. Vollmann. 1991. "Transaction-Based Overhead Considerations for Product Design." *Journal of Cost Management*, Summer, pp. 7–19.

This article raises key points about product design that managers and accountants should consider. While much emphasis has always been placed on product design and process design, the authors also emphasize the concept of knowledge workers (engineers, planners, designers, and software programmers) and how to account for these people. Accounting models for allocation may be dysfunctional for controlling overhead costs. The concept of "transactions" is explained very well, along with a list of typical transactions. A brief case study is included.

Garner, C. Alan. 1994. "Capacity Utilization and U. S. Inflation." *Federal Reserve Bank of Kansas City*, Fourth Quarter, pp. 5–21.

This well-written article contains a defense of the classic computation of capacity by economists and of the notion that inflation will start at about 82% plant utilization. The author rejects the notion that reengineering has led to a new order.

Guttikonda, Rama R., and Doris M. Cook. 1991. "A New Look at the Old Problem of Overhead Cost Allocation." *Collected Papers and Abstracts of the American Accounting Association's Southwest Regional Meeting*, March 13–16, pp. 190–96.

The recent developments in the overhead cost allocation area are summarized in this working paper. Presented in a very readable fashion, the authors' focus is on such topics as activity-based costing and the treatment of various forms of overhead costs under the theory of constraints and related models.

Hallbauer, Rosalie C. 1989. "The Evolution of Normal Costing," Working Paper 89-12. Florida International University.

This working paper gives an excellent and very readable synopsis of the English literature of normal costing for the 19th and 20th centuries. Normal costing, which by definition entails an analysis, definition, and treatment of capacity and idle capacity costs, is still used by companies such as Caterpillar to stabilize cost estimates and ensure that tactical strategies for resource deployment are realized.

Hansen, Stephen, and Robert P. Magee. 1993. "Capacity Cost and Capacity Allocation." *Contemporary Accounting Research*, Spring, pp. 635–660.

While this article requires econometric training for full comprehension, the authors do an excellent job in relating their findings. They feel that the traditional cost allocation procedure does approximate the opportunity cost procedure as full capacity is approached. A key note is "An obvious alternative is a fully dynamic rule in which the manager's cutoff varies with the remaining capacity and number of pending product proposals. Unfortunately, this rule requires a large number of cutoff values and no single closed-form expression is possible" (p. 640).

Hill, John, Ricardo Cost, and Eduardo Jardim. 1992. "Strategic Capacity Planning and Production Scheduling in Jobbing Systems." *Integrated Manufacturing Systems*, Vol. 3, No. 3, pp. 22–26.

These authors stress the need to establish a finite notion of capacity for very flexible jobbing firms, using a brief case study to illustrate their solution. Key comments are: "It is usually difficult (and often misleading) to calculate their capacity. Bottlenecks tend to shift according to the product mix and so vary the capacity available" (p. 22) and "...the central feature of the package is a discrete simulation algorithm which allows schedules to be prepared according to rules incorporated in the system" (p. 23).

Kee, Robert. 1995. "Integrating Activity-Based Costing with the Theory of Constraints to Enhance Production-Related Decisions." *Accounting Horizons*, December, pp. 48–61.

The capacity model developed by this academic integrates the basic concepts of the theory of constraints and ABC models to generate a mathematical, least-cost solution to the capacity utilization issue. Employing a mixed-integer programming approach, this model gives the optimal production mix subject to the capacity of the individual activities making up the firm's production schedule. The key features of this unique, well-developed model are that it uses mathematical modeling to solve for optimal capacity utilization; effectively combines both operational and financial views of the capacity problem; can easily be added to existing ABC applications; when at least one bottleneck operation exists, provides a superior solution to a pure TOC or pure ABC methodology; and uses marginal revenue as its decision basis. This article is recommended reading for practitioners and academics alike.

Klammer, Thomas. 1996. *Capacity: A Manager's Primer*. Arlington, TX: Consortium for Advanced Manufacturing-International.

This document reviews the CAM-I capacity model and states that the model's primary concern is to support the strategic decision process by helping managers understand and define the many states of capacity, measure these states, and then communicate them in a simple format. Built from activities at the operational level, the model is a collection of capacity data that includes the supply of capacity, the demand on that capacity by specific products, and the constraint within a process that limits the production of good units. The primary features of the model are that it integrates capacity data across many dimensions, ties to the financial reporting process, details responsibility for capacity losses, and uses time as a unifying measure. The book is recommended reading for managers planning to implement capacity reporting.

Konopka, John M. 1995. "Capacity Utilization Bottleneck Efficiency System—CUBES." *IEEE Transactions on Components, Packaging and Manufacturing Technology,* Part A, September.

This article presents a detailed view of the CUBES model developed in conjunction with Sematech, the industry consortium for the semiconductor industry. Deployed at companies such as Texas Instruments, this model integrates financial and nonfinancial data, builds from activity-based costs, uses theory of constraint logic, and provides a dynamic and least-cost analysis of capacity deployment. Representing one of the new views of capacity analysis developed using simulation programming capabilities, this model breaks the analysis of capacity utilization into 11 components: nonscheduled time, scheduled downtime, engineering time, unscheduled downtime, standby/idle time, other time losses, tool speed loss, batching losses, quality losses, and actual CUBES efficiency against theoretical capacity. This article is recommended reading for anyone wanting to review the state-of-the-art in capacity cost reporting and analysis.

Mackey, James T. 1983. "Allocating Opportunity Costs." *Management Accounting*, March, pp. 33–37.

This article presents a linear programming solution within the traditional costing framework for costing both bottleneck and nonbottleneck departments. A brief case study is included. Some key statements: "A linear programming model is used because it can be used in capacity planning for production systems and can be used to establish both optimal production mixes and estimations of opportunity costs.... The only productive capacity that has a positive opportunity cost is the fully utilized, constraining department(s). But it is precisely in this situation, at full capacity, that the lowest application rate is applied to work-in-progress inventory" (p. 33).

_____. 1987. "11 Key Issues in Manufacturing Accounting." *Management Accounting*, January, pp. 32–37.

This excellent article deserves a very close reading. It was based both on a detailed questionnaire and field interviews. There are many items to note. "...[T]he technological world is changing and accountants do not seem to be meeting the challenge. There seems to be a group of problems that have well-developed solutions in theory but are not being implemented in practice" (p. 32). "Bottlenecks occur when machine capacities are not perfectly balanced to production demand" (p. 33). "With a job shop's highly variable demand, both the capacity and the bottleneck machinery change with the product mix" (p. 33). "Certain amounts of work-in-process represent stored capacity, and are used to protect against perturbations in production activity and demand surges with semi-finished products" (p. 33).

"Reduction in inventories creates situations where, increasingly, short-term manufacturing flexibility will be used as a substitute" (p. 34). "Economic theory would say that this kind of downscaling reduces the number of internal transactions that a firm would make. Consequently, the need for accounting numbers to provide prices for internal decisions would be reduced.... Because of the high cost of automated and robotic machinery, accounting systems as a matter of practice should be generating variances that reflect the cost of carrying underutilized capacity.... Such a preponderance of fixed, long-term costs makes incremental pricing hazardous at best" (p. 35). "The conclusion that seems to come through is that variances are used by higher-level managers to control the plant manager's activities and not to evaluate individual responsibility centers within a production unit" (p. 36).

McLaughlin, Robyn, and Robert A. Taggart, Jr. 1992. "The Opportunity Cost of Using Excess Capacity." *Financial Management*, Summer, pp. 12–23.

The authors place the capacity decision in terms of an option model and show another model, equivalent annual cost (EAC).

This article should appeal to financial managers and add another dimension to decisions on capacity.

McNair, C. J. 1994. "The Hidden Costs of Capacity." *Journal of Cost Management*, Spring, pp. 12–24.

This article details the basic issues surrounding measuring, managing, and analyzing capacity and capacity costs. Starting from a definition of capacity as "the resources available to do work," the central theme is the various forms of waste embedded in existing approaches to capacity cost management. Key thought: "In the race to gain a sustainable competitive advantage, companies have to find ways to use their existing resources better...redefin[ing] capacity to focus management's attention on wasted resources rather than on the output of the plant. Since waste is hidden in existing definitions and approaches to capacity management, it never goes away and often increases. This robs companies of their ability to respond to the challenges of a global marketplace. Continuous improvement begins with an understanding of what is possible—that is, how much value can be created with existing resources" (p. 12).

McNair, C. J., and Richard Vangermeersch. 1996. Statement on Management Accounting 4Y, "Measuring the Cost of Capacity." Published in collaboration with the Society of Management Accountants of Canada, Hamilton, Ontario, which issued it as Management Accounting Guideline #42.

Endorsed by the IMA, the SMAC, and CAM-I, this seminal guideline details current best practices in capacity cost reporting. Comprehensive in scope, the document focuses on the core issues defining capacity cost management, 12 different models being used by companies to measure and manage capacity, and the role of management accounting in defining and implementing capacity reporting. Within the document, the separation of idle capacity costs from actual product costs is once again defined as the MAAP for the field.

Mills, David E. 1990. "Capacity Expansion and the Size of Plants." *RAND Journal of Economics*, Winter, pp. 555–566.

This article presents an econometric look at the capacity decision in the framework of an investment-time game. Once again, certainty in the capacity decision is elusive. Key notations are: "Even if small plants impose higher average costs when producing at capacity, the time intervals over which they become viable may be shorter as demand grows, depending on the trade-off between cost and capacity" (p. 556) and "This makes it hard to predict *a priori* whether capacity expansion in industries is predisposed to large, infrequent additions, small additions in quick succession, or some mixture of plant sizes and gestation periods" (p. 556).

Myers, John. 1994. "Fundamentals of Production that Influence Industrial Facility Designs." *Appraisal Journal*, April, pp. 296–302.

This excellent article was written by a professor of industrial engineering technology and hence can add much more insight to capacity than just the real estate appraisal issue. The author brings out some key notes for capacity management. "Manufacturing subcomponents is a production headache for most manufacturers and a company avoids doing so if possible.... It should be understood that there is no perfect layout for a production facility" (p. 297). "One crucial component in the appraisal of a manufacturing center is familiarity with the entire history of the property" (p. 297). "Another concern is environmental factors. ... The production capacity of a facility is usually monitored in the industry by a document known as a master production schedule" (p. 298). "Although all companies should have master plans, generally only the more progressive companies have them" (p. 299). "When this (JIT) approach is compared with that of the traditional U. S. philosophy of manufacture-to-stock, which requires more work-in-process, handling, and storage than JIT, the floor area requirements can be dramatically different" (p. 301).

Noreen, E., D. Smith, and J. Mackey. 1995. *The Theory of Constraints and Its Implications for Management Accounting.* Montvale, NJ: Institute of Management Accountants.

The authors of this well-written monograph detail the key features of the theory of constraints (TOC) model and its impact on management accounting. The objective of the TOC model is to support continuous improvement throughout the organization. Essential to this improvement process is the effective deployment of constrained resources. Focused on throughput capacity, or the maximum flow through a process given existing physical or "invisible" constraints, the model identifies the optimal trade-off between throughput investment and operating expense. In approaching capacity costs, the model suggests that idle capacity is not an opportunity cost unless customer orders are not being filled. The key features of this model are that it emphasizes company profitability over keeping people/machines busy; highlights key constraints inhibiting process performance; is useful in plants or processes using TOC in their management approach; provides a solid baseline for action; and has a strong record of effectiveness. The authors' integration of TOC with management accounting is comprehensive. The monograph is suggested reading.

Orr, James. 1994. "Has Excess Capacity Abroad Reduced U. S. Inflationary Pressures?" *FRBNY Quarterly Review*, Summer-Fall, pp. 101–106.

This article explores the theory that excess capacity in such countries as Japan, Canada, Germany, France, Italy, and the United Kingdom would lessen U. S. inflationary pressure because of stable or lower prices on imports. The author concludes that the rise in the relative dollar price of imports from Japan because of its strengthening currency offsets a large part of the decline in the dollar price of imports from Western Europe and Canada and hence limits overall import price declines.

Pindyck, Robert S. 1988. "Irreversible Investment, Capacity Choice, and the Value of the Firm." *American Economic Review*, December, pp. 969–985.

An econometric model of investment in capacity with an opportunity cost of investing underlies this article. While the author concludes that managers probably cover such an opportunity cost by allowing for an arbitrary risk factor, he does raise some very important issues. Items to note are: "Most major investment expenditures are at least partly irreversible; the firm cannot disinvest, so the expenditures are sunk costs. … When investment is irreversible and future demand or cost conditions are uncertain, an investment expenditure involves the exercising or 'killing of an option'—the option to productively invest at any time in the future.... The value of the unit must exceed the purchase and installation cost, by an amount equal to the value of keeping these resources elsewhere alive— an opportunity cost of investment" (p. 969).

"In effect, a unit of capacity gives the firm an infinite number of options to produce, one for every future time, each with exercise price equal to production cost, and can be valued accordingly.... These 'operating options' are worth more the more volatile is demand, just as a call option on a stock is worth more, the more volatile is the price of the stock" (p. 970). "...and, in markets with volatile and unpredictable demand, firms should hold less capacity than they would if investment were reversible or future demands were known" (p. 983).

Raddock, Richard D., and Charles E. Gilbert. 1990. "Recent Developments in Industrial Capacity and Utilization." *Federal Reserve Bulletin*, June, pp. 411–435.

The appendix in this article traces the history of the Federal Reserve Board's attempts at measuring capacity. It is important to note these caveats: "Capacity is an ambiguous concept, and capacity and utilization estimates are often rough approximations. No census of plant capacity exists.... Even for a single plant, a range of capacity concepts applies. At the high end of the range would be an engineering maximum based on the rated speed of machinery in place and operated with minimum downtime. At the low end, economic concepts relate a firm's capacity to a quantity of output that minimizes its unit costs or beyond which its costs rise unacceptably.... Asking what the practical capacity of a plant is may be like asking how much water a bathtub can hold without overflowing: It depends on who is in the tub at the time and what he or she is doing" (p. 425).

Siegel, Joel, and Mathew S. Rubin. 1984. "Corporate Planning and Control Through Variance Analysis." *Managerial Planning*, September/October, pp. 35–39, 49–50.

This article falls into the trap of treating the volume variance and idle capacity variance as the same but otherwise represents one of the more thoughtful pieces on overhead variance analysis during this period. "The standard should be established depending upon the corporate goal to be achieved" (p. 36). "An unfavorable labor efficiency variance may arise from idle time caused by manufacturing bottlenecks or delays such as that caused by deficient sales orders or raw materials on hand" (p. 35). "The overhead volume variance relates to the utilization of plant capacity. A continual unfavorable variance may be due to having excessively large plant. Management may get a better look at cost under-utilization of production facilities by computing lost contribution margin than looking at historical cost incurrences.... One must note that variances are interrelated" (p. 37).

Staubus, George J. 1987. "The Dark Ages of Cost Accounting: The Rise of Miscues in the Literature." *Accounting Historians Journal*, Fall, pp. 1–18.

The author, a highly respected researcher in financial accounting, applied his talents to cost accounting in this article. It reviews the explanations for the dark ages of cost accounting: (1) John Maurice Clark, (2) Paton and Littleton, (3) American Institute of Accountants' Definition of Depreciation Accounting, (4) the direct costing literature, and (5) criticisms of allocation. Key comments to note are: "The comatose state of cost accounting's conceptual theoretical development is especially remarkable when one compares the stagnation in that field with the progress that has been made since World War I in microeconomics, finance, and general accounting theory" (p. 6). "*An Introduction to Corporate Accounting Standards* [Paton and Littleton 1940] may deserve a share of the blame for the failure of cost accountants to develop a clear concept of cost" (p. 9). "These definitions imply that depreciation expense may be arbitrary and is not a measurable economic phenomenon" (p. 12). "On the whole, direct costing literature is now a handicap to the development of cost accounting" (p. 14). "Allocation lacks theory. Accounting for the value of resources used in the enterprise is based on microeconomic theory, the theory of finance, and the decision-usefulness theory of accounting" (p. 15).

Surdell, Gregg J. 1991. "Capacity Planning Applies to Warehouses Too!" *P&IM Review with Apics News*, February, pp. 42, 47.

This article is a very good reminder that capacity management applies to the distribution function as well as to manufacturing. Key notes are: "Upon the receipt of a shipment forecast, the distribution center manager must know how his key resources and critical work centers will be affected" (p. 42). "A distribution operation can be managed similar to a manufacturing concern. Just because distribution is not producing a finished good does not mean that they do not have to know what their daily shipment capacity is" (p. 47).

Uchitelle, Louis. 1994. "Fed's Move Reheats Debate over Job Growth and 'Capacity.'" *Providence Sunday Journal*, August 21, pp. F-1, F-2.

This newspaper article illustrates the political aspects of the capacity figures of the Federal Reserve Board.

Veral, Emre A., and R. Lawrence LaForge. 1990. "The Integration of Cost and Capacity Considerations in Material Requirements Planning Systems." *Decision Sciences*, Vol. 2, pp. 507–520.

This article brings capacity constraints into a MRP system through use of the master production schedule (MPS). Key notations are: "It is well known that the basic logic of material requirement planning (MRP) is insensitive to capacity considerations.... Lack of capacity to execute the manufacturing plan adopted by a firm could result in missed due dates, higher than anticipated in-process inventory, and/or a weakening of the firm's competitive position.... Consideration of capacity in a closed-loop MRP environment can take place as the MPS is being developed and as an extension of the MPR processing logic" (p. 507). "In general, the Dixon-Silver algorithm is designed to determine lot sizes for multiple items that are processed through a single facility such that inventory-related costs are minimized, no backorders occur, and capacity is not exceeded" (p. 509). "As the projected load exceeds normal capacity by a greater and greater amount, the feasibility of the manufacturing plan becomes more and more questionable" (p. 513). "The results strongly suggest that master scheduling is the primary influence on the trade-off between inventory-related costs and work load variability" (p. 517).

Vollmers, Gloria. 1996. "Idle Time, Idle Capacity." Working paper. University of Maine.

This working paper is an excellent review of the literature from 1920 through 1960. It is an extremely thoughtful piece that explores both the transitions in the treatment of idle time and idle capacity reporting and potential explanations for the shift in these practices over time. Recommended reading.

Wise, Timothy M. 1990. "An Assessment of Capacity Management." *Internal Auditing*, Spring, pp. 75–81.

This very important article provides a sample audit program for capacity issues. The author uses data processing services as his base but any other function could be substituted for it. There are very key notations: "Capacity management plays a major role in maximizing computer resources and projecting future resource requirements.... Internal auditors should periodically audit for the efficient use of capacity management" (p. 75). "Capacity planning focuses on determining the resources required to process future work loads and satisfy service levels. This future-oriented objective is accomplished by analyzing projected work loads and reserve capacity. Capacity planners must also be familiar with trends in information technology and the impact of these trends on the corporation's operations" (p. 76). "The staff must understand how users interact with the data center and the relationship between user work load and DP resource consumption.... Although not indicators of capacity or service, utilization thresholds will indicate potential service problems" (p. 77). "Another task during the audit survey is to identify the operational components that support capacity management" (p. 80).

INDEX

T

U